# GUNNAR FEHLAU

# the recumbent bicycle

**Out Your Backdoor Press**
**SECOND EDITION**

ISBN 1-892590-58-1

Second Edition Copyright 2003; First Edition 2000; Out Your Backdoor Press.
Jeff Potter—Editor and Publisher. Printed by Color House Graphics, Grand Rapids, MI.

Library of Congress Control Number:   2003114739

The original version of this book was published under the title "Das Liegerad."
© Moby Dick Verlag Kiel/Germany, 1996.

A copy may be ordered by sending $20 postpaid to:

Out Your Backdoor, 4686 Meridian Rd., Williamston MI 48895;  ph. 800-763-OYBD (6923)

For information on other OYB titles, see catalog at back of this book and
the full service website at... **OutYourBackdoor.com**, which hosts:
• OYB Press title details and ordering info • 500+ free homegrown adventure articles
• OYB magazine ordering info and back-issues • textfiles of OYB books
• OYB bookstore (for 100's of related titles) • OYB & Local Spirit Travel Forums
• links to other do-it-yourself culture websites.

---

**Gunnar Fehlau** is president of the Bicycle Press Service in Germany, available at
www.pressedienst-fahrrad.de.

**Jasmin Fischer** was the English translator for this book. She is available at
www.jasminfischer.de.

**OYB Acknowledgments:** Enormous credit goes to Jasmin Fischer for her translation
of this book from the original German. She pulled through wonderfully where others failed.
And I thank Martha, my wife, for letting me do this project and encouraging me through it.
I look forward to seeing her and our youngsters more often! —*Jeff Potter, editor*

*Front cover photo:*
Laurie Smith, editor of the *Easy Riders Recumbent Club* magazine, rides her "Tour Easy,"
the classic by Easy Racers (www.easyracers.com; www.geocities.com/e_r_r_c/;
Michael Berry photo).

*On the back cover:*
Racer/designer Bram Moens rides his sleek M5 low-racer creation
(www.m5-ligfietsen.com; Frans Lemmens photo).

# Contents

*Dedicated to my father,*
*without whom this book would not have been written.*

# Preface

Although the recumbent bicycle was invented before the turn of the century, it has, like many other alternative bike concepts, spent its existence in the shadow of the 'normal bike,' which is based on the Rover Safety Bike of 1885.

As early as 1869 there was a model that resembled a modern recumbent. However, continuous development of the mode only started in the early 1890s.

Recumbents were actively developed up to the late 1930s, and they often put the upright racing bike into second place in competition. But after achieving its best results, the recumbent was banned from further competition by the UCI (the international bike sport association), and, not coincidentally, declined in popularity.

Success in sport always has a big influence on the use of a product. As a result of the ban, sales figures deteriorated quickly. Soon the recumbent disappeared from the world of cycling.

Today, the situation has changed. Apart from a small number of racing enthusiasts it is mainly everyday cyclists and tourists who enjoy the advantages of these flat fliers. The beneficial aerodynamics, design diversity, safety and highly adjustable, comfortable position make the recumbent an ideal vehicle for a wide variety of distances, uses, speeds and rider types. Its manifold construction possibilities overcome any problem whatsoever with rider position, and potentially improve even the problems of traffic congestion.

In the middle of the seventies, the IHPVA (International Human Powered Vehicle Association) was founded in the U.S., and the previous lull was broken. Two parallel developments converged at that time: Engineers from the West coast, whose goal was

to reach the highest possible speed, and activists from the East, whose intent was to build a safe, muscle-driven bike to help solve the transportation crisis.

It was the IHPVA's goal to develop the full potential of cycling regardless of UCI limitations. Air and water vehicles are being aggressively developed within the organization as well. In the sector of ground vehicles, the laid-back position and the chain drive dominate.

In the more than 25 years of continuous development since then, significant progress has been made. Any interested person can now buy a recumbent that professionally meets any of dozens of needs, and is not forced to build one himself, which was the situation not so long ago. But homebuilding is still done, and to a high level, with much freely shared advice and not much complexity for the tinkering enthusiast.

Recumbents are still often accused of great weaknesses: they aren't maneuverable, they cause your legs to fall asleep, they can't climb hills, they're dangerous around cars. These prejudices are directly due to lack of experience and knowledge, and have more to do with ignorant fear of the unknown than with reality or facts. As we shall see.

This book delivers the basic knowledge you need to approach the recumbent from any direction. (Note that it offers a complete overview of the 'one-track' vehicle, as distinct from trikes.)

The following areas covered should be enough to set anyone on their way: comparisons of major features, history, physics, racing, touring, city-use, design, homebuilding, fairing info, and useful shopping and riding appendix resources.

—*Gunnar Fehlau*

# What is a recumbent anyway?

Compared to popular bike types such as the racing bike, the touring bike, the mountain bike, the foldable bike, or the tandem, the recumbent is exotic, indeed!

It is the only type of bike which differs from the others not only in widely varying frame design, but also in the way you are seated. Your position on all other bikes is vertical, or leaning forward, and the angle between your upper body and legs depends on the use of your bike: Your position is flat forward on a racing bike and rather upright on a Dutch city-bike. The root principle, however, is the much the same with very little variation: Your legs step down on to the pedals to drive them.

On a recumbent, the legs are in a different position. You pedal horizontally, and much more closely to the ground, in general. And your body position can vary tremendously.

The recumbent form of bike design exists largely as the result of efforts to make a bicycle faster, safer, more comfortable and more diverse in function, to put it in a nutshell.

Nearly all recumbents are laid back in position. The typical laid back recumbent uses your back, hips and broad parts of your rump as contact surface. The crank is positioned in the front, and your body is tilted back between 15 and 75 degrees, depending on the model.

However, there is a rare variant that should be mentioned: the prone recumbent, or "belly bike." With this bike, your front chest and belly area serve as the contact surface and the crank is behind you. These can be fast and exciting to ride.

We can also differentiate between two basic forms of construction: the long and the short recumbent. The common abbre-viations for these are LWB for "long wheelbase" and SWB for "short wheelbase." The wheels and the bottom bracket position are important for this categorization. If the front wheel is positioned in front of the crank, we are talking about a long recumbent; if those two are reversed, we are talking about a short recumbent.

To summarize, we differentiate between four main types:

- •back recumbents
- •belly recumbents
- •long recumbents
- •short recumbents

...And the variations on these themes are endless.

Compact, or medium wheelbase, models (CWB) are an effective, popular hybrid.

Low recumbents, often called lowracers, are a variant with extremely low seats and the crank in front of the front wheel—these are presently dominating unfaired racing.

The many different construction and design variants—mainly distinguished by frame format and steering position—are the result of the multiple options that recumbent or "horizontal" bikes offer.

These options exist largely due to the separation of steering, power and support functions, which in upright bikes are tied together. You might think the resulting constructions look odd and alien, but regular bike shapes are diverse as well—and growing more so every year. Just think of the differences between a classic racing bike and a full-suspension mountain bike; between a fully loaded touring bike, a foldable bike and a tricked-out carbon-fiber monocoque triathlon bike.

We are only starting to realize how much variety cycling has to offer!

# Ch. 1 / History and Stories

*Francis Faure on the Mochet track recumbent with small rear fairing. (photo: Mochet)*

# The Long Journey of the Recumbent Bicycle

Until the end of the 18th Century, people only had their feet, the horse and cart, and the ship as the means for travel and transport. The locomotive came into being in 1789 as the first new transportation system of the Industrial Revolution.

The "running wheel," made in 1817 by the Baron of Drais, served as the initial pattern for the construction of all other bicycles. The Baron had been looking for some kind of transportation which would enable him in his job as a forester to maneuver in between closely standing trees. As far as he knew, no appropriate vehicle existed, and as a horse did not seem suitable, he built something himself. The machine he had in mind had to be narrow, so he avoided the traditional side-by-side wheels construction of the wagon: the gyroscopic force of the wheels alone prevented his craft from falling over.

With the invention of the crank drive the real bike was born, because the rider no longer had to have contact with the ground. A treadle was mounted on the front wheel, allowing immensely higher speeds. In order to increase speed even more, the front wheel was enlarged. The rear wheel was made proportionally smaller so that the machine would not be too long.

The riders sat at dizzying heights atop their bicycles, which were aptly called highwheels (also Penny Farthings and Ordinaries). It was an art to mount a highwheel, and to be able to ride it even halfway gracefully. The highwheel was suitable only for the small population of people who had good enough balance and skill to keep the unstable bicycles on the road. Even experienced and daredevil riders easily passed their limits, with frequent accidents and injuries.

In 1884, two Englishmen, Starley and Sutton, were responsible for the next decisive push in the development of the bicycle, the technical possibilities of the highwheel having been exhausted.

They invented the chain drive, which provided the solution for constructing a bike that was easy to drive...and faster yet. The crank was shifted from the front wheel to the middle of the bike. It was attached to a sprocket, which transferred power to a cogwheel at the rear through a chain. This cogwheel was initially fixed directly to the rear wheel, but later it was replaced by the freewheeling hub which allowed coasting. The wheels were also now the same size.

The new center of gravity was no higher than that of someone walking, making riding easy. Learning how to ride the new Safety Bicycle was possible for everybody. The highwheel of a few daredevils was now a mode of transportation for the masses.

The magic word for speed was "translation." Translation—the result of stepped-up gear ratios—created the necessary increase in rotation speed despite the smaller wheels. This technical improvement was also beneficial to sports. Competition with the new bike was faster and more thrilling.

*In the widest sense, this crank-arm bike from 1869 can be seen as an early recumbent. At this time there was tinkering in many directions, but most of the ideas were cast aside after conception. A successor to this model or another producer who was inspired by this creation is not known. (photo: Museum of Engineering and Traffic, Berlin)*

For strength and simplicity, frames were typically triangulated in a pattern that has caused the design to come to be known as a "diamond" frame.

Apart from numerous inventions in the realm of sport, there were also endeavors to develop bikes as utility vehicles. The bicycling mail carrier and baker's bicycle are historical examples. The sporting aspect, however, was almost invariably the most fruitful ground for technical development. In the field of accessories, everyday bikers had the higher development potential.

Due to the continuing efforts of sports people and builders, the importance of air resistance was finally appreciated. This insight was responsible for the creation of fairings and several new riding positions in the early period.

The first illustration of a recumbent bicycle was printed in 1893 in the *Fliegende Blätter* ("Flying Pages"), a humor magazine from Munich. We see a rider sitting in a kind of a lounge chair between front and rear wheel, smoking a cigar. His forward motion is produced by a crank attached directly to the front wheel, but there is no form of steering apparent. In the background, you can see two safety riders whose faces show more strain than the "pilot" of the recumbent bike.

That same year, the "Fautenil Velociped," which is considered to be the first recumbent bicycle in the world, was built, using balloon tires.

In the following years, a large number of developments were made in the recumbent bicycle. In 1894, Joseph Turncock, an Englishman, applied for a patent for a recumbent bike. This bike had a rocker-arm drive. It was steered directly from a lying position. It had a reclining seat above the rear wheel. Its appearance was very similar to the "Jaray Bike" that was popular in the 1920s.

In 1893, the armchair-bicycle from the

*This caricature from the magazine* Fliegende Blätter *("Flying Pages") of September 10, 1893, marks the actual invention of the recumbent. From this year on, horizontal pedaling was pursued with different models, mainly in France, Germany and the U.S.*

Swiss producer Challand was much admired at the bike salon in Geneva. It had two equally-sized wheels, and an arm-and-leg drive. The seat was above the rear wheel, a little in front of the axle. I. F. Wales secured the U.S. patent for this bike in 1896.

At a time when there was no one dominating type of bike, experts discussed all these ideas with interest and an unbiased perspective. One of these was Paul von Salvisberg, who wrote the following in the newspaper *Radsport in Bild und Wort* ("Bicycling in Pictures and Words") in 1897:

"An engineer from Geneva named Challand recently invented a new bike, which he has modestly named the "Normal Bicyclette," as in his opinion the driver is sitting in a normal position. The attached sketch, however, does not evoke an impression of normalcy, but rather creates feelings in the viewer similar to those evoked when people lean back in their chair as an aid for digestion while eating. If it continues like this, footstools and loveseats will soon also be furnished with foot-driven sprocket and chain drive.

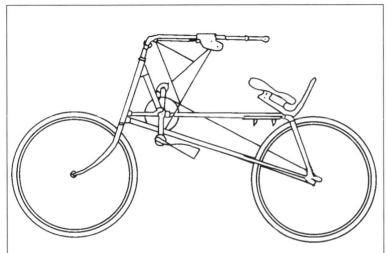

*In 1895, the producer 'Challand' went public with his recumbent, which apart from a novel driving position also had a revolutionary full body drive.*

*The Challand production from 1897 appears to be a lot more practical. Foregoing the full body drive in favor of a pedal crank is a gain. This machine fascinated the press. (Drawings based on article in Olms Press.)*

"But let's listen to what the inventor himself has to say about the advantages of his new machine: The main power comes from the above-mentioned basis at the back of the seat, which the driver presses against less with his weight than with the strength of his legs. This is done with horizontal rather than vertical leg action.

"In an upright, even reclining, upper body position, with a stable seat and completely uncramped organs, the rider can produce a force with his thighs which is approximately, and this is the inventor's conviction, three times his body weight with each leg. So for instance 2x3x150 kg, thus 900 kg, simply amazing! (...)

"Moreover, the rider does not sit very high. A fall is less risky and less likely to happen than before. He easily steers with one hand, with the other one he can just as easily catch flies or eat apples. The brakes are not less unique, e.g. they have been replaced by a brake shoe which is sensibly mounted to the rear wheel. The powerful backpedaling option, by the way, makes braking seem to be an extreme stopgap action.

"At the last exhibition in Geneva (1896), convincing tests were supposed to be conducted with this flying sofa: in spite of the enormous [?] translation of 4.52 meters, the machine, which was at the time constructed only with wood, ran extremely easily. The latest 1897 model is made of steel and weighs 26.5 lbs. The seat is adjustable, as the positioning of the legs at an angle of about 45 degrees from the horizontal was realized to be most optimal.

"Coming to the ladies' bikes, the matter is a little more tricky, and thus the beautiful sex is brought from the horizontal position to a more vertical one by a seat that is tilted forward more. This is supposed to be better against strong winds. (...)

"Now there is nothing more left to to watch the happy inventor recline through the world for a few thousand kilometers on his Normal Chaiselongue.

Hail! v.S."

Soon after its first salon appearance, the experts recognized the advantages of the recumbent construction method. Even if there were some errors in their judgments (for instance the supposed advantages of shorter stroke lengths and improved aerodynamics of the vertical position on the ladies' bike—women being able to ride with skirts was probably the actual motive), you can find an overall view in favor of the recumbent bike, or at least a neutral opinion. These reviewers do not only give theoretical evaluations, they try to swing a test ride as well.

At the turn of the century inventors like Challand and Brown laid the groundwork for the successes of recumbent bikes in the 1930s.

Even in the 1800s there was a clear connection between the discoveries of aerodynamics and the development of drive mechanisms. Often the vehicles on display at shows would have some surprising new lying position or a totally novel drive.

Furthermore, from before the turn of the century, up to the 1920s, there were attempts to develop a comfortable armchair-bicycle based on the regular diamond frame bike with 27" or 28" wheels.

In 1897, a "Mr. Darling" entered the scene with such a model. His belly-recumbent bike was based on an already existing low-frame "diamond" bicycle that he modified. Two frame-tubes were soldered to the frame as extensions of the chainstays. At their ends they met to place the bottom bracket behind the rear wheel. From there a tube bent upwards around the rear wheel to the seat tube, and halfway there it was supported by two stays leading to the rear dropouts. Instead of a saddle, a belly rest was mounted to the top tube.

The steering setup common to racing bikes was replaced by a fork mounted directly to a touring style handlebar without a stem. This design made very cheap production possible, as it was based on a regular bike frame and special parts were mostly not needed.

Although belly bikes (or prone recumbents) played a large role in the de-

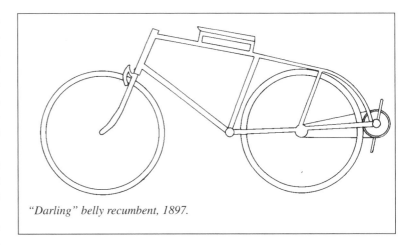

*"Darling" belly recumbent, 1897.*

velopment of aerodynamic land vehicles, they have never stepped out of the shadow of the others. One reason for that might be their biomechanics. Neither the rib cage (and thus the lungs) nor the bowel or stomach function well under the burden of body weight; however, today's best prone designs shift the pressure points to hips and shoulder.

Prior to the 1990s, the last production of belly recumbent bikes took place in 1955. The Italian world-champion Enzo Sacci tested a model of Italian origin, but without particular success. There have been admi-

*This sketch is the only thing known about the American "Brown" recumbent, 1901.*

rable recent designs and race results, but no production models.

Far more successful were the designs where riders used their buttocks or back as contact surface. These designs were comfortable and quick. They could compete very well against safety bikes. Just as the "Darling Bike," the American "Brown Recumbent" was based on a modified diamond frame. It consisted of the front part of a ladies' bicycle and the rear part of a men's. A tube from the top of the men's seat tube led to a shortened seat tube of the front part. A second tube connected the chainstays and seat tube with the down tube of the front assembly. In this lower meeting area one found the bottom bracket. The seat was mounted to the bent men's top tube. The handlebar was oddly shaped, but it was mounted for normal direct steering to a reversed stem through a headset to the fork.

Riders sat relatively upright on the Brown, the view of traffic and scenery was relaxed, and the center of gravity was at a usual height and position. The Brown was also exported from the U.S. in 1901, some models being shipped to England.

The recumbent of Englishman P. W. Bartlett was presented in the September,

1905, edition of *Scientific American*. Bartlett announced the bike to be as "comfortable as a rocking chair." The bike was very compact: the driver sat on a leather seat above the rear wheel and drove the cranks, which were 18" lower and between the two wheels at the height of the rear wheel hub. The handlebar was mounted under the seat. Stopping the bike must have been tricky as the seat was beyond toe-touching, at 30" above the ground. On the other hand, the

| "Brown" Recumbent | |
| --- | --- |
| Front wheel: | 25 inches |
| Rear wheel: | 28 inches |
| Gearing: | 2.134 meter |
| Weight: | 30 lbs. |
| Steering: | direct |
| Wheelbase: | 67 inches |

short wheelbase in connection with lack of steering lock-up allowed for a very tight turning radius.

Prior to WWI, all attempts to mass-produce a recumbent in Europe came to nothing. The interest of the media and sports fans was more focused on cowled diamond-frame racing bikes.

The first European production recumbent was built in France in 1914. In frame shape and construction, it very much resembled the Brown. This un-pedigreed bike is attributed to Peugeot, but there is no evidence for this theory. The wheel sizes were very unusual for this period: 22" in front and 26" at the rear. Moreover, the bike had one of the first shifting mechanisms.

In the 1920s, the Jaray recumbent bike from the Hesperus factories in Stuttgart was sold successfully without being intended for sports. It was also distributed in Holland and Switzerland. The unusual rocker-arm drive of the bike should be noted. Paul Jaray (1889-1974), the German zeppelin builder and inventor of streamlining, oriented his

*The first mass-produced recumbent: France 1914. (photo: Museum für Technik and Verkehr Berlin)*

frame design toward the contemporary normal bike frame. The driver sat on an extra-cushioned seat above the rear wheel. The rocker arm drive was run by a kind of "triple gearshift": three pairs of foot rests which were mounted to the lever of the rocker arm could be chosen to produce the desired speed. Additionally, it had either a 2- or 3-speed Torpedo multi-shift hub at the rear wheel. In this way, six or nine different gears could be selected. The variety of shifting made the J-Bike special, and can be seen as a reason for its (relative) success. The less-powerful recumbent position demands quite a variety of shifting mechanisms, with wide gear ratios, and many producers could not do justice to this requirement.

The company Weiss & Co. Reform Fahrradwerke from Stuttgart also produced in the 1920s a recumbent that was very similar to the J-Bike. They opted for the proven chain drive. By strongly ovalizing the front chainring, the engineers created an energy-saving way of powering the bike.

Symptomatic of all recumbent bike development until the 1970s is the absence of commonality. Cooperation among engineers was unheard of through the early years. Nor were new designs developed from already existing ones. The development of the recumbent bicycle correspondingly proceeded slowly and went up in smoke time and again.

## Georges and Charles Mochet

A milestone in HPV history is found in the inventions of Frenchman Charles Mochet. Before WW2, he built light vehicles with either engines or pedal drive. One day, he made a cart with a pedal drive for his son. His wife had encouraged him, because she thought that ordinary bicycling was too dangerous for little Georges. Papa Charles tested his construction and fell in love with the ecstasy of motorless speed. He soon realized that a market for bikes like

*The "Jaray" bike was the first recumbent that had commercial success in German-speaking areas. Ladies' versions were available with a child's seat.*

this existed, because automobiles were still too costly for most people, although they certainly longed for a vehicle with the comfort of a car.

He made vehicles with a pedal drive designed for two people sitting next to each other which were to be much cheaper than an automobile, and for which the maintenance work would only be that of two bikes. The result had four wheels and a lightweight body made of sheet metal.

At the beginning of the 1930s the demand for his vehicles was rising continuously and development proceeded apace. Charles Mochet's plans were always very lengthy, but then everything was also thoroughly thought through. He himself said: "Something that looks simple is beautiful."

Discussions with the public eventually caused Georges Mochet to produce a vehicle with three wheels, and later with just one seat. That recumbent tricycle had a wheelbase of 57" and 19.5" wheels. The crank bearing was behind and above the front wheel, and power was transferred from the crank to an intermediate drive under the seat then to the rear wheel.

A two-wheeled model was also built and called the "Velocar." It had a seat 22" above the ground, which was tiltable and horizontally adjustable, right in front of the rear wheel. The crank was located a further 3" higher. A shaft connected the 15"-wide handlebar with a universal-joint at the top of the headset of the fork.

At first, French bike racer Henri Lemoine tested this bicycle. Whether it was because of the ridicule of his sports comrades or the bike itself, Lemoine lost his interest after a few rides and turned back to his racing bike.

Then Francis Faure tested the bike. He is said to be the first pro racer who was really interested in this type of bike, and the first who was willing to train on it.

He received only laughter from his friends as well, but when he accelerated on this bike, he left everybody behind, even though he was only a second-class track racing professional. His colleagues could only follow him with their eyes, flabbergasted: there was no draft. The low construction made riding in the lee impossible.

After testing, Mochet wondered whether his bike might conform with the official rules of bicycle racing. On October 26, 1932, he wrote to the UVF (L'Union Velocipedique de France) to find out which conditions his machine must fulfill in order to be admitted to the record races and racing in general. The officials of the UVF eased his doubts in a reply on December 27, 1932, and approved the bike, because it did not have any device for reducing air resistance, which would have been forbidden according to the rules.

Georges Mochet now set out to beat the one-hour record held by Oscar Egg. Faure, his driver, accomplished this on July 15, 1933 at the Parc des Princes Velodrome in Paris. On that day, Faure rode 27.9 miles (45.1 km)—a triumphant new world record. Five years would pass before a racer on an "ordinary" racing bike was able to reach an average of 28 mph.

The record is so much more amazing when you take into account that Francis Faure did not belong to the cycling elite. *Cycling* magazine described him as "having no pretensions as a star speedman."

The record lasted barely two months. On September 9, 1933, Marcel Berthet, who was already 47 years old, managed to go 48.604 kilometers on a faired ordinary racing bike. This record caused some people to question the UCI whether such bicycles complied with the rules for admission.

At this time, Charles Mochet wrote a letter to the UCI in which he stated his posi-

*Construction sketch of the Velocar (drawing: Bernd Kessler)*

| Mochet: Touring model of 1936 | |
|---|---|
| Wheelbase: | 57" |
| Seatheight: | 22" |
| Wheel diameter: | 20" |
| Handlebar height: | 40" |
| Seat width: | 14" |
| Crankarm length: | 170 mm |
| Chainring: | 46 tooth |
| Intermediate gears: | 18/22 tooth |

tion about their impending decision. He thought it was unjust that the rules should be changed. "What is the recumbent bicycle being reproached for? That its rider lays on his back? Advancements are characteristic for technical sports, that is but natural, and everybody benefits! Everybody can pick his bike, buy a recumbent model, build one or have one built. The idea of special races for recumbent vehicles is unjust, because races exist to find out who and what is better. If the races are separated, it will be impossible to show that the recumbent bike is better! Therefore it should be allowed to participate. A prohibition violates the rule of fair play and simple logic. How can any titles be distributed in the future, if one knows that there are new and better things? If the recumbent bicycle is a mistake, it will disappear just as it has arrived, and it will be soon forgotten. But if Chance decides that it represents progress from which riders benefit, then I am sure that the UCI does not want to take responsibility for preventing the recumbent bicycle from proving itself! In this hope he [the delegate to whom this letter is addressed] should act accordingly!"

Even in street races the unfaired "Velocar" was successful. The professional Spanish racing cyclist Paul Morand was engaged by Mochet in 1934 and won the Paris-Limoges race against ordinary racing bikes.

On February 3, 1934, a questionable discussion took place at the 58th UCI Congress, followed by a vote. The debate was about the rules which were to define the form and character of racing bikes.

Martin, an amateur racing cyclist, rode a recumbent bicycle around the conference table to demonstrate that such bikes were comfortable, safe and usable. A representative from England predicted a great future for this design.

But the Italian Bertolini held a different opinion. "This is not a bike," he said, but he could not give a reason for his opinion when

*The 'HPV people' knew already in the 30s that a trip into nature on a recumbent was great. (photo: Mochet)*

the others inquired after his motives. The Frenchman Rousseau supported the Italian. He also thought that a recumbent bicycle did not conform to the definition of a bicycle.

The recumbent bicycle, as well as many other bicycle concepts, was excluded at this time from official races by a new definition of the racing bicycle. From this point on, a separate category was made that applied to bikes which failed to comply with the usual bicycle regulations. The category was thus divided into two classes, one for vehicles with aerodynamic adaptations, the other for those with no adaptations, but limited to diamond-frame ordinaries. These changes were ratified by a vote of 58 to 46.

Even then, there were nagging rumors that the vote might have ended differently if Mochet and Faure had united a bigger lobby behind them, or if famous riders had achieved the records.

To assess the situation at that time, one has to remember that the recumbent bicycle was admitted in 1932 by the UVF with the remark that it did not have any added aerodynamic parts. In 1932, when the bike had only briefly and insignificantly been in the

*Plassat, Lemoine and Francis Faure, held by his brother Benoit Faure, at a velodrome on February 20, 1934. Probably this was one of the last races of recumbents against racing bikes, because six weeks later the UCI prohibited mixed competitions. Boxing world-champion Al Brown fired the starting pistol. (Photo: Mochet)*

spotlight, the officials did not see a reason for a prohibition. In 1933, when the bike achieved a sensational record, suddenly things looked different, and this "weird" bike condemned all subsequent models to

*Caricature from* Auto, *February 20, 1934.*
*Speech balloon: "Live happy, live horizontal!"*
*Caption: Francis Faure, winner of the Vel d'Hiv' race, agrees to his fate.*

live in its shadow. Admitting the "Velo Horizontale" might have meant the end of the "Diamond Frame" era.

In the press, especially in the biweekly French bike magazines of high circulation, the decision by the 58th Congress of the UCI was thought to be important, even before the vote. Caricatures and sarcastically-humorous articles questioned the appropriateness of the recumbent bicycle, or gossiped about the hunchbacked bikers on "old-fashioned" racing bikes, or they depicted Faure sleeping on his Velocar at a record-setting pace.

While the majority of the UCI voted against the recumbent bicycle, the print media offered a different picture. Advocates and enemies used the weapons of reporting and commentary. Thus the interested reading public of cyclists whose sporting future depended on the decision, developed a multilayered and wide field of opinions.

In the German magazine *Der Radfahrer* ("The Cyclist") issue of December 20, 1934, the column "Peter Pedal" from an English magazine was discussed. It told of a "revolutionary deed that will not be without consequences in the field of biking." Additionally it remarked: "In any case, one is convinced that the Velocar is, in France and Paris, the bike of the future, and that it will replace today's bike types. Maybe the French are correct in their assumptions, especially when we think back to all the difficulties the high bike had to fight against when it was introduced."

Some papers performed thorough research and made sensational discoveries. A newspaper article from December, 1933 mentions a recumbent bicycle that was seen, according to the text, in Paris in 1914: "The origins of the horizontally-ridden bike, even today, have not been traced. It is known for certain that this machine dates back to a much earlier period than two years ago, when professional racing on it became more common. The photo which we have reproduced here should assuage all doubts. In 1914, a young Italian named Guglielmo drove to Paris equipped with an awkward device that clearly reminds us of our Velocar. As he could not make his invention flourish in Italy, he tried to market it in Paris. He met a Monsieur Benaben, who laid the foundation. But then the war came. Monsieur Benaben, a captain of infantry, was killed right at the beginning, and the invention lay fallow...."

Despite the UCI's decision, which came into force on April 1, 1934, Charles Mochet continued to experiment and construct. He died on June 3, 1934. From then on Georges Mochet continued the work. He built a special recumbent bicycle to be used with a fairing. The front wheel was made smaller and the seat was lowered to only 12" above the ground. And again it was Francis Faure as test rider on the racetrack at the Vel d'Hiver in Paris....

On this four-kilometer-long track he made his first run without a fairing. It took him 5 minutes and 20 seconds, which put him at the pace of a racing cyclist.

For the next attempt Faure used the fairing. With this change, he gained 2 mph, and he managed at the end to reach a speed of 30.8 mph despite of the weight of the 22-pound fairing.

Francis Faure was surprised by the good handling of the horizontal bike even though it was so heavy and, due to the fairing, so big.

The fairing was altered once more for the next attempt—the openings toward the ground were minimized. Now, the 4 km test track could be ridden in 4.32 minutes (33 mph).

Mochet realized the significance of the fairing and tried to gain more seconds by continued optimization. The lacquer fairing surface was smoothed and polished. Thanks to such slipperiness, the 55 kmh-hurdle (34

*"A bicycle, as ridden by Francis Faure, enables you to practice in the horizontal, half asleep." (from a badly-preserved excerpt of a Danish paper)*

*"I like this position a lot, but isn't it possible to put a small engine underneath?" (from a French newspaper)*

*Three-quarter profile of a Velocar "Tourist." (photo: Ingo Kollibay/Bike Museum Einbeck)*

mph) was surpassed by 0.4 kmh. Now an official record attempt was supposed to follow, but it failed because the air stream caused problems with the pilot's eyes, since his head was exposed outside the fairing. For sensitivity—and more speed—it was decided that the pilot should ride with a fairing that encompassed his head.

With the final model of fairing, Francis Faure was able to achieve a time of 4 minutes and 20 seconds (56.5 kmh / 35.1 mph) on the Mochet recumbent.

Before WW2 there was a duel for The Hour called the King's Competition. Berthet, the former professional race cyclist had set the world record at 49.994 kmh (31.1 mph) with a fully-faired upright racing bike (Velodyne No.1) in 1933. Who would be the first to exceed 50 kilometers (31 miles) in an hour? Mochet and his rider and Berthet each wanted victory for their side.

On March 5, 1939, Faure and Mochet went to the official racetrack of Vincennes, close to Paris. Francis Faure was victorious, finishing a distance of 50.337 kilometers in sixty minutes. At the end of the 1930s, an ordinary unfaired racing bike had only reached an average hour speed of 45.84 kmh (28.48 mph).

This record remained unbroken until 1971. Georges Mochet was satisfied with the success and decided to produce the Velocar for sale.

The demand rose during the war years, when people had even less money for a "real" car but were still looking for a vehicle that was more advanced than a normal bike. This demand was also taken advantage of by the few other recumbent bicycle producers who arrived on the scene—Triumph Moller, Cyclo Ratio and Sofacykel.

*A Chopper/Cruiser from the 30s, the Danish "Sofacykel" from 1935. Not a real recumbent in the true sense, it nonetheless had a special position on the bike market and can, historically-speaking, be categorized as a semi-recumbent. The handling is extremely slow due to the shallow head-tube angle. A spring dampens fork-flop when turning.*

# Other European Producers of the 1930s

The activities of Charles and Georges Mochet dominated the 1930s. However, there were numerous other recumbent bicycles in France and the rest of Europe. From the Velocar's homeland came the "Sport-Plex" long wheelbase (LWB) recumbent. Also, a Frenchman named M. Villard made a recumbent that was specially tailored for transporting and delivering newspapers. The basic construction resembles the Triumph Moller. Under the steering tubes, there is a box for papers. The low position of the paper carrier puts the center of gravity close to the ground, for easy on-the-job handling.

Companies in England also experimented with the idea of riding bicycles in a lying or sitting position.

The British have always been innovative bike developers: the pedal drive, the first butted steel frame tubes, and the crossed spoke can be attributed to them. In August, 1934, the technical expert of the English bike magazine *Cycling*, A. C. Davidson, presented a homemade recumbent bicycle which consisted mostly of standard bicycle components. Only two weeks later, F. H. Grubb went public with what he claimed to be the "first English recumbent cycle." He was a well-known British frame builder. His bike weighed approximately 30 lbs., had two 20-inch wheels, and a wheelbase of 60". At 75 degrees, the head tube angle was relatively steep. The fork trail added up to 2.5". The bike was a long wheelbase recumbent with indirect steering and an upright seat only 16" above the ground. Since the crank was even lower than the seat the pedals could touch the street during turns. Leg-length adjustment was accomplished with an adjustable seat. The bike was sold under the name "Kingston Recumbent."

In the summer of 1935, Jack Sibbitt built

*Velocar "Tourist"—close-up of the steering joint, which was delicate and used to wear out easily, resulting in a lot of play in the steering. (photo: Ingo Kollibay/Bike Museum Einbeck)*

a recumbent prototype. In October of the same year, *Cycling* reports the following about the Paris bike salons: "On display were a multiplicity of horizontals as well as the Alcyon horizontal tandem."

In Denmark, Holger Moller, who had been working in the automobile industry for 20 years as a steering expert, developed a

*Velocar "Tourist"—close up view of an intermediate drive. To adjust chain tension, you could slide the cogs on the main frame-tube. (photo: Ingo Kollibay/Bike Museum Einbeck)*

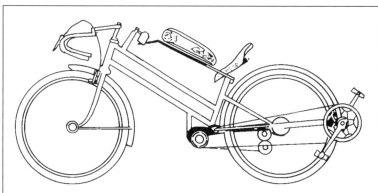

*According to the press, this belly recumbent from the Dynacycle company was supposed to be an improvement of the famous Velocar. In practice, however, it did not succeed.*

long recumbent with a steering wheel. A steering shock-absorber gave a quiet ride on the rough roads of the time. Clever construction enabled riders to adjust the bike to their size. The inventor called his bike a "family bike," and it was built by the Grant company. The bike museum at Oldenburg displays a model with wheel suspension. In cooperation with an English company, this bicycle was also distributed in Britain under the name "Triumph Moller."

In 1934, one could also buy the "Cyclo" in England, which was a long recumbent bicycle with over-seat steering and 20-inch wheels. The technical innovation of that model was that it had the first Cyclo two-speed chain shifter.

In the same year in which the Triumph recumbent entered the market, the Cyclo Gear Company itself presented a short-wheelbase recumbent bicycle. This model was sold under the name "Cyclo Ratio." It was based on the "Ravat Horizontale" from France which had already been successfully marketed there.

In 1936, Frenchman F. Albert Raymont registered the Ravat as a patent in England. He exhibited it at the Bicycle Salon in London. However, it was driven from the market by the Cyclo Gear Company.

The pilots on the Cyclo Ratio were very good at track competitions and could also readily climb the British mountains, not the least because of the high tech equipment of the bikes. These bikes were equipped with the excellent Cyclo four-speed shift. An eccentric, adjustable crank bearing (used nowadays on tandems to adjust chain tension for the synchronization chain) sufficed for the fine-tuning between rider and bike.

The rear brake was also very interesting and resembles Shimano's aero-brake of the 1980s.

Taking into account the necessarily longer chain, builders found it difficult to provide enough chain tension. This problem caused

*The 1934 Cyclo recumbent had 20-inch tires and two gears. (photo: Mark Hall Cycle Museum)*

| *Ravat: "Cyclo Ratio"* | |
| --- | --- |
| Rear wheel: | 27.75" |
| Front wheel: | 18.4" |
| Seat height: | 27" |
| Crank height: | 28" |
| Handlebar height: | 47" |
| Wheelbase: | 32" |
| Tube diameter | .75" x .4" (oval) |
| Frame length: | 66" |
| Weight: | 32-35 lbs |

builders to add an intermediate gear-shaft, turning one long chain system into two short, manageable ones. In general, the front wheel was smaller than the rear and frame dimensions evolved in the direction of higher stability.

Both British models had a seat which was a combination of a regular saddle and a simple backrest. All models sold badly in England. The 1936 "Kingston" was not an exception, as the tall wheels, low seat and intermediate shaft created a look that racing cyclists loathed.

Apart from commercial attempts, there were private initiatives. The British Arthur Baxter, for instance, hand-produced some recumbent bikes. He drafted plans for the rocker-arm drive, creating three different models ("Town," "Country," and "Racing").

When it comes to racing, one should mention Oscar Egg. This legend of bike racing developed his own one-off recumbents for record-attempt rides at about this time.

Throughout the 1930s, the "Sofacykle," created by Hænsler, was available in Denmark. The position while riding on this bike is basically an evolutionary midpoint between the regular bike and the recumbent. The chainstays are 25" long, the seat-tube

*Triumph Moller, 1936: The semi-recumbent position of this stately bike is coming back into style these days. Back in the 30s, it garnered a lot of attention, especially in Scandinavia.*

angle is a very relaxed 40 degrees, and the handlebar is extremely high, reaching far back. It is reminiscent of the stretched-out cruiser popular on the beach scene today and hints as well to today's models of 'semi-recumbent' bikes.

*Advertised by the frame builder F. H. Grubb as the first British recumbent, the Kingston recumbent was sold in 1934-35. The main traits of the modern recumbent are recognizable.*

*In the year 1936, Cyclo Gear Company presented the "Cyclo Ratio," a short recumbent with an improved four-gear-shifter.*

*To handle the play in the chain, an intermediate cogwheel was added. (photos: Mark Hall Cycle Museum)*

# Why did the recumbent disappear?

One of the most interesting questions for recumbent bike historians is why it disappeared so completely from the end of the 1930s to the 1970s, despite its commercial production and the great interest of the media. It is difficult to come up with conclusive answers. It seems as if various circumstances coincided. One of them is certainly that the quality of roadway was seldom ideal for a recumbent without suspension. The common cobblestone pavement and dirt and gravel roads did not make laid-back cycling a smooth, easily-controlled pleasure. Recumbents also need multi-gear shifting, which only existed with at most 4 or 5 gears in the years before and after World War II. A gearshift in those days made a bike expensive and required high maintenance—two characteristics an everyday vehicle should not have, not at that time, nor today.

Today, the problems with recumbent bicycles from the 1930s are solved. Existing gearshifts leave no wish unfulfilled, the streets are of high quality, and recumbent suspension options are equal to the best offered among all bike types.

The breakthrough appears to be happening, but is still somewhat bogged down. Why is that so? The prohibitions of the UCI and the triathlon federation are a factor—they prevent direct comparisons and deny the chance for widely known sporting successes.

On the other hand, the stable appearance of the diamond-frame ordinary bike, which has shaped people's perception for 100 years, causes skepticism about strange designs. It is difficult to overcome this uneasiness. Riders, builders, clubs and shops for recumbent bicycles know about this problem only too well and untiringly perform pioneer public relations work.

Other trends seem to be working in favor

of recumbents. Wild shapes and special functions are popping up and becoming popular in the road, triathlon and mountain-bike scenes. So much so that normal diamond frames are losing market share to monocoque, composite, beam and Y-shaped frames. The establishment is finally becoming more open-minded. Lastly, the physical stresses of riding uprights are becoming more apparent and a rider is often looking for ways to relieve a painful back, butt, hands, feet or neck—which points to recumbents, with their reduced pressure-points.

## Paul Rinkowski

While the activities of the builders and tinkerers in Europe sharply decreased after the war and recumbent bicycles were only available intermittently, American activities were much more constant. Even after the war, Americans had recumbent bikes. The upright bicycle has at times been as popular in the States as in Europe. But the role of armchair-bikes was still much smaller than that of diamond-frames. Still, recumbents survived, in a marginal way, through various major bike fashions (e.g. the Cruiser in the 1950s) for decades until the U.S. recumbent renaissance of the mid-Seventies.

During this period, in postwar Europe, Paul Rinkowski of Leipzig, in the former East Germany, played a surprising and singular role in the fields of recumbent research, development and production—with results that had great impact on bicycles in general.

Rinkowski, born in 1915, put all his efforts into increasing bicycle efficiency and making it a viable alternative to the automobile. Although his designs achieved his goals, and would've been appropriate for mass production, the socialist officials of the German Democratic Republic did not see

any need for such a vehicle and rejected the idea. Nonetheless, the design quality of existing prototypes are testimony to the innovative talent of their inventor.

Rinkowski can be seen as the most important developer of HPVs during the post-war era because of his untiring work, for which he sacrificed all his spare time and money. It is without doubt that his family, in particular his wife, deserves praise for enabling Rinkowski's successes.

Rinkowski's engineering studies (1931-

*Paul Rinkowski   (photo: Rinkowski)*

34) built the basis for his work on the recumbent. Even before the foundation of the GDR, Rinkowski started to develop his bikes, beginning in 1947.

He experimented with full-body drives, because 15 percent more power could be generated. During a day of bike racing in the Bruno-Plache Stadium, he demonstrated such a bike. During the first lap laughter echoed from the stands. With a sprint in front of the stands, he completed the second round to bravos and applause. Eventually, he dropped the idea of a full-body drive, because only few riders could handle it. Wrist-controlled steering contributed to the difficulty, so that the second, improved model could still only be handled by two riders.

For almost four decades, he contributed to recumbent bicycle development and created his own concepts, disregarding existing recumbent approaches. Actually, he worked on his bicycles without knowing that the rest of the world was researching the same subject. He was completely alone and unsupported in his field and in technical production. The supply situation in the GDR was as horrible as one might expect, especially for private people who wanted to do their own "little tinkering." This forced Rinkowski to rely on his creativity and improvisational skills to produce or find the necessary parts.

For uniform stability he chose 20-inch wheels for front and back. The greater rolling resistance of the 20-inchers as compared to the usual 27/28-inch wheels did not discourage him. On the contrary, he tried to minimize this resistance.

To improve the everyday user-friendliness of the bikes he decided to forgo the use of tires with inner-tubes. To achieve both amazing goals—reduce rolling resistance and improve reliability—there was only one option: build the tires himself. The result of this project would revolutionize wire-rimmed bike tires.

Rinkowski's tiny bicycle garage soon resembled a giant spider web as he worked on creating his tires—the world's first radials. A hundred meters of thread crisscrossed the workshop. First the thread was dipped in rubber solution then led through innumerable guideways. In this way the solution had sufficient time to dry and to acquire the required degree of hardness. He also had beaded clincher rims turned from wood.

He secured his research with a GDR economic patent in 1954. Rinkowski's radial tire for bicycles was determined to be superior to the diagonal tire. He developed the radial tire long before it entered the automobile industry. Tests showed that two-tube tires of ordinary construction and size had a rolling resistance of 6 Newtons. To overcome the resistance of Rinkowski's tires only required 3 Newtons. He himself stated the following figures: "The patented recumbent bicycle tires under burden have a resistance of about 240 grams, while a pair of tube tires has a resistance of at least 420 grams. I know this so accurately because I

photo: Rinkowski

have developed a rolling-resistance measuring device that is now the property of the DHFK-Academic Sports Club in Leipzig."

Rinkowski's design resulted in 1.5 miles more per hour in practice compared with a racing upright, if the bikes were powered with 60 watts (which equals riding 12-14 mph on an upright). This includes the general advantage of the improved aerodynamics of the recumbent position.

He stayed with and perfected one basic design of recumbent until the end of his life in 1986. The design has been protected by patent since 1953. "After the basic configuration was determined, development did not stop. Test rides were conducted for many years to collect data as to frame, fork and nodal-point stability," as details were ever more fine-tuned. "We did long treks with traveling days of over 200 km—it goes without saying that the street quality greatly differed from today."

But Rinkowski was not only occupied with recumbent bicycles. He also built three- and four-wheelers, children's bikes and a camping bike, which is telescopic so that it would fit into the trunk of Trabants (very small, locally-built GDR-era cars)—it had telescoping forks and the legendary tires, and was created circa 1963.

Around 1958 he motorized some of his recumbents with Mokick engines—they whizzed at 35 mph through the countryside.

On the "Day of the Republic" in 1956, one Rinkowski recumbent was allowed to participate in a local county bike race. Dieter Schipke started free from any serious competitors and crossed the finish line after a solo ride with a margin of seven minutes. Such a showing of new technology, speed and sports potential only resulted recumbents being banned from racing with normal bikes.

The foreign press interpreted the innovation a little differently: the West-German

*Model with full body drive. (photo: Rinkowski)*

magazine *Radmarkt* ("Bike Market") reported about the Rinkowski recumbent after the IFMA bike show in 1962 that "...regarding all the novelties and further developments which were presented there was nothing that could compare to the recumbent bicycle that the Leipzig engineer [Rinkowski] has been working on since 1948."

Unfortunately, the Western appreciation did not help him very much as his field of activity was limited to the GDR due to political reasons.

Only a circle of personal friends, relatives and people of like mind appreciated his achievements. From time to time the press mentioned this "crazy" engineer and made use of his small sensations and curiosities, with TV appearances in 1981 and 1984. But overall, Paul Rinkowski remained misunderstood in his intention and his work by officials and the media.

Rinkowski's four-wheeled vehicle was loaded with technical finesse: indexed shifting, reverse gear, independent four-wheel suspension and a differential drive for the rear wheels were standard equipment. This

HPV, which he called the "Sesselvelo," had a complete fairing made from frame tubing and sheet tin. It was a high speed fairing like that on Mochet's racing Velocars, but the aim was a different: a bike for everyday use.

He did extensive aerodynamic research, as well, and soon achieved good results—which were put into regular practice only years later.

For instance, he equipped his Sesselvelos with disc wheels in 1955 to make cleaning easier and to perfect the aerodynamics. It was another twenty years before disc wheels were first used in international bike races.

The GDR bicycle sport federation finally became interested in his talents, and he did research for their racing bikes. One of his ideas was flat-bladed spokes, which have become common in the meantime, and which help to bring about the decisive thousandth of a second sometimes necessary for victory.

Using meticulous hand work, Paul Rinkowski built super-light and fast tubular sew-up tires to the great delight of the biking elite of the GDR, and with these, too, he contributed to their international successes. His tires had an excellent reputation and were lovingly called "Rinkis."

In this way, Rinkowski finally became a sought-after man in GDR bike sports. However, there was still neither support nor understanding for the genius of his recumbent designs.

In 1962, a Rinkowski recumbent was used to ride the 50 miles between Leipzig and Chemnitz in 2 hours 45 minutes. That might not sound very fast today, but the roads back then were in very bad condition, with all the smoothness of mountain-bike trails.

The following year a comparison race between a Rinkowski recumbent and a racing bike was supposed to take place. Rinkowski was confident. But the race was canceled by bike sport officials: they certainly had the touring race of 1956 in mind.

GDR race organizations continued to refuse to authorize a strong racing cyclist for recumbent test rides on the track. Paul Rinkowski had built a track model in 1955. It had suspension, a handlebar mounted under the seat and an extremely small, handmade cogwheel. He calculated that his bike would be 4 mph faster than a normal track bike.

Rinkowski decided to equip his bikes with suspension since bumps are transmitted more directly to one's body on a reclining bike, and because the body's natural biomechanical springs in the form of spine, knee and arm joints cannot work due to such a position. Small telescoping springs inside the fork and rear supports, meticulously built by hand, provided convenient comfort. The easily adjustable, thin plywood seat was air-cushioned with old inner-tubes until the builder managed to get hold of some foam rubber.

One has always to highlight the circumstances under which Rinkowski realized his ideas. In all areas, material was scarce, especially for private projects.

In dire straits, he sent a petition to the office of Walter Ulbricht with a request to support his work with 830 East German Marks. He also attached a request for financing the production of more of his recumbents. Both pleas were rejected.

# David Gordon Wilson, Chester Kyle and the IHPVA

While the tinkerers and bicycle-freaks in Western Europe were each working on their own, a group of enthusiasts in America got together under Prof. Chester Kyle with the goal of breathing life back into the pre-war idea of finding extra speed and function in alternative bike designs.

They founded the IHPVA (International Human Powered Vehicle Association) on March 28, 1976, and they're still active. The association's aim is to promote and develop muscle-driven ground, water and air vehicles without any kind of limiting regulation.

Kyle offered a seminar on bicycle engineering at the California State University of Long Beach in the summer of 1973. Despite the great number of students enrolled (two!), the seminar started. Kyle directed the main focus to be on rolling and air resistance. The goal was to determine the resistances of the various bike types.

Within the university building, the researchers proved their zeal by setting up a test track. They equipped a long corridor with electronic ground sensors to measure elapsed time.

They soon demonstrated that a faired bike was faster and rolled farther. In 1974 the students and Prof. Kyle finished building a full fairing that they mounted to an ordinary racing bike, completely enclosing it (but for wheel-holes) and smoothing all its exposed area into an aerodynamic shape.

In November, 1974 the American Olympic athlete Ron Skarin reached a speed of 43 mph in the 200-meters sprint on what they called the "Faired Bike." That year, Kyle met Jack Lambie, who was working on aerodynamic bikes at the same time, and who had calculated that it was possible to reach 50 mph in the 200-meters-sprint. The

two agreed on a meeting to further test various bikes—and the International Human Power Speed Championship was born (April 5, 1974).

To reduce air resistance further, it was necessary to reduce the frontal area of the bike to a minimum. As the faired possibilities of the traditional racing bike were limited by an extensive frontal area, the group turned to the recumbent bicycle. Here they had no preconceived frame designs or construction principles—just an empty field for research and experimentation.

The tinkerer's and do-it-yourself-builder's main interest was at this time still focused on the high speed sprint. These engineers worked towards the ultimate speed which is possible to attain with human power on earth.

By 1977 a fully-faired recumbent bicycle built by Bill Watson reached 46.1 mph.

*David Gordon Wilson on the Avatar 2000. He is the pioneer of the safe bike. His research soon led to the long recumbent. (photo: D. G. Wilson)*

Shortly afterwards the sports doctor Allan Abbott reached 49.1 mph in his "cigar" bike. With his self-built high-speed vehicle he demonstrated that he had mastered the art of aerodynamics. He had already satisfied his desire for pure speed four years earlier, when he rode a bike for one mile at 139 mph in the sheltered zone behind a race car at the Bonneville Flats, on August 15, 1973.

Years later he surprised experts with the construction of his Flying Fish. He developed this hydrofoil water-HPV with a friend and reached speeds that were higher than those of a world-class sculler.

Events went head-over-heels when the builders put their vehicles on three or four wheels. This allowed vehicles to be built much lower. Seats dropped down between the wheels almost to the ground (a seat-height of one inch wasn't uncommon). The pedal radius was also lowered almost to ground level. Additionally, builders experimented with arm drives and tandems or triplets. Riders were positioned every which way to try to make the most aero shape with the most power.

Reports from the IHPVA during this pioneer time evoke the impression that this era was all about speed. This impression must be partly revised. In doing so, one has to consider the work of David Gordon Wilson above all. In 1968 he announced the "Man powered land transportation competition." Bikes were supposed to be improved in every sense, and speed was not the primary criterion. Safety and usability were top priorities. Two participants from Poland brought creations to the competition. Stanislaw Garbien presented a fully-suspended recumbent bicycle with medium-long wheelbase and two equal-sized wheels.

Kazimierz Borkowski demonstrated a recumbent bicycle equipped with a rowing drive. Borkowski was an employee of the National Bike Factory of Poland.

The competition was won by a recumbent bicycle named "Bicar Mark III" by W. G. Lychard. The bike had two 16-inch wheels and a shaft drive with an elliptical crank chainring. It was furnished with a pneumatic seat and direct over-seat steering. The relatively low seat height of 16" was remarkable. David Gordon Wilson then modified its plan and sent a drawing to Fred Willkie in Berkley, California, who had had an exchange of letters with Wilson earlier, asking him for more ideas for bikes.

Wilson enclosed some money provided by a fund for the support of muscle force development, set up by Paul Dudly White, who had died in 1965.

Willkie built the bike, tested it and got pains in his upper thighs. In a nutshell, he didn't like it. It was a short recumbent, resembling the Cyclo Ratio or the Ravat. He called it the "Green Planet Special I." Historically, one can see this bike as a link between today's short wheelbase bikes and the short recumbents of the 1930s.

Wilson revised the plan a second time and got a second report: Willkie greatly enjoyed riding the new vehicle. However, a move prevented him from riding it much, and he sold it to Wilson, who then forgot about it, taking it out years later only to show it to his students as a design example. That evening he risked riding it home from campus and was pleasantly surprised.

After some modifications the "Green Planet Special II" turned into the "Wilson-Willkie." It was still not perfect and was prone to a nose-dive while breaking hard.

In 1978, frame-builders Richard Forrestall and Harold Maciejewski constructed the "Avatar 1000," an improved Wilson-Willkie short recumbent. Despite a 25-cm longer wheelbase, the bike was still front-heavy. 62% of rider weight rested on the front wheel. The construction was thought over again and what came out was the "Avatar 2000," a long wheelbase recumbent, born only of the attempt to create a safe, everyday bike.

These two criteria, "safe" and "everyday," describe the aims of a small number of developers and researchers who have merged with the IHPVA. They have not succumbed to the ecstasies of speed of the founders and many present members. They work for the development of the bike as an everyday vehicle, as an alternative to or replacement for the automobile, and as a safe vehicle. This is an orientation with many historic precedents, and which has a great future ahead of it.

The idea of the practical long recumbent bike was received enthusiastically. The Avatar 2000 was launched in 1979 with no advertising but lots of media interest and soon hundreds were sold. Copies or further similar developments quickly followed—like the Swiss "Wiglet" from Fateba in 1982, or the bikes from Radius in Germany, among others.

*The first "Vector" in European hands. In 1982, Wolfgang Gronen got hold of a model like this and dominated the European HPV sprinting competitions with vice world champion Gerhard Scheller for a long time. (photo: Mochet)*

| Vector '80 | Singletrack | / Tandem |
|---|---|---|
| Length: | 116" | 151" |
| Width: | 25" | 25" |
| Height: | 32" | 33" |
| Weight: | 51 lbs | 75 lbs |
| Frontal area: | 0.424 | 0.437 |
| Cw-value: | 0.11 | 0.13 |

The Wilson-Willkie animated a lot of bicycle "freaks." Milt Turner's "Hypercycle" entered the market at about the same time with a frame-set for the sensational price of $200, and sold about 1000 units by the beginning of the Eighties. He had prototypes in existence in 1978-80. Turner builds the "Laid Back" today. The Hypercycle and Avatar 2000 were sold from the Sports Warehouse in Ohio (which later became Bike Warehouse...then Bike Nashbar). Production of the Hypercycle ceased in 1983.

In this early period three companies were launched whose first bikes, despite all the amazing change since then, are all still popular: Easy Racers' "Tour Easy," Lightning's "P-38" and the RANS "Stratus."

# Faster, Faster...the History of HPV Races and Records

The racing cohort of the American IHPVA was greatly inspired by the Abbott Prize in 1978. Allan Abbott promised to award $2500 to the first HPV which would exceed the national speed limit of 55 mph (88.5 kmh) in the 200-meter sprint. The prize could also be won if a single rider beat 54 mph.

It's worth noting that for upright bikes the records have remained fairly stable at 46 mph for the 200-meter sprint, 35 miles for The Hour, and 533 miles for the 24-Hour (22.2 mph). (The UCI Hour record was relegated back to 30.7 miles in 2000, as set by Eddy Merckx in 1972, now slightly improved by Boardman. A new "Absolute" category was added for bikes limited to other UCI specs, then changed again to

"Best Performance." Confusing, indeed.)

The victorious HPV, "White Lightning," built by students from Northrup University, who made use of the aeronautic engineering department's know-how and in-house wind tunnel, far-surpassed the prize's speed limits to claim the cash. White Lightning was put together with more than 2500 man hours—and cost about $3000. The bike is 18.5 feet long, 36" high and 23" wide. The three student designers—Chris Dreke, Don Guichard and Tim Brummer—used a symmetric NASA wing profile to give the vehicle its form. Brummer is the inventor and

| Specifications of *Blue Bell:* | |
| --- | --- |
| Length: | 115" |
| Width: | 23" |
| Height: | 56.5" |
| Weight: | 42 lbs |
| Frontal area: | 0.424 sq meter |
| Surface area: | 6.67  sq meter |

producer of today's popular Lightning line of recumbents. Butch Stinton and Jan Russell rode this tandem vehicle on its record run. It was the first HPV to exceed the 50-, 55-, and 60-mph barriers with 61.04 mph/94.34 kmh.

A year later, in 1979, the first single rider vehicle beat the 50-mph-barrier piloted by American Fred Markham.

In 1980, the "Vector," a child of the team coordinated by Al Voigt, a major designer in the airplane industry, approached the 65-mph mark. The Vector tandem (Grylls/Barszewski) sprinted up to 62.889 mph—only 2.111 mph under the target.

The two "pilots" sat back to back. While the front pilot steered, the rear pilot also drove a crank with his hands. This theoretically produced 17 per cent more energy.

In this sport, you'll notice a mix of terms coming from different sports. In superfast HPV racing, handling these bikes is something like piloting an airplane—with taxiing, take-off, and use of landing gear. Many riders and builders have an aviation background. (The popular RANS company builds recumbents *and* small airplane kits.) Three-wheeled, fully-faired, fully-suspended HPVs also sometime feel more like race cars than bikes! It was still cycling, but many fields have added their expertise—and terminology—to the world of HPVs.

Markham and Chris Springer gave an impressive demonstration in the Vector tandem when they "drove" California Interstate Highway 5 from Stockton to Sacramento in 49.40 minutes for an average speed of 50.5 mph over the 41.8 miles. This ride took place in highway traffic!

The media attention caught the eye of big business for advertising purposes. The British bike shop chain Halfords, auto accessories producers Brimax, Shimano and DuPont all have supported teams.

In the meantime, the speed wave spilled over to Europe. In 1981, the Aspro Speed Challenge took place in Brighton. And European racers came on strong. For example, the 200-pound English trike "Poppy Flyer" reached a speed of 46.442 mph ('delta' trike: two wheels in rear). The impressive British tandem trike "Dark Horse" gave a convincing ride with 45.129 mph.

Despite these achievements the prize money of 5000£ at this event was won by the dominating U.S. Vector team. "A fine race. It just had the wrong winner," remarked Kyle. "I would have liked a British winner, because competition improves technology. And we want progress!"

A production vehicle attracted attention at this event: the British "Windcheetah." This tadpole trike (2 front wheels, one rear) invented by Mike Burrows, and piloted by Andy Pegg—who uses the bike on a daily basis—won third place in the sprints.

In 1982, Kyle's wish finally came true:

the British "Blue Bell" was the fastest one-man HPV of the world at the 8th IHPSC in Irvine, California. In a 200-meter sprint, it narrowly beat "Easy Rider" and the then-current world champion Vector three-wheeler, with a 1st place speed of 61.91 mph.

A prototype of the Blue Bell fairing had earlier proven that the developer team was on the right track at the IHPVA Speed Trials in Brighton, England. At an average of 46 mph in a longer event it ranked third after Vector and Poppy Flyer.

To come full circle: hiding under the Blue Bell fairing...was an Avatar 2000. This made the victory a sensation among experts. How was it possible that a recumbent bicycle made for everyday use could be faired and beat the Vector which was designed from ground up for maximum human speed?

The secret was that the fairing had amazing aerodynamics. Derek Henden and the Nosey Ferret Racing Team had no access to computers or wind tunnels, but nevertheless they built a fairing that was superior to all others.

It all started in the summer of '82 when the underlying bike was bought by Richard Ballantine, an innovative cycling journalist. The former Australian judge Tim Gartside was to be the pilot. He was unknown in the HPV circle. Up to then he had only participated in two regular bike races.

The gear ratio of the Avatar was modified to be quickly changed by installing a second set of cogs in the form of an intermediate drive, so that it could fit the needs of racing instead of the demands of street riding. The gearing and cadence jumps resembled each other in both versions. Thus a rider who'd trained on the streets could quickly adapt to the highspeed conditions of racing.

The Blue Bell fairing was very light compared to the others, only 6.8 kg, and thus the whole vehicle was lighter—this reduced

*At the beginning of the 80s, the "Poppy Flyer III" was a main competitor of the American Vectors in European races. (photo: Mochet)*

the necessary acceleration power immensely.

The Blue Bell fairing was built precisely to the size of the wheels and of the rider. The bike was equipped with a 17-inch high performance Moulton front wheel instead of a wider mass-produced 16-inch model commonly used. They used a lightweight 700c rear wheel and high pressure tire. The seat was very narrow to reduce the overall width. For the same reason the thumb gear lever was replaced by a handlebar end switch. A 1:8 gear-ratio (thanks to the intermediate drive), wheel covers, and an early-era computer-speedometer finished the bike.

After the competition, the Blue Bell fell twice and was repaired. On the following weekend, the Nosey Ferret Racing Team's baby won the first prize in the San Diego Velodrome Pursuit Race. In the victory lap after the race the rider crashed and the machine was almost totaled.

The reasons for these wrecks were obvious. The fairing had a large side surface area, and the tail was not rounded. Side-winds had an easy target. Additionally, modifications

*Professor Schöndorf teaches vehicle construction at the engineering college in Cologne. Together with his students he built four-wheelers at first, then three-wheelers, and finally he focused on two-wheelers. His "Muscooter" models with suspension ended up being the basis for a serial production recumbent. He says about his own developmental work: "Had I known about the work of Paul Jaray and Charles and Georges Mochet, I could have saved ten years."*

Giving up a wheel had the advantage of a smaller rolling resistance. Moreover, a trike has aerodynamic disadvantages, as air gets compressed and whirled around in the flat zone between vehicle and ground. Valuable seconds are lost.

Two-wheelers are slim—19" wide is usually sufficient for a rider, which is 8" less than a three-wheeler.

At the 1983 Thamesmead Festival of Human Power, near London, another English construction showed the optimization of the single-track idea. "The Bean" by John Kingsbury caught attention, but created even more of a stir later in 1990.

At the 1983 championships in Indianapolis, Blue Bell lost its position as fastest HPV of the world. "Lightning II" by Tim Brummer won the competition at 54.78 mph.

In 1984 the chemical giant DuPont put up a prize of $18,000 for the first muscle-driven vehicle to exceed 65 mph (105 kmh).

The rules were the standard IHPVA rules which stated that tailwinds had to be under 5.5 fps and that a downhill grade could not exceed 0.6667 percent.

*The Hobbythek TV editorial staff sent out almost 70,000 construction plans for this bike in 1985—a boon for the recumbent which has never been repeated.*

for the race changed the distribution of the weight on the wheels from 31/69% to 25/75%, front/back. The front wheel tended to lose traction. In cornering, during braking, or on sandy or wet pavement the problem only got worse.

But with the success of Blue Bell a new era of HPVs began: two-wheelers took over from three-wheelers.

## 1980s Street-Savvy R&D

As an aside, we should state that, again, HPV development in this early period wasn't just about racing. There was global innovation in the 80s in everyday practical bikes. Three excellent European models were also available in addition to the American powerhouses of Easy Racers, Lightning and RANS. These three represent the amazing diversity breaking into the scene.

The Danish "Leitra," a three-wheeled fully-faired recumbent developed by Carl Georg Rasmussen, is remarkable for its orientation toward practical use, for a clever aluminum body that tips forward to allow entry, and for its great safety. Over 125 Leitras now drive around over the world to-

day. The Leitra is still one of only a very few practical multi-track velomobiles on the market. ("Velomobile" meaning an HPV designed to do the work of a car.)

Secondly, there was the "Roulandt" from the Netherlands. This long recumbent bicycle has indirect steering under the seat. Despite good sales, acceptable ride quality, moderate weight and an inexpensive price, the maker had to stop production. A quality error in a supplier's frame-tubing had caused a wave of frame failures.

The third important model of the early Eighties came from Belgium. Under the name "Veleric" Eric Anbergen distributed an extremely well-calculated everyday HPV. The design format is nowadays called a "lowracer" and competes in races with great dominance at the present time. The seat was located between the wheels only 8" above the ground. The chain was led around the 16" front wheel by the 20" high crank which drove a 20" rear wheel. This bike was offered with an optional full fairing with unbreakable Macrolon panels. The drag-coefficient Cw-value was, according to the manufacturer, 0.18. Unfortunately, this bike was also unsuccessful, so production facilities were sold to the German Michael Kügelen. He had the frame produced in Germany and exhibited at the IFMA (1982). Here, the Veleric appeared absolutely exotic. Kügelen remembers: "It took such an effort to explain, that we just could not cope with it. You'd explicitly explain the advantages of a recumbent to one visitor, and you were hardly finished when ten other people asked the same questions over again." He sold about 250 units right after the show, half of them with fairings—amazing for that era!

Yet another recumbent was way ahead of its time. In the March 1984 issue of *Tour* a fully-faired recumbent prototype from Gazelle was presented. The "SST," as it was called, strongly resembled the Veleric—low

seat, high crank—only a rocker-arm drive differentiated the two bikes.

Gazelle was not the only large company with activities in the HPV sector. The producer Union Fröndenberg had contracted with the Italian designer Colani. He developed tandems and single cab vehicles with three and four wheels. But none of these got further than a prototype.

In a surprising turn of events, in 1984 the German TV show "Hobbythek" caused a recumbent sensation which has never been surpassed. A recumbent bicycle was demonstrated on the show, and a simple do-it-yourself plan could be ordered from the TV station. 70,000 plans were sent out in the area of transmission! In the aftermath there was a lively exchange of letters between viewers and the TV station as tinkerers described their improvements, ideas and modifications. As a consequence, the station produced another show about recumbent bikes.

The TV station editors, Peter Brückner and Burkhard Fleischer (today the publishers of the German magazine *ProVelo*) then picked five examples from all the letters

*Karl Georg Rasmussen and his Leitra. More than 125 HPVs of this type are used every day.*

with special ideas and modifications. After the second show 70,000 people again demanded further information, as offered.

In 1985, a circle of friends dedicated to the special mix of sport and innovation that drives the HPV spirit, formed the association "HPV Germany."

Already in 1983, Germans Andreas Fortmeier and Peter Ronge were occupied with recumbent bicycles. They started with short recumbents and arrived—similar to David Gordon Wilson—at the production of a long recumbent. Their customers wanted a bike that was suitable for the city as well as for touring. They fulfilled their goals in 1985 with the "Peer Gynt." Since then, these bikes have attained cult status. In the first year only six bikes were sold. A year later, in 1985, the number rose to 35 bikes—not really a basis for a company, but publicity work and persistence paid off in the years to follow.

In 1992 their company, Radius, reacted to the demand for sporty recumbent bicycles and presented a short model. Then after more than 10 years, they replaced the "Peer Gynt" with a successor model "Viper" in the fall of 1995. Viper has adjustable rear wheel suspension and 20" wheels. Radius was sold at the end of the Nineties.

Also, in the mid-80s, Kurt Pichler of Karlsruhe, founder of Pichlerrad custom bicycles, sold the first of his recumbents.

# More Speed!

In the early summer of 1986, news broke about the winning of the DuPont prize. The dashing American Fred Markham (called "Fast Freddy" ever since) scorched for 200 meters in 6.832 seconds along California Highway 120...for a speed of 65.486 mph. The victorious "Gold Rush," built by Gardner Martin, followed the trends of the time in being one-tracked. The rider could only mount the bike with the assistance of two other people and even so had to twist, as the opening was too small for his shoulders.

An immense amount of work was hidden behind this record. Gardner Martin had used his famous Tour Easy touring recumbent model as the basis for the Gold Rush, although he modified it greatly.

Front end and handlebars were reduced to a minimum so that the rider pedaled while bending far forward. This made for a lower vehicle height, and let the arms pull to increase power as in a regular bike sprint. An aluminum frame, ultra-light Kevlar fairing and other special equipment made for a total weight of only 30 pounds! (14 kg) Markham, who had raced in two Olympics on upright bikes, lived close to Gardner Martin and had already been "team driver" for years. At the end of the Seventies, he was the first solo rider to exceed 50 mph—on a belly bike built by Martin. His biggest rival in the race for 65 mph was thought to be the Allegro delta trike team from Don Witte, which held the 200-meter record with 62.98 mph.

After the Gold Rush was finished, there

*"Hornet"—a fully-suspended short recumbent by the Radius company.*

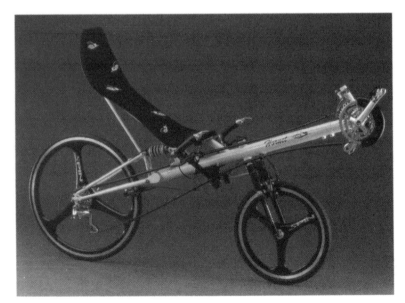

was a first attempt on Columbus Day 1985, which failed. The second weekend in April 1986 revealed a stubborn barrier to breaking the record: the wind could not be stronger than 5.5 fps. Spring breeziness prevented qualifying under IHPVA-regulation conditions.

The weekend of May 9-11, 1986, was supposed to bring the record. Until Saturday night a strong breeze dashed all hopes. On Sunday even the smallest chance was ready to be taken advantage of. At 6 a.m., everybody was on the track...and until 7 p.m. rough winds swept through the valley. But with sunset the wind stopped. Only a tiny breeze accompanied Markham when he made a test ride. Finally the wind said farewell completely, and nothing stood in the way of a record. Fast Freddy dashed at 65.486 miles per hour along the highway and he knew during his ride that he had won the DuPont prize: the drumming inside the fairing had never been so loud.

With the conquering of this barrier, industrial interest in the HPV concept unfortunately sank out of sight. The hand-craftsmen and engineers again had to rely on their own finances for materials and labor.

In 1987 Gerhard Scheller launched an impressive demonstration in the Mosel valley, Germany. He had placed second in the upright UCI World Time Trial championship of '81. He wanted to singlehandedly beat the world 100 km speed record held by a Russian four-man Olympic squad.

On his dramatic ride, set up in a Vector, Scheller managed the distance in 1:31:24. This is 28 minutes less than the four-man team time trial. One has to add that our pilot had to handle rain, valley winds and twisty village streets.

This new Vector team continued the hunt for records, and at the highest bike track of the world, in Bolivia, they started to set new top marks.

The one-track trend continued at the an-

nual European championships in 1988 in Nümbrecht/Cologne. The English Blue Bell (which should have been called Black Bell because of its new color) finished the first of three 200-meter sprints only 0.04 seconds slower than Vector's top time of 8.04 seconds. The second ride was more thrilling: the stopwatch showed 7.92 seconds after Glen Thompson brought Blue Bell through the sensors.

The face of Vector team leader Wolfgang Gronen changed drastically: Nobody had expected an outcome like this. The throne of the Vector hadn't been shaken since the Vector was first brought to Germany in 1982 and since the unbelievable Cw-value of 0.07 (as listed by its builder) had been pared down even further.

Another single-track model contributed to this disturbance, not by its speed of 52.51 mph, but rather by the circumstances of its creation.

"Sweet Surprise" was not only prominent because of its beautiful fairing, but also because of its prehistoric technical components (steel cottered cranks). It was the product of Maciek Kaczmarek of Poland, who had built his cowling extremely accurately and to a high aerodynamic level.

Bad Polish components spoiled the first ride, because the gear shift went on strike at the start. At the end of the event, an ar-

*"Veleric" sold 250 models in 1982. With an extremely high crank bearing and a very low seat it is actually a low recumbent.*

chitecture student named Kosinski, who had only been planned as an emergency backup, replaced the real driver after a fall, and took an unofficial turn around the track. He himself fell and slid through the electric eyes. But an unofficial manual timer showed 58 mph! What remained was the thought of how "Sweet Surprise" would have done with its original driver and proper equipment.

This idea was such a horror to W. Gronen that he engaged Kaczmarek then and there to build a similar vehicle for Vector and his sponsor Union Fröndenberg.

Only a year later, Scheller was riding the new single-track Vector at the European championships in Münster, 1989. But again there was a bike that could easily compete with him. The Dutchman Joost Conijn set the top pace in the 30 km criterium with his early-era home-made carbon-fiber recumbent frame and a windsurfer-sail fabric fairing. Only long racing experience finally got Scheller the victory. He let the Dutchman ride ahead, stayed in the back himself, and only took the lead two laps before the finish. Trailing by a few meters and with an

---

*Easy Racers: "Gold Rush"*

Bicycle weight: 19 lbs—6 speeds, titanium parts, spokes and crankset, aluminum frame, Cro-Mo fork, ultra-high pressure sew-up tires (8 bar front, 10.3 bar rear), polyester plastic shell fairing.
Fairing weight: 10 lbs
Fairing fasteners weight: 2 lbs
Gears: 92 x 11-19 (700c rear wheel)
Height: 51"
Width: 19"
Length: 96"

---

*Results we saw at a recent event...*

| | |
|---|---|
| 5000 m in 5:25:40 min. | = 34.38 mph |
| 1 mile in 1:17:04 min. | = 46.10 mph |
| 1000 m in 42:37 sec. | = 52.80 mph (flying) |
| 500 m 19:88 sec. | = 56.27 mph (flying) |

---

impressive final average of 29 mph the young Dutchman rolled exhausted across the line.

Not only were the racers remarkable in the late-80s period of HPV development, amazing things could be witnessed once again in the everyday bike.

In Germany, the main recumbent maker Radius had so far only competed with imports from England and America as well as Pichler and the Swiss Fateba. But now there were numerous small producers who offered enthusiasts short recumbents which were fun and fast even without a fairing.

There were the Mertens brothers, who accessorized their short racing recumbent and produced a run of 10. There was also the "Kingcycle" by Miles Kingsbury, a short recumbent with 17" and 24" wheels, linen seat and triangulated split-frame design.

In the Netherlands, Bram Moens (M5) and Derk Thijs (Thijs Design) both launched models which are successful to today. Moens' mainstay is a lowracer. But Thijs takes the prize for most distinctive design with his highly-refined *rowing* bike. His Rowingbike frame is a clean mono-tube beam along which the feet slide together, back and forth. The steering looks like a conventional pivoting stem model, until you realize that a cable attached to the bars lets you apply power with your arms as well, while still enabling steering. Thijs has won open marathon events against team upright racers with a faired version of his impressive bike.

This producers' push was completed by Christian Uwe Mischner from Munich, who introduced his Flux short recumbent in 1989. Only a year later it was put into production. From the start he impressed experts with its ride quality, smart detail solutions and quality control. This bike was even equipped with a front brake in the style of a modern V-brake that Mischner made himself.

1989 was not only an exciting year for European everyday bikes. The American HPV racing scene achieved two very big successes.

In August, a relay team of four cyclists participated in the Race-Across-America. RAAM is the longest bike race in the world. Almost 5000 kilometers long, it runs non-stop from the West to the East coast. Not only is the distance tougher than any other race, but drafting is forbidden.

Since all bike types are admitted, Michael Coles, Bob Forney, Jim Penseyres and his brother Pete—two former RAAM winners—chose to race an HPV as a team. They started with a faired Lightning F-40.

The Lightning excels with high practicality, fine mountain-climbing capability, high speed and low weight (about 25 lbs). With the highspeed X-2 fairing, a speed of 57.8 mph was reached in the 200-meter sprint in 1985.

The Gold Rush team was also at the start. They led the race until about 130 miles before the finish. The four Lightning pilots pulled ahead and arrived after 5 days, 1 hour and 8 minutes. The HPVs were almost three days faster than the fastest racing upright cyclists, and averaged 24.02 mph for the whole enormous distance.

In September of the same year "Fast Freddy" set a new Hour record of 45.338 miles aboard the Gold Rush.

The next year, 1990, on a brisk, windless evening in September, Freddy's record was broken on the Millbrook Proving Ground, England. The British "Bean" dashed for an hour over a two-kilometer course and achieved a proud 46.96 miles with Pat Kinch at the helm.

The high-speed two-wheel Bean, devel-

*Chris Huber behind the "Cheetah" record-holding machine. (photo: Chet Rideout)*

oped by Miles Kingsbury after years of intensive work, had already appeared at the Thamesmead Festival and won many victories in the following years.

Then in 1994, the Dutchman Bram Moens rode to a new world Hour record with a distance of 47.92 miles. It remained unofficial, however, because he did not wear a helmet that conformed to the rules. He used an M5 bike from his own company. He is the only HPV champion who developed and built the bicycle that he piloted to a record.

## "Gold Rush" versus "Cutting Edge"

Long wheelbase one-track vehicles replaced three-wheeled craft as record-setters in the middle of the Eighties. The two-wheel "Gold Rush" had won the much desired DuPont prize. Before that "Blue Bell" and "Lightning" had already marked out ruling claims. After the success of "Gold Rush," Fred Markham remained unbeaten in head-to-head racing. This all changed when Matt Weaver, only aged 20, livened up the American scene with his vehicle "Cutting Edge." In 1990, at the 16th Human Powered Speed Championships in Portland, Oregon, he dashed away from "Fast Freddy" and won the 20-mile criterium.

The race was very exciting. Markham and Weaver quickly left the field behind and fought a duel on the tight course. Weaver noticed that Markham lost speed in every corner. He was slowed by washboard ruts in the raceway pavement made by the cars which usually raced there. But the unevenness did not disturb Weaver. He felt that braking put him in more danger. His only chance was overtaking in a turn and taking the lead. Markham always started wide then swung tight to the inside of the curve. Only a small pass-through on the outside ever remained in any turn. Weaver finally jumped around and finished the race with a 47 second lead.

Young Matt developed and built his soon-to-be-influential vehicle by himself in a small shack behind his parents' house, while being supported, like Markham, by Gardner Martin's Easy Racers company.

Fast Freddy commented on this engineering achievement: "He did what a lot of people with a lot more engineering background could not do."

But Weaver's success did not come out of nowhere. His father had been involved with building soap-box derby racers, which are highly technical projects nowadays.

Before Weaver started construction, he calculated with his computer the ideal frame and, as far as possible, the ideal fairing.

This lengthy research by the former Berkeley student resulted in an HPV plan from which the frame and fairing was minted— the first of the truly low lowracers. The low height wraps the legs close around the front of the bike and fork. The carbon fiber frame has an outrigger boom from head-tube to crank, located directly in front of the front wheel. Turning is restricted to about 8 degrees each way. In round track races, the low center of gravity makes up for that, and maintains enough turning capacity. One of the most unique twists of this design is that of the two main frame tubes, one leads *over the right shoulder*, allowing the rider to be positioned lower than with any other design. The over-shoulder tube supports two fasteners for the fairing. The steering is a directly-operating handlebar. The necessarily huge gear development results from a 70-tooth chainring leading the single chain to a tiny package of cogs on a 28-inch rear wheel.

Weaver's winning first frame inspired the

*Matt Weaver's "Cutting Edge," built in 1988 was the most radical design of the time. The driver lies extremely reclined and extremely close to the ground. This causes a problem that usually only occurs with UCI bikes: the pedals can touch the ground in curves. (photo: Jon Schwartz)*

*Specifications for Cutting Edge:*

| | |
|---|---|
| Length: | 114" |
| Width: | 16" |
| Height: | 35" |
| Wheelbase: | 52" |
| Bike Weight: | 24 lbs |
| Fairing Weight: | 12 lbs |
| Total Weight: | 36 lbs |
| Frontal area: | 0.26 sq meter |

Europeans. Bram Moens, Walter Ising and Peter Ross rode similar bikes at the 7th European Championship in Munich in 1992. However, they did not take Weaver's philosophy of "sitting low and in between" quite as far.

As for Weaver, he has continued to push the furthest limits. He made an assault on the recent prizes with his new bike, the "Virtual Edge." Weaver designed this new bike from start to finish digitally, using the latest CAD software. He views the road by way of video—previously said to be impossible to do—and he manages the interior oxygen level. He says he also gets significant gains from close-fitting wheel-shrouds which reduce energy-robbing air-pumping by the wheels. However, Easy Racers now pilots this bike, renamed "Virtual Rush," while Weaver keeps building newer ones!

# Innovation & Integration

The striving for high speeds, all-weather capability plus everyday usefulness—and all three together—continues even now. As always, the result is an individual interpretation of "everyday," "weather" and "speed."

In this context one can consider the Dutch "Flevo Bike" that in spite of the enormous effort needed to learn to ride one, was selling a few hundred bikes a year until recently. People decide that its advantages are worth it to them. It has unique leg steering by way of a hinging frame which allows a very simple front-wheel-drive, and a very natural riding style once one gets used to it. But it's very odd until then! It is a robust and simple design, with fine ergonomics, reliability and maintenance, and so fulfills the 'all-round' demand of its particular set of owners.

The new short Bacchetta line and the classic long recumbents from Easy Racers and RANS each show a good approach to achieving all-around popularity. They give preference to everyday usability, and are certainly well-made. There are many other unique designs which represent individual interpretations in the quest for the ideal compromise between speed and utility. If one test-rode the wide variety of recumbents offered today, one would find an amazing range of ride experiences.

Although one can state that there are broad general streams in the development of recumbent bicycles, the designs still remain all so different from each other, just as the mountain bike is different from the racing bike which is different from the city bike and the BMX.

*Fully-suspended wheels are not just a trend in the mountain bike sector. Suspension has been used on recumbents since the beginning, and it improves a wide variety of uses.*

*Fully-suspension, encapsulated drive and one-sided wheel-mounting: bikes like the "Green Machine" by Flevo show one approach to the velocipede future. A modified version went on the market.*

*Velomobiles are a big part of the HPV scene. Trikes are a common platform due to their stability. The Flevo design team does a lot of work in this area. Their new "Versatile" (pictured) offers deluxe features in contrast to their fast "Quest" and simple "Mango." (photo: A. Vrielink)*

Three big trends are certainly low seat height, higher crank bottom-bracket, suspension and the city-bike. New producers recently seem to focus on either low or compact (medium-length) recumbents. This should not lead to the idea that the long recumbent is the 'vintage' type or that its potential is exhausted. (Short, medium, long and high and low models were all explored from the beginning.) The short ones are rather said to be more sporty and are somewhat in fashion. Lowracers are winning races, especially in the stock unfaired divisions, and are very fast "out of the box" for the fast riders. The sporting aspect of recumbent riding seems to be catching on. Certainly the short construction has advantages in city traffic that the lowracer does not. High-racers also offer a fast and safe option—these are very reclined bikes but with larger wheels. Long bikes offer great comfort and stability. Long models are still popular and could surpass short versions with just the discovery of improved designs. Compact models are coming on strong with new bikes from the largest companies such as Cannondale and Giant. It's a fluid market and arena for invention, with significant

shake-ups and shake-outs almost yearly. In the field of accessories, producers are doing a lot with partial fairings—both front and rear tailboxes—which find application in everyday use as well as in races.

Off the street an interesting tendency is noticeable: producers like Schwinn, Cat Eye and Life Fitness offer very popular hometrainers in recumbent design. Brochures point out the great comfort and training opportunities which protect the back. The big question remains: When will these companies realize that you can also exercise outside on the street...?!

The ideal frame form and aerodynamic shape has not been found yet, nor do the HPV clubs regulate anything in this sector. A free field for enthusiasts remains open.

Based on what has recently been developed, we should eagerly anticipate what will appear on the HPV scene in the future.

The Internet, since its beginning, has been a great way for HPV cyclists worldwide to share ideas, photos, plans, methods, and race and ride reports as soon as they happen.

Recently much work has been done by weekend sportsmen with fairings made of the common, cheap corrugated plastic sheeting called Coroplast. Fairing and trunk plans and videotape how-to kits are being shared worldwide among cooperating clubmates.

Cyclists are discovering the advantages of HPVs especially in centuries and open-field ultramarathon events—thanks to their comfort and protection from the sun, wind and climate (not to mention their increased privacy at crowded rest areas).

A hard-racing HPV is nowadays often used in everyday training on open roads. This new breed is relatively easy to build, easy to maintain, easy to ride in all weather, and very robust, so that it can withstand bad roads and the occasional fall. Cargo space for groceries and optional lighting are almost necessary. —And of course the rig has to be fast enough to get good results in the races.

Another option is that a team builds two bikes with the same geometry. One is for racing, the other is called a "mule"—a trainer built out of quick, crude materials, perhaps without a fairing, which gets a racer uses on open roads to get used to any design quirks of the real thing.

Developers also work on including protection that's extensive enough to protect a rider in a crash or if his HPV is struck by a car. This concept can include roll-bar, wrap-around cage and seat belt.

A fascinating new area of home-building focuses on the "tub" format. The frame is built into the fairing, simplifying construction. The rider sits low, basically on the "floor." The vehicle is simple and can be lighter than other variants. Very low fairings which are stiff enough for the "tub" concept, and strong enough to stand on, can be made with such simple materials as fiberglass laid over both sides of glued blue 1" foam panels, such as are used in house construction.

## Recent Racing Action

All categories of HPV racing have seen extensive refinement and rapid improvement—stock, partially-faired, utility, fully-faired and unlimited streamliners. And an extensive series of races of both pack and individual time trial formats has developed in the U.S. and Europe.

At the '96 HPV world championships in Las Vegas, Dean Pederson raced "Coyote," a partially faired street legal bike, and won the overall long distance road race in very windy conditions with an average speed of 30 mph—while competing against fully-faired streamliners. His clever fairing includes a roof for rain protection but is able to be entered without opening any doors. It was built around a stock bicycle by Steve

Delaire, of the Rotator line, in California.

Production lowracers are becoming very popular and dominant in unfaired and semi-faired HPV racing worldwide. Major brands include M5, Lightning, Reynolds, Birk, Optima, Challenge. Their speeds are becoming phenomenal, especially with tailboxes. In 2003, M5 lowracers with tailboxes won significant open races against upright

### 365 days of the year...

I love the way people always react to my recumbent bike even if these reactions have not really changed over the years.

In pedestrian precincts and shopping areas only a flying saucer would attract more nosy parkers. And if there are two or more velomobilists on their recumbents, you can watch an amusing puzzlement spreading at the roadside, mixed in with the disbelief, amazement and respect which otherwise only acrobats enjoy.

It is equally entertaining to watch the reactions of automobilists when they discover a recumbent in their rear mirror going 50 kmh. They double-check with disbelief first their speedometers and then again the rear mirror—or they self-consciously speed up. Of course, you also meet some occasional obvious dislike if you can't maintain the 50 kmh which is permitted in inner cities.

But in general most people seem to enjoy the 'performance,' and you can ride the roads without being constantly honked at. Especially enjoyable are country roads of smooth asphalt. You glide along swiftly, wind around your nose, effortless, almost as if you were flying....

*—Klaus Schroeder*
*(of Scooterbike and Aeroproject)*

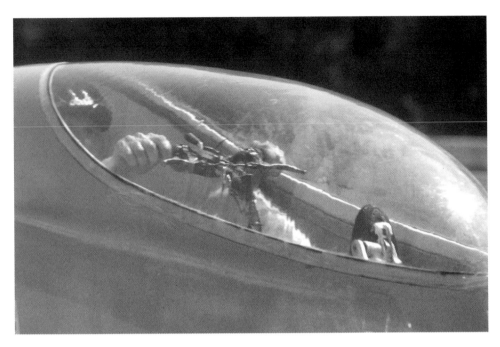

*Lars Teutenberg in "White Hawk," Vector's latest winner. He holds the current world records for the Hour and 100 km with this bike, with 51.33 miles...and a scarcely-slower 50.32 mph. (photo: G. Fehlau)*

bikes—the Dutch "Free" time-trial championship and an 80 km Swiss amateur race. Frederik van de Walle was allowed to enter the 3.2 km prolog of the 2000 UCI Tour de Seine et Marne on his Challenge "Jester" with tailfin...and won by 10 seconds, riding 32 mph.

In 1997 Andy Wilkinson set a new overall record for the 861-mile End-to-End race in England on a faired Windcheetah trike in 41hrs:4min:22secs, besting his previous upright world record by 4 hours—and hitting 70+ mph on some downhills!

More upright events are including recumbents. The USCF now allows unfaired 'bents under 2 meters long—the same (pointless) rule as for uprights—in time-trials. This boosts popularity and innovation even more. Recent results are encouraging.

At the 2003 USCF time-trial championships, Tim Brummer, owner of Lightning, won his 45-50 age-group riding a U-2, a modified, unfaired M5 lowracer he sells. His time of 52:22 for 40 km also gave him 5th overall, for an average of 28.5 mph.

There have been other gains on a smaller scale for recumbent racing within the USCF.

In 1999 Andreas Weigel took 2nd overall (behind pro Shawn Wallace) on an unfaired Lightning R-84 in a USCF TT in San Diego, with 26:46 min's for 20 km, for 27.8 mph.

That same year Jeff Potter (publisher of this book) was allowed to race a Michigan USCF criterium on his lowracer (built at the WISIL club's Skunkworks) on a 'noncontender' basis and proceeded to lap the all-classes field.

In 1999, two major prizes arrived to motivate builders and racers. The $25,000 Dempsey-McCready Prize for the first single cyclist to break 55 miles in one hour, and the .deciMach $24,000 Prize for the first rider to surpass 75 mph in the 200m flying sprint, at sea level—82 mph at altitude.

Sam Whittingham and Georgi Georgiev have so far made the biggest speed news. At the 2002 World Speed Championships, held at the high altitude of Battle Mountain, Nevada, Whittingham in Georgiev's Varna "Diablo II" topped his multi-year streak of record-breaking runs with a new official HPV world record of 81 mph! Note that he broke his record of the previous year by 8 mph! ("Only" 1 mph more is needed to claim the .deciMach prize.)

Varnas at Battle Mountain seem to be breaking as many records as the limited pavement allows—including a new women's record of 64 mph by Andrea Blasecki. Blaseckie and Ellen Van der Horst both have raced past 60 mph at Battle Mountain. Van der Horst holds the current women's Hour record at 46.46 miles.

A winning situation for the Varnas seems to be the athletic talent of the riders combined with their small size. Reducing the size of the HPV while keeping great sprinting power inside seems to be key.

The long experience of Georgi Georgiev, Varna team designer, also is critical. He builds the Varna bikes on a very low budget, using no wind tunnels or computers. He says he gets the inspiration for his shapes from nature and animals.

The popular Battle Mountain event has attracted many top new-breed racers, including Matt Weaver, Sean Costin, and Jason Queally—as well as up-and-coming recordholding teenagers Tanya Markham and Mackie Martin.

Weaver feels his ultrasmooth HPVs achieve significant amounts of "attached flow," enabling 80+ mph—with the potential, he says, of 100 mph!

Costin hosted the inaugural weeklong event at the unusually flat and quiet course found by Weaver. Amazingly, Costin, an Illinois resident, also raced, piloting the only other "camera bike," the "Coslinger Special" to 62 mph. The bike was inspired by Weaver's radical video concept and built as an ultralow "tub" fairing-as-frame design.

UCI track champ Queally came with a heavily-funded British race car project, Blueyonder, and left cheerfully impressed by the friendly superiority of the micro-budget record-setters.

The event is known for a spirit of cooperation. Racers help each other between runs and share speed insights while often working overtime in adjusting, modifying, and keeping their vehicles ready for the daily runs of the annual affair. It also has a reputation for cheery relations with the rural community, which goes out of its way to make the event possible. The racers have staged popular presentations for the local school children, letting kids get into the HPVs and putting them all on display. Many media people attend the event, including several documentary makers who have made films and TV shows of the event.

*A front view of "White Hawk" showing the shape needed for record speeds today. This shape is still shifting, but the best today are small and very smooth. (photo: G. Fehlau)*

## Life-thoughts of a recumbent commuter

I think it is really pleasant to lie back on my recumbent after breakfast, to chose my riding style depending on personal preference and weather, and to arrive at our bike shop for work, all warmed up after the 30-minute ride. If I had taken the car, I would have arrived five minutes earlier, had I taken the bus, I would have arrived ten minutes later.

The average speed for these 8 urban miles is about the same for both HPV and car, but the recumbent produces lower costs—for me personally and for society on the whole. It restores a chronic lack of exercise, improves my health, and enables me to experience nature and my surroundings. As a result of many years of using an HPV, I now ride a recumbent in any weather (using either the Slapstick or Aeroproject). With the passage of time and the purchase of adequate accessories and clothing, a sphere of contentment developed for me that has a very special value.

Common judgments hold that if you ride an HPV, hills are torture, and your first semi truck will be your last, because low recumbents can easily be missed. I can only tell you that I prefer riding up mountains on a recumbent to standing up on a normal bike, and that inner city traffic is not a place to take a nap no matter what bike you're on. With careful driving and an eye on the rear mirror you can very well manage the car chaos around you.

I would also like to say something about the fellows who cannot imagine having a quality of life beyond their 16 valves, eight speakers, and stop-and-go trophies as they blast through inner cities and on highways: quality does not exist in cities full of polluted air, but in cities which pulsate with life.

Los Angeles, Amsterdam, Luebeck and other cities have already determined to go in a cleaner direction. Individualized traffic with Otto engines are supposedly going to be a thing of the past in these cities. Instead, electric busses and trams as well as human powered vehicles are to replace cars.

Electric power is sometimes a questionable decision; this is well-known. However, it is relatively unknown that despite all the cars on Earth, the largest part of transit is still done by muscle power. In Asia alone, more bikes move people than all cars on this planet added up. There are also signs in central Europe that speak of the fact that the velocipede is a contemporary means of transportation. Not for everybody—but for more and more people.

*—Klaus Schroeder, bike shop owner,*
*bike manufacturer, HPV pilot,*
*true believer*

# Ch. 2 / On Parade with the Recumbent

## Everyday use and city traffic

As traffic slows and becomes more congested and car parking becomes difficult, more people prefer bikes for everyday transit. They share the view that bikes are more practical for short trips in the city than automobiles or public transportation. However, their bikes differ widely from each other. Preferred steeds range from the British 3-speed or Dutch flier—a cult object bought for $50 at a flea market—to the carbon racer with tri-bars and clipless pedals.

Their owners believe that they have found the ideal bike for daily use. And indeed they have—ideal for themselves, their expectations, their city, their demands and their purse. (One could have the most wonderful everyday-bike, if only money didn't matter....) When purchasing a city-bike or everyday-bike, most people at this point in time do not yet consider buying a recumbent. However, it offers marvelous opportunities for such use.

A recumbent HPV can result in a great increase in range, and offer improved safety, cargo capacity, and dreamy comfort.

### The recumbent as everyday-bike offers these advantages:

- comfortable position (no pressure points for butt, hands, neck or back)
- eye-level eye contact with car drivers
- low falling height
- faster on flats and downhills
- no pedal strike in corners
- legs as impact crumple zone rather than head
- the ability to keep pace with synchronized traffic lights up to 30 mph (with strong legs and fairing)
- open, relaxed posture for chest and belly

- unusual appearance offers "security plus"—while riding and while parked
- natural "heads up" position improves both close-range and far-ahead field of view
- greater trip-distance range
- keeps up with flow of auto traffic easier, due to speed
- warm in winter, as exposure is much less with fairing
- cool in summer, as brightly colored fairings reflect sunlight and offer shade
- rain protection, with fairing and integral fenders
- dirt protection of machine and rider, with fairing
- good all-round weather protection
- free choice of clothing (no special gloves, shorts or jersey needed)
- better all-round protection in case of an accident—for bike and rider

### Disadvantages & Limitations

- horizontal position bad if exposed during rain w/o special protection (side-zip jacket)

*Weather protection and storage space characterize everyday recumbents.*

*A children's trailer is fun for all.*

recumbents. Here, we will look at a rough classification of the two basic goals. (Personal modifications and changes are excluded.)

### *"Fast on the road"*

The term "fast" is open for interpretation, of course. We are mainly addressing here all those who prefer a racer to a Dutch city-bike, and who would tend to use a diamond frame racing bike for daily pedaling. If they're riding in low traffic conditions, then a low, lightweight recumbent with racing wheels and tires, and appropriate high performance gearing, might be best for them—possibly also short-travel, firm suspension to improve comfort and control at top speeds and in intense cornering. Add a tail-fairing trunk and away you go.

Racers mostly forgo lights, rack and fenders. On the HPV market, a number of small retailers provide fast models which have been adapted to daily use, and are a compromise between racers with a very low center of gravity and those with a more traffic-appropriate eye height. Seat height should be no less than 15". Wheelbase tends to be under 44". Emphasis is directed towards speed rather than comfort and cargo capacity. Prominent in this category are the brands Lightning, Rotator, Bacchetta, Optima, Challenge, M5 and Windcheetah.

- turning of the head to see behind difficult w/o mirror
- long or faired recumbent can be heavy and harder to park
- no bunnyhopping up over curbs possible
- can't stand up or unweight off seat (very far) for bumps, sprints or tricky maneuvers
- wobbly start-up w/ some models
- slower hill-climbing
- heavier
- can't attach bags to handlebars
- might have lower eye-height
- can't wear backpack
- fairing windshield can fog or obscure by rain
- potential of foot entrapment under seat suggests clipless pedals and extra caution

In reality, the recumbent has to be treated like any bike type: each of the numerous varieties is suited for a specific purpose. He who wants to benefit from the general advantages of a recumbent bike has to analyze where, how fast, and under which conditions he rides or wants to ride in order to find the best corresponding recumbent type.

The chapter "Basics of Recumbent Design" contains information about the design characteristics of different types of

### *"Comfortable on the bike path"*

As opposed to the speedbikes, this type has a very comfortable character. They are cut for the former British 3-speed users. They have wide tires, one of which, at least, is suspended. The wheelbase is usually longer and the gearing is widely variable to meet the demands of slow, uphill riding (with cargo) as well as rare bursts of speed. The best-known makers of these bikes are Easy Racers, RANS and Radius.

Then there are hybrids that combine both philosophies along with extra notions, similar to industry blends of mountain bike with racing bike. These concepts are very promising and represent the efforts of the biggest companies involved. These typically use the Compact wheelbase format, and even a revival of the semi-recumbent position. BikeE was the best example of this type so far. Its place has been taken over by entries from mega-makers Giant, Cannondale, and Sun, as well as Burley, Cycle Genius, HP Velotechnik, and Flux.

One versatile model that needs mentioning is the Lightning F-40, which is a light, short P-38 with a fiberglass nosecone and full cloth fairing to create the high speed F-40. It is fast, easy to handle, and comfortable. The bike can be ridden "naked" as a stock P-38, with nosecone only, or with complete fairing. This is similar to the "Hornet" by Radius, with fairing, rear trunk fairing and nosecone that can all be bought separately, or combined to make a full fairing.

The Easy Racer's Gold Rush replica with Zzipper windshield and cloth fairing is another convertible. Also, the "S-Comp" by Flux, a construction that should rather be called a low-flying airplane. The seat is 18" high and one pedals 8" above the seat—a great way to get an aerodynamic position. The narrow above-seat steering reduces exposed frontal surface still further.

I believe that in this sector one can expect unprecedented developments—especially as suspension is now being added in so many models, and at ever-lower prices.

However, if price is no concern look into the Lightning R-84. This carbon-fiber bike has full suspension, 24 gears, hydraulic brakes and above-seat steering. It weighs only 20.2 lbs and costs $3500 for the frame. $7500 will get you the complete fully-faired F-90 variant.

A further innovation in the field of rethinking the bike appeared in the Flevobike from the Netherlands. With front-wheel-drive, leg-steering, and full suspension,

these two- and three-wheelers were appreciated by many HPV pilots, even though the bike demands a new form of navigation. The steering is done through the hips, due to a rigid front fork and a pivot in the mid-section of the frame. It only takes a week to learn and then it's second nature like any other aspect of cycling. This is the height of cleverness—simplicity—in design.

There is no single ultimate city-bike in this field nor an everyday model accepted by the masses, but instead a large number of solutions that address different priorities. The active upright cyclist who rides a lot in the city seldom rides an over-the-counter bicycle, but instead uses an individualized model that has been modified based on experience. It is exactly the same when it comes to recumbents. The smaller number of producers often results in more do-it-yourself work from the customer, but the number of models which strive to be complete out of the box city-bikes is quickly increasing. One can chose among a rainbow of frame styles and materials, wheel sizes, and seat variations. Once the decision for

*Giant claims their new "Revive" recumbent isn't one. Really, it's a semi-recumbent. The enclosed drivetrain, rear shock, fenders and other commuter features—along with budget pricing—make it a good city-bike.*

*Fully packed and with a Zzipper on snowy Scandinavian roads demands a knack for driving. A recumbent protects you from falls with serious consequences with its low height. (photo: Francoise and Bernard Magnouloux)*

which general format is made, the small, time-intensive, costly detail modifications begin. They give a bike its final individual appropriateness and style.

## On Tour...via Recumbent

Vacations are part of the modern way of life, with destinations as varied as the means of transportation. Each mode of transportation is good for a journey. The bike offers its own wide range of strongpoints: it allows enjoyment of nature, direct contact with people and countryside; plus it offers thrift, reliability and an amazing blend of independence and community.

To my mind, the recumbent represents the best and most mature variation of bike. It is fast and pain-free, so it increases one's range significantly, and the heads-up view improves the natural experience. The recumbent combines a safe, pleasant seat position

with an energy-saving, small frontal area.

The position on the recumbent is wind-evasive and allows an unimpeded view of traffic, the environment and nature. All other bike types fall short of this. None of them combine comfort with such beneficial aerodynamics and safety. Not even the fashionable triathlon aero-bars can compete, as their usage confines the chest and puts the weight forward.

One can readily add fairings for touring and use faired luggage trunks, which get a lot of development attention in the HPV field.

Note that most of the special aspects of the recumbent in touring will cross over to everyday use. Recumbenteers, at this point in time, do face relatively more specific challenges across the board than do upright riders, so to an extent the rules of life on the road will apply to you at home as well.

Your well-being on a recumbent is guaranteed, provided the bike fits the rider. Nor is the psyche neglected. Traveling by recumbent puts one in touch with the inhabitants of different parts of a country. If a loaded recumbent crosses the countryside, it is usually quite an attraction. More than for uprighters, a recumbent draws positive response from motorists, kids and even teenagers. It can sometimes even be difficult to leave a nice chit-chat with friendly, curious locals under the shadow of a big tree. Kids come and eye the weird vehicle, challenge you to race or simply laugh about "that thing." Two questions later and you end up in a conversation about life, the universe and everything. Local dishes and drinks are served—rejection would mean insult. This messes up your touring plan, but it is also what constitutes the charm of recumbent journeys. It is nice when you can at this point give a little gift to your host: the best might be a picture of your fully-packed bike and family. Perhaps some year, though, the world will be as used to 'bents as to uprights.

The stretched-out, open position on a recumbent leaves plenty of space for the inner organs. The lungs work easily and the intestines and stomach are not compressed. In practice, this offers significant advantages. After a power-breakfast in the morning you don't have to wait to start your long touring day, you just get on the bike and go. Stomach and intestines have enough room to work despite pedaling. This open position might not enable you to do mountainous passages at "Tour de France" speed, but it prevents superfluous stomach aches.

The comfortable seat, the lack of pressure points for hands and neck, allows for low-stress touring for long distances.

Adaptation, lighter models and further innovation then help us improve on the mountain-climbing side of the equation!

Bernd Kerke reports about a journey through Australia on his Radius recumbent:

"The streets are often only unpaved gravel roads but as we are fully suspended, it's no bother. Overall, touring on recumbents is sheer pleasure. After about 300 km, our muscles are used to the different kind of strain, and the suspicion of going nowhere leaves after checking your cyclometer. Compared to previous bike tours in Europe we are about 15 per cent faster, but hardly ever exhausted in the evenings. It is a fabulous feeling to have your eyes turned to the scenery, and to ride a bike without any bone-twisting. No tense shoulders, no blisters or boils on your hands or rear, but still we manage to go 170 km a day with 30 kg of luggage without falling down dead afterwards. Riding with luggage and on bad roads is easily adapted to."

## Luggage

The recumbent's construction makes wearing backpacks nearly impossible, except for the option of wearing a rucksack on your chest for quick trips in the city.

A sensible alternative is a messenger bag, the carry-on of bike messengers, which can be worn across your back, over the seat. Many recumbent-specific, and even model-specific, seat-bags are now available as well, often in aerodynamic format.

Regular racks and panniers often work just fine. Occasionally special rack mounts are needed. Specially fitting racks and panniers for various models are also offered.

As an external possibility, consider a trailer. Especially when you travel with children, a trailer gives you plenty of capacity.

## Loading

A vehicle on tour undergoes heavy strain, as with an increasing load the strain rises. This is predictable and inevitable. It is important, however, that weight distribution is even. If there is too much luggage on either rear or front wheel, the handling degrades. Braking and steering can become treacherous. Tires become unevenly worn. A test ride on a loaded bike is absolutely necessary. If the road-contact area of one of the tires is flattened hardly at all, you should change the weight distribution. Use a weight-scale to further verify that you've kept the same wheel-weight ratio. This maintains the desired ride quality and safety, and prevents flat tires, rim damage, as well as broken hubs and spokes.

Light, one-track trailers (such as the B.O.B.) are especially versatile. They do not impair maneuverability, offer plenty of space and bear a lot of weight. Beware of the combination of trailer and a recumbent with rear suspension. The rear shock can begin to shimmy under even light loading of a trailer.

## Tire Width

With sufficient air pressure and civilized asphalt, 32 mm tires are sufficient for touring. A wide tire is naturally the simplest, easiest and cheapest 'suspension' for a bike. Moreover, it is likely to be problem-free, and special parts are unnecessary. With any type of fully faired HPV, especially a high-speed model, you'll not want to experience a blow-out. The event is dangerous and the repair is time-consuming. Many recumbenteers are opting to ride the new breed of wide, slick, low rolling-resistance tires which, even though they are heavier, seem to be designed with recumbents in mind, and which are now offered in most typical HPV wheel sizes. Thankfully, 'bents today finally have a wide variety of quality tires to test and choose from, to determine what works best for your needs.

### Gear Ratios

Load-weight, desired speed, geography of the route, and your riding style all combine to determine your needed gear-ratios. Recumbents tend to need smaller gears than usual for climbing, especially when loaded (as you can't stand and pedal). And if you wish to take advantage of increased down-hill speeds, you'll need a big gear to match. Depending on construction, the 'translation' (distance traveled per crank rotation) of a recumbent can vary widely. Fast 'tall' gears can be combined with mountain 'granny' gears using a 3x7 internal gear shift plus external derailleur without any problem. Your preferred cadence plays an important role here, and gearing has to be oriented towards that. Expert advice, experience and adaptation will help greatly.

### Pedals and Shoes

Efficient energy transfer pays off on long rides. In order to achieve this, a firm connection between pedal and shoe is needed, for the foot hangs vertically from the pedal when riding a recumbent. Every bump tends to bounce it out of regular toe-clips. That is why a clipless pedal is almost essential for performance cycling. It guarantees a secure connection between shoe and pedal, and ensures safety in traffic.

If a foot falls off the pedal and touches the road while under way, one risks injury. The foot can get sucked under the front of the seat, resulting in a twist or even broken bone.

I prefer racing shoes on tours that mainly take place on smooth roads. They transmit power the best and are comfortable en route. I prefer "in sole" systems like SPD on tours with bad roads or tours that include hiking passages. Mountain-bike shoes come with

*The "Roadster" by Human Powered Machines of Eugene, OR, has relaxed chopper styling with tires and frame geometry suitable for dirt road riding.*

a recessed cleat and rubber sole which is usually easy to walk in and offer reasonable transfer of muscle power. Combo-pedals and those with twist-straps have proved their worth in city traffic.

## Spare Parts

Recumbent bikes should be thoroughly checked-out before any journey. That is self-evident, but not sufficient. On journeys, one has to anticipate every "impossibility": theft of bike parts, sabotage, accidents and failures. Then everything depends on the question: Where do I get a spare?

This problem is greater when it comes to the special parts of recumbents.

To start, simply avoid special parts wherever possible. Small recumbent front wheels are a disadvantage. Bacchetta and ZOX make 26x26 sports models which make tire-buying a breeze. Only the 20"x1.75" wheel common to the folding bike and BMX bike is reliable for spares in faraway countries. Note that the 406-mm BMX rim is not to be confused with the uncommon 451-mm version called a "road 20."

Ever since the mountain bike conquered the world, the choice of a 26-inch rear wheel is advisable. The variety of tires that fit on a 599-mm rim (MTB 26 inches) range from a narrow 25-mm slick to a 2.5-inch knobby. This offers the advantage that tires can easily be matched to terrain. A lot of these models are available as light, space-saving fold-ups with Kevlar beads, ideal for carrying along. And when in a pinch one can always ride knobby tires on the road. This is certainly better than waiting for days for new tires. If smoothness is preferred over top speed, then wider rims are a good pick.

If one wants a large wheel but not a 26", one has to know about the customs in the country of destination to make a decision between the 27-inch, which is rare in Germany, for instance, and the 28-inch. I was stuck in Ireland for a week once because I

photo: Francoise and Bernard Magnouloux

needed 28-inch tires (only the inner tubes are interchangeable with 27-inchers).

What holds true for tires is also appropriate for brakes and other components. A very precise set-up of the bike, even in the tiniest details (oiled cable housings, deburred threads) is crucial. Furthermore, the components should be sensible. Forgoing lightly-built parts that might wear out prematurely is a good cost-savings measure and greatly improves reliability. Robust, long-lasting parts are much better. Commonly available sealed-bearing hubs, pedals and bottom bracket are characterized by complete freedom from maintenance and great reliability. V-brakes offer much higher-power braking with much less hand-effort, but set-up and maintenance can be trickier. The popular new disk brakes are easy to set up, powerful, weatherproof, and tolerant of many wheel-rim mishaps—all wonderful things—but repairs for their own internals won't be available in every town.

All components should be commonly compatible with a wide variety of local makes. Indexed STI or Gripshift gear shift levers, and even the amazing new Schlumpf crank-drive and new-era hub gears, are asking for trouble once you're out of town. They demand dozens of manufacturer-specific parts, cogs, chainrings, chain, hub, cable-knobs. This is especially true for 8-, 9- and 10-speed groupos. Bar-end or thumb-shifters are better because their indexing function can be switched off. They do their work independently from the choice of cog, chain and shifter. If you get entangled in an accident on a remote part of your journey, or if you change your gear for some reason, you simply mount the first cog that fits, switch off the indexing function and continue riding.

### Tools

Tools must be chosen to fit your array of bike parts. If you carry along all needed tools for complete repair, you won't be dependent on farmers and gas station personnel. Those who do not want to be burdened with the weight of that freedom should be carefully selective when it comes to the choice of bike components. Using Mavic hubs, Mavic headset, Edco internal bearing, the Sugino "Out-tex" crank arm replacement

screw, as well as Dia Compe 986 Cantilever brakes, all greatly minimize the number of necessary tools. In the once-heavy tool bag, you might now only find 2-6 mm Allen keys, a 12/14 and 8/10 mm cone-wrench set, and a light Parktool crank puller. Chaintool, gear puller, spokewrench, Swiss Army Knife and Leatherman Tool complete the list. Or you can opt for an amazing new multi-tool such as the Topeak McGyver, with its 30+ bike tools in one small unit. Glueless patches now make tube repair easy. (Let's not forget recent progress in tubeless tires!)

### Daily Range and Day-Trips

The toughest riders can manage days of more than 500 km on their recumbents. This style of bike boosts the typical range due to great comfort, free breathing and undisturbed digestion. Take it as you like it, but riding 60-100 miles a day with a recumbent is not a problem at all.

### Ferries, Planes, Busses and Trains

If you want to take your recumbent by plane, you have to announce that in advance and prepare well, and you must not exceed the weight limit with the rest of your luggage, otherwise it gets expensive. Not all trains offer the opportunity to take bikes along. Loading your bike in and out by yourself is rarely permitted and so bikes can get damaged. Taking a bike along on buses depends on exterior racks or the good will of the driver. Outside of Western culture it is usually only a matter of negotiation.

Whether on big ocean liners or a small 5-person ferry, you will usually find plenty of space for a bike on a boat. Small ferry docks can sometimes be too narrow for wide loads and handlebars, but physically carrying a loaded HPV will be difficult, so stay alert. If you have a long bike, you should make sure that the extra length won't cause a problem.

*The long recumbent often gets used as a travel bike, as it is more comfortable than a classic bike. This Ryan is a real 'Cadillac.' (photo: Vanguard)*

Generally speaking, the current uniqueness of recumbents gives you an ace up your sleeve. Coupled with a little charm, the bike itself opens up some bus doors and ferry gates. With exact info from tourist bureaus and an ability to negotiate, a lot of things are possible.

## Theft

Last, but not least, some words about the potential nuclear meltdown of any bike tour: theft.

A bike trip without a bike—that does not compute. It is not, however, very easy to steal a recumbent. The thief ends up operating as if he were on a stage. In front of a supermarket a recumbent is quite an attraction and is watched a lot. Here, it is difficult for the thief to break a lock unheeded. Additionally, he is confronted with probing questions, because he is thought to be the owner of this weird vehicle.

For quick parking, a cable lock and a parking place in the middle of the crowd is sufficient. If you are going to be absent in an urban setting for a longer time, a U-lock is advisable.

It is a little different with panniers: they are easily removable, and their contents are just as important on tour as the bike. Therefore one should tightly affix them to the rack and secure with a cable lock. Naturally you should take out valuables when away from the bike.

If the bike's gone nonetheless, the obviousness of your vehicle will be extremely helpful. After reporting to the police, go to the nearest local radio or TV station and hand a photo to the editor. For them it is a small sensation that emphasizes public service for the station and also helps a deprived biker. Go to newspapers with the same information. Of course, it is simple for the police to stay watchful for an extraordinary recumbent bike.

## Test Tours and Rides

Organized recumbent bike tours or day trips are advisable for all those who want to try out a recumbent before buying or making one yourself. Ideally, these would involve a variety of models. Many HPV bike

*A trailer is a sensible addition to panniers on tours with a lot of luggage.*

shops allow one to rent a bike for a time, or even loan them overnight. They certainly encourage a wide range of test-riding on what they stock. They know that recumbents often involve more learning than usual.

On a group testing-tour guided by experts, you'll ride with others of similar interests: most riders are on tour to get to know a new feeling of riding. The advantages of these laid-back floaters can be ideally experienced on such test trips. Addresses can be found in the advertising sections of bike magazines, especially *Recumbent Cyclist News* and *VeloVision*.

# 13 Years of Building Recumbents

"Ultramobile"—I could not think of a better name when I was twelve and I screwed my broken, chain-driven toy vehicle to the front end of a broken foldable bike. The result was an agile three-wheeler which was less apt for moving ahead but perfect for having fun. A few broken pieces, one idea and two screws had amounted to quite something.

Six years later, I bought an arc welder, and new possibilities opened up. My creativity was not limited to nuts'n'bolts. Water pipes, steel furniture, and bike spare parts were the components of a really usable three-wheeler. A terribly wind-vulnerable long recumbent was my next project. It had indirect steering, though, which unfortunately broke after the first bump in the road. I also used this bike during the first German HPV competition, in 1986. The sheer abundance of ideas and apparent perfection that I met there was impressive. But the "everything's-been-done" frustration soon turned into action, and at a closer look, all the constructions I had seen did have a flaw. Thus I continued to build alternatingly two-wheelers and three-wheelers.

In the meantime, I had learned how to weld and had discovered thin-walled tubing. I used these frame tubes to build my first good recumbent: a short model with a rear wheel suspension. This bike also got a fiberglass nosecone fairing, and bike and rider were covered with an aerodynamic and really colorful cloth fairing. This way I surprisingly won my first racing bike competition and participated in the Tour-de-Sol '89. I perfected my concepts on the following bike and became the European Vice-Master in Muenster in '89.

Bernhard Klar, whom I met during this time, provoked some great ideas for me. During long afternoons, when I was supposed to be attending lectures, we got rid of each other's conventional concepts and developed a simple, light and beautiful frame. The "fastest bike in town" concept was born. We built ten of these bikes manually until we realized that the concept was not fit for serial production. Nonetheless we collected some valuable experience.

In 1990, I and five people from southern Germany had the idea to build a high-speed vehicle. But being discouraged by the cost of the project, we tackled the problem of developing an every-day-fairing instead. Everybody contributed experiences, skills and materials—this is how the "Z-2" fairing was born. The concept was designed so universally that it would fit a lot of riders and a multitude of stock bikes. We had reached a shared compromise of ideas— thus the fairing really proved to be as universal as we had wanted it to be.

Besides, it was fast and safe. Our expectations were fulfilled. Experts in plastics further improved the following model.

The "Z-2" fairing was very successful— especially for the talented Walter Zorn who won uncountable races using this fairing.
—*Martin Staubach*

# Ch. 3 / Recumbent Bicycle Sport

The recumbent is the product of the desire to make cycling safer, more comfortable, more enjoyable—and faster.

After participation of recumbents in "normal bike" races was forbidden in 1934 by the UCI Congress, no separate sporting division for recumbents was formed. As a result, recumbents disappeared from the sporting stage for a long time.

Even today, the statutes of most bike associations are formulated in a way that it is difficult to construct a recumbent that meets the requirements and still possesses the advantage of a safe, aerodynamic body position.

However, times are changing. It is fascinating to see how quickly triathlon handlebars have become accepted in the racing scene, even though they offer only the advantage of aerodynamics and some shock absorption rather than any improved human muscle power, and they impair safe handling.

Many race organizations also accept innovative frame designs such as the Softride beam and Trek's Y-Frame. (However, the UCI disallows these frames, and tri-bars in mass start events, in addition to sub-15-pound bikes.)

Also, the American USCF gives its officials the discretion to allow recumbents into races and has no measurement rule against them—however, their 2-meter overall length limit is a needless barrier. At this point, time trials and training races are the likeliest place to gain access with the USCF. Planning ahead with officials and proving your skills to them on group rides, or on upright bikes in the regular racing circuit, all can influence their decisions.

The question remains as to why the biggest organization, the UCI, suppresses a bike variant which allows so much diversity of position and fit and so many more potential advantages than a normal bike.

Due to their newness on today's scene, in some events recumbents might not be banned via specifications; they might simply not be allowed. In events where they are given their own class, fairings might not be allowed. Events and associations seem to be taking a "let's see what people want" attitude, at best. They're not always biased against recumbents, but every new class adds more work to their already overwhelming schedule. Recumbents and faired HPVs are also an unknown to some organizers who question their safety and who are responsible for everyone involved. People also get impressions from seeing a few awkward riders and judge the whole type on that basis.

Century rides, which are wide open for informal racing, seem to be completely accepting of any type of bike or fairing. As a result, in this scene we're presently seeing an explosion of 'bent riders. The sport-

*Unfaired racing performance has risen dramatically over the last years, with production lowracers dominating. In the top group, average speeds of 30 mph are the rule. (photo: www.tim.be)*

rider's grail of a sub-4-hour 100-mile century has proven very feasible for fast recumbents and gained them acceptance here.

Since the middle of the Seventies, recumbent races have taken place in the U.S. under their own various club headings. Several series have been developed, such as today's HPRA, but the main races are organized primarily by the IHPVA, which was founded in 1974. This organization puts no restriction on vehicles. Two bylaws, however, are the only exception: the vehicle must not store any power, and it must not be a danger for rider or participants. Any further restrictions result only from "sports Darwinism"—unfit or unusable innovations disappear from the track pretty quickly. Developmental experience, imagination and smart engineering determine the real "limits" of what is possible.

A second contingent of velo riders has gathered under the HPV roof: the daily cyclists. They loathe the traffic jams of the big cities and they have realized that the bike is the ideal mode of transportation for distances up to 10 km. They use their bikes for shopping trips, ride to work or visit friends. But the traditional bike is not comfortable or fast enough. Some activist antagonists of MIVs (motorized individual vehicles) who champion the daily rider have developed recumbent events to highlight the utility aspect of bikes. There is fierce, but friendly, competition here, too!

The main thing about HPV sporting events, though, is their diversity and sense of camaraderie. There will be many kinds of bikes and skill-levels on display, and on the track at the same time. And a convivial air both on and off the course.

Many HPV people are, nonetheless, mainly interested in transforming their energy into high speed action. They want to demonstrate recumbent fun and superiority with incredible racing thrills and success. Today many events have sprung up to express the whole range of HPV performance:

- 200 m sprint
- 500 m sprint
- time trials (on road and track)
- ultramarathons
- hour races
- hill climb races
- circuit races, criteriums, road races
- stage races
- season-long point series
- everyday vehicle utility tests / maneuverability contests
- drag-races

The following is how these events basically are run....

### 200 meter sprint

The 200m sprint has a running start. The cyclist gets either an unlimited run-up or 600-meters (depending on which record they are after) then flashes past an electric eye to start the timing. A finish-line eye is passed after 200m, followed by a sufficient cool-down distance. The vehicles may be pushed until the driver finds his or her bal-

*Young people, too, participate in HPV sports, often with other family. Here Tanya Markham gets ready for a run. She holds the record for junior women with 52 mph in the "Gold Rush Le Tour." Mackie Martin holds the junior men's record at 60 mph in the "Virtual Rush." (photo: F. Markham)*

ance. The short timeframe and high speeds make selection of building material extremely important. Nowadays there is a battle over materials in which private persons can hardly participate without an affluent sponsor.

The Varna Team's record is standing strong, but high speed buffs are investing all their ambition into toppling it in an effort to claim the $24,000 .deciMach Prize which will go to the first rider to break 75 mph in this event (or 82 mph at altitude). To succeed, you need a vehicle with very low air resistance and great power transfer efficiency. Without a doubt, a top athlete must also be at the pedals. Record-holders like Sam Whittingham, Chris Huber, Fred Markham, and Lars Teutenberg were and are all top UCI racers.

The choice of sprint vehicles today tends unequivocally toward the two-wheeled bikes called 'inline' or 'single-track.' They offer the smallest possible frontal surface. Furthermore, the rider only has to overcome the rolling resistance of two tires, not three or four, and there's no additional turbulence that occurs under the big floors of multi-track bike fairings.

Constructions like the Varnas of Canada, the Bean of England, and Vector's German White Hawk teach the three-wheelers to be afraid of the single-tracker in this event. (Trikes come on strong today mainly in distance events.)

To shave that thousandth of a second, sprint-bike builders make use of all possibilities. Their precious "eggs" are tested in wind tunnels, and frame and fairing are tailored to each rider. Each millimeter of frontal surface area is involved in the struggle between aerodynamics and power transmission. Drivers twist and turn, helped by assistants, to mount their vehicles. Door cracks are sealed with the thinnest possible tape to avoid any additional turbulence. Inside, only the finest components of the racing sports

*Drafting with unfaired recumbents results in higher speeds—but it takes practice. (photo: Djouadi Arezki)*

are used. The bike/rider package is then rolled to the start and held up for the launch.

Basically, you make the shell and frame as light and stiff as possible. Thus the choice is often made in favor of unconventional, experimental and usually more expensive components and accessories. Frames made from aluminum honeycomb, covered with carbon fiber, for instance, make it possible to build a fully-faired sprinting machine that only weighs 28 lbs (Nilgo III).

*Production lowracers, like this Optima "Baron" (with Aerospoke wheels) allow citizen racing at speeds on par with faired models...and UCI bikes. (photo: Aerospoke)*

### 500m and 1km sprints

The 500m and kilo sprints are the big brothers of the 200m sprint. They are only offered at bigger HPV events. If a velodrome is not available, it is difficult for organizers to get clearance from local officials to occupy the 2000m stretch of smooth road that this event requires. It's easier to get permission to use roads for shorter closed events or for open events where traffic is allowed and all laws must be obeyed.

The famous new Battle Mountain course in Nevada has enough room for several major records to be won in a single run. Today's top speeds require such long build-up distances (several miles) that several records can be broken at once, as Sam Whittingham did in his Varna.

### Time trials

A common event for many distances and time limits. However, in HPV racing, time trials aren't always awarded trophies. Often they are used to split participants into groups of similar abilities. Seeding racers in heats for subsequent main events prevents the danger of a fast rider colliding with a slower one. Most events don't find it popular to have a rule outlawing drafting, likely because drafting simply isn't such a big factor in HPV results. The pure TT format is often reserved for record attempts.

### The Hour

The fascination of The Hour gets ahold of the fans of both traditional bikes and HPVs. The records of Boardman, Moser and Company delight the UCI world, but only drag a tired smile from HPV enthusiasts. Their vehicles broke the 33.5 mi UCI record as early as 1939. As of 2002, the HPV Hour is 51.33 miles, set by Lars Teutenberg in the Vector White Hawk.

The speeds which could be achieved by the best professional cyclists are almost unimaginable if they would only lend their legs to the HPV cause for a short time.

Today, whoever breaks 55 miles (90 km) in an hour can claim the $25,000 Dempsey-McCready Prize!

Hour races with lots of vehicles on the track present a special thrill. If drafting is allowed, groups form which quickly achieve the speed of fast trains.

### Stock Racing

HPV racing is made up of several classes, which vary in definition between the U.S. and Europe. Unfaired and semi-faired records for what in the U.S. are called Stock and Superstock classes are presently being discussed. These classes allow for a popular and simpler form of racing that's a lot like regular UCI racing, and are even allowed to mix with USCF racers on occasion. Races and championships have been held for years already, with results that surpass many UCI efforts. Most importantly, manufacturers are readily able to provide bikes for this breed of HPV racer. These makers are represented mostly by European builders like M5, Optima, Challenge and the gorgeous Birk lowracers, with and without their stylish tailboxes and nosecones and other fairing, depending on class. In the

U.S., Bacchetta, Lightning, Barcroft and Reynolds offer strong race options. Homebuilders, and of course teams, can easily participate. Sometimes streamliners race the unfaired class on the same day simply by removing their fairing.

### Stage racing

At the only stage race (held twice) for recumbents, the "Tour de Sol" in Switzerland, you got a chance to participate in mountain stages. Mountains are a top challenge for humans and materials. The toll of racing heavier rigs for days on end also adds up. In stage racing, especially in mountains, all weak points stand out strongly. "Points" events over a weekend are also a form of stage racing.

### Criteriums

Short-course criterium races with plenty of turns held in areas suitable for easy spectating are certainly the most popular events at HPV festivals. Speed and bike-handling, without concern for traffic and other dangers, makes biker hearts beat faster. A com-

mon distance is about 20 miles. Depending on topography, the average speed of unfaired packs can reach 35 mph. Pilots who want to win in a faired class should work toward a 30-40 mph average.

### Distinctions and similarities between HPV and UCI racing

The construction of racing HPVs demands a different approach from that used in traditional races. The tricks, and trick parts, which bring victories for UCI-conforming bikes are not worth a lot in recumbent races. One of the main reasons is the absence of a jump out of the saddle. There is less close-quarters explosive sprinting during the last few meters. There is more focus on pure rider strength in HPV racing, since there is much less drafting to conceal weakness.

The rider has to take into account the weight of a faired vehicle when he wants to overtake. Strong riders might need a long 200-300 meters to pass each other. The heavier the vehicle, the more time required to accelerate.

*A record-setting recumbent "Varna" bike gets taped. Georgi Georgiev, designer of several record vehicles as well as everyday bikes, is in center. Taping the edges and openings prevents the disruption of air streams —indispensable in record races, superfluous in everyday-life.*

Regular bike parts only have to stand up to the forces of body weight and strength of arms, plus a certain amount of speed abuse. The forces on highspeed HPVs require some parts to be much more robust, while other parts become less relevant. Accelerating a recumbent puts large forces into the seat back. Heavier forces in general are put on the seat, and parts of the frame near the seat, because weight is focused there and a rider can't unweight for bumps. A faired vehicle has to handle powerful forces of a wide variety, without damage or flex, at speeds far exceeding normal bikes. Riding in a strong sidewind, for instance, can require one to lean hard to the side—like hiking out on a sailboat—greatly stressing tires, wheels, fork, handlebar, frame, fairing and mounts. Thus a 'light' homebuilt HPV suitable for safe racing (and everyday riding) at 30-60 mph on bumpy, mountainous roads, in strong winds, would tend to weigh 45-70 lbs. If you use an 'exoskeleton' tub bike with frame and seat seamlessly integrated into the fairing so that every element shares the others' loads, you can build a lighter strong vehicle.

A standard racing bike's gear-range is not very useful on a heavier faired recumbent. The recumbent has to replace the missing 'jump' and 'honking' without losing adaptability to terrain, by having small jumps in gear ratios, as well as both higher and lower overall range. Eightspeed rear cogs and/or triple cranksets are a good choice. There are some examples in Chapter 5, on Design, of sensible gear ratios for touring, racing and everyday city use.

The more tight turns a course has, the more important it is to get away right after the start to avoid bottlenecks. Any 'accordion effect' of braking in the rear of a pack hurts HPVs worse than it does UCI bikes.

On a mountainous, hilly or uphill courses, only a lightweight recumbent will make a rider happy. Unless momentum is conserved—as with rolling hills—aerodynam-ics in the hills plays a less important role. Overall weight as well as good seating and pedaling angles are more vital.

In the EU, a high crank is preferred: up to 11 inches higher than the seat. But riders in Northern California seem to find that for big, long climbs, a more-upright seat angle with somewhat lower bottom bracket is more effective: and their famous designs reflect this in the Tour Easy and P-38. Their experience seems to be that a high bottom-bracket bike ends up with the rider pedaling on his head, as it were, up a big hill. If you start out in a more upright position on the flat, as the ride gets steep your angles become more performance-oriented. A position which allows one to pull on the handlebars while climbing also seems to help.

Recumbents with suspension and fairings can easily accumulate excess weight. For uphills, a bike (and its rider!) have to be light and able to 'fly' up the slopes, otherwise chances for a victory evaporate.

It is different on a flat course with easy cornering. Here aerodynamics play the biggest role. Once the bike is accelerated the goal is simply to get to the finish line without many speed alterations.

Three-wheeler pilots are also pleased about an open, gentle course. Their vehicles are often heavier than single-trackers and thus they have more difficulty driving through or accelerating out of sharp corners. The three-wheelers do have it easier at the starts, to be sure.

### Skills and Strategy

Drafting is common but risky. The drivers of partly or fully-faired recumbents have only a limited view of what happens directly in front of their vehicles, below the nose of their fairing. This blind spot extends, depending on fairing, from two to four meters ahead. If drivers want to use the scarce slipstream offered by the drivers in front of them, they are forced to come so close that the leading HPV's rear comes into the blind area. The pilot has to know the dimensions of his bike exactly, and he must memorize the shape of the rear of the vehicle in front to keep a gap between the two vehicles. If he is not up to this task, severe and material-destructive accidents can be the consequence, especially due to the high speeds. Unfaired recumbents have a much smaller blind spot, or none at all if the feet pedal in a low position. Therefore their collision risk is much smaller. However, these riders use this fact to ride up even closer behind their front man. The crank arm of the follower on a short bike with high pedal rotates very close to the leader's rear wheel. The distance between the two bikes is then only a few inches.

All recumbents have limited rearward visibility as well, requiring the use of mirrors. Even with mirrors, it is quite easy for faired bikes to lose track of where riders are behind them, or to not notice when they're being overtaken by faster riders. This requires alertness for safety as well as tactics.

After considering the differences from racing regular bikes that come from heavier, faster vehicles with narrower field of vision, we come to the similarities.

HPV racing at its highest levels is like other bike racing in many ways. Clever pacing can be vital. Drafting is often important, and becomes more so the less fairing a race class allows. Elite unfaired Stock bike races most resemble regular bike races. Cornering technique is standard, with the shortest, smoothest line being the best. At top speed on narrow roads, use the whole road—start wide, dive to the inside, then carry wide again, as fast as traction will allow. Pedal through, if you can. The faster the bike the more road you'll use in curves. Experience in a wide range of regular bike racing is always a plus.

Fully-faired racing can give you the thrills and sensation that come with auto racing. Being jostled around in the interior of a vehicle, white-knuckling it through turns, run-

ning in a long line of top performance vehicles, feeling your suspension working at its max to smooth out the washboard and give you traction, hearing the loud thrumming of wind and chattering of parts—it all makes you feel like you're in a car race as much as a bike race! You might even forget the effort you're making, what with all the other demands on your reflexes and senses: the corners come fast and furious.

### Mixed Events

There are a few races in which recumbents can compete against racing bikes. Neither tourist rides nor ultra-marathons are subject to the UCI regulations. These include such events as RAAM, at 5000 km, and the "Paris Brest Paris" Audax in France, at 758 miles (1219 km), neither of which is likely to be everybody's cup of tea, but recumbents are making amazing inroads here.

Pete Penseyres led the '95 PBP overall aboard a Lightning F-90 until a malfunction stopped him halfway. In '99 Bob Fourney finished 14th overall in 47 hours.

Traditional-length amateur races now also see recumbents as front runners. In 'unrestricted'-classes which are supposed to catch the interest of high-end and pro riders, it can be possible to start with a recumbent bike. It only depends on the good will of the club that organizes the particular non-UCI event.

Furthermore, the USCF (United States Cycling Federation) finally reduced the 80-year old technical rules to only two. Only the length (200 cm) and the width (75 cm) are restricted. All fairings except for wheelcovers are still forbidden. Thus recumbents can be allowed to participate in USCF races. However, officials have sometimes used a simple trick: they switch standards to UCI instead of USCF. Officials always deserve to have the final say regarding riders and machines they don't know. More officials do claim to be receptive today, but all of them probably need to be assured of the skill of the particular rider trying to enter. Race safety, especially in pack racing, is their first obligation, so we can't fault them. Progress here can only be earned on a case by case basis.

When racing in mixed events with upright bikes, it's usually best to work with small groups, or at the front, back or to the side of a larger peloton. It's not pleasant, safe or strategic to be low-down in the midst of a big upright pack. Visibility then is nil. When working with small groups, though, eye contact comes easy, since your eyes are at about the same height as the upright racers in the drops near you. The difference in overall posture is then hardly noticeable and fast action comes naturally!

### *Utility Prize*

Fans of the everyday utility bike get a chance to compare skills at the World Championships at least. Events for them are not so common otherwise. The event is comprised of several skill, function and cargo tests, including balance tasks, which resemble everyday situations and which have to be mastered without mistakes in the short-

est time. Riding without mistakes is not a problem on a daily basis. But competition demands a style that does not waste a single second. Little mistakes sneak in easily and chances for victory disappear. In this discipline as well, vehicles are severely tested for quality. Sometimes there is a 2-m-long seesaw in the course which already has the deaths of bike frames on its conscience. Furthermore, all brakes and gears have to be perfectly tuned, because quick braking saves time as does quick shifting.

Everyday unfaired riders used to dominate these skill tests. But recently a new type of cyclist is challenging them. This is the racer who uses his racing HPV on a daily basis. These riders master their elite vehicles in traffic, in difficult and risky situations. This makes them strong competition for all defenders of comfortable everyday bikes. However, the organizers examine and judge the bikes themselves for everyday usability, including lights, fenders, cargo-capacity and daytime visibility measures. Here the bikes are compared according to settled criteria. Often participants themselves assess the bikes.

## HPV Speed Records... ...current as of October 2003

| Discipline | Start | S/T | M/F | Mi/hr | Time | Date | Driver | Vehicle | Designer |
|---|---|---|---|---|---|---|---|---|---|
| 200 Meter | f | S | M | 81.00 | 5.523 s | 10.02.02 | Sam Whittingham | Varna Diablo II | Georgi Georgiev |
| 200 Meter | f | S | F | 64.74 | 6.190 s | 10.02.02 | Andrea Blaseckie | Varna Mephisto | Georgi Georgiev |
| 200 Meter | f/arm | S | M | 32.60 | 13.803 s | 05.12.95 | Jacob Heilveil | Chairiot | GM/AV/Forsyth |
| 200 Meter | f | T | M | 68.405 | 6.540 s | 10.03.02 | Maynes/Doherty | Bearacuda | UC Berkeley |
| 200 Meter | f | T | F | 47.59 | 9.4 s | 03.05.80 | Bowen/Sandlin | | Tom Rightmeyer |
| 1 km | f | S | M | 79.79 | 28.037 s | 10.06.01 | Sam Whittingham | Varna Diablo | Georgi Georgiev |
| 1 km | f | S | F | 47.31 | 47.558 s | 07.27.99 | Andrea Blaseckie | Varna II | Georgi Georgiev |
| 1 km | f | T | M | 63.73 | 35.100 s | 17.09.93 | Markham/Whittingham | Double Gold Rush | Gardner Martin |
| 4 km | s | S | M | 42.70 | 3.29.56 m | 07.29.98 | Robert Lafleur | Lafleur IV | Robert Lafleur |
| 10 km | s | S | M | 47.29 | 7.53.02 m | 07.22.98 | Paul Buttemer | Varna | Georgi Georgiev |
| 100 km | s | S | M | 50.32 | 1.13.05 h | 07.27.02 | Lars Teutenberg | White Hawk | Vector/IKV |
| 1 Hour | s | S | M | 51.33 | 1.00 h | 07.27.02 | Lars Teutenberg | White Hawk | Vector/IKV |
| 1 Hour | s | S | F | 46.46 | 1.00 h | 08.20.02 | Ellen van der Horst | White Hawk | Vector/IKV |
| 12 Hour | s | S | M | 31.46 | 377.6 mi | 04.14.95 | Axel Fehlau | M5 Lowracer | Bram Moens & Derk Thijs |
| 1000 km | s | S | M | 26.68 | 23.17.21 h | 05.06.95 | Axel Fehlau | M5 Lowracer | Bram Moens & Derk Thijs |
| 24 Hour | s | S | M | 26.44 | 634.64 mi | 05.06.95 | Axel Fehlau | M5 Lowracer | Bram Moens & Derk Thijs |

f = flying start         S = Single         M = Male         arm = only arm power

s = standing start       T = Tandem         F = Female       D = Drag race measuring from Start

Records current as of: 10.15.03

# Ch. 4 / The Physics of Aerodynamics and Handling

The overall handling qualities, steering traits and powering of a recumbent depend on the same physical laws as a traditional bicycle. However, there are some differences which should be elaborated on.

Simply starting to ride a bike is a complex physical process, because the state of standing still gets changed into a state higher of energy, the state of moving.

The recumbent position prevents standing up and shifting body weight to help get under way. Inertia has to be overcome by seated muscle power alone. Starting is thus more precarious and energy-consuming than on an upright bike. Of course, this is most noticeable when you have to start up often, as in traffic, in the mountains or with luggage.

It is similar when it comes to acceleration: short 'jump' sprints, as are common in upright racing, are more difficult on a recumbent. Steady, controlled speed is more important on a recumbent than on an ordinary bike.

When going slowly at a lower height the stabilizing gyroscopic effect of small wheels is smaller, so the bike is proportionally more unstable. For safe starts, and also at slow speeds, one's center of gravity has to be kept directly above a bike's support line—the theoretical straight line between the contact points of the front and rear wheel. Sloppy starts and lazy riding, which are fine on an ordinary bike, are riskier on recumbents— the more so the lower the seat and the smaller the wheels. An over-the-shoulder bike with two-inch seat-height and dual 16" wheels, for instance, is a tippy starter indeed!

In all cycling, if your center of gravity falls off to one side, you steer in that direction to "catch" it and right yourself.

A good analogy for the start-up stability of upright versus recumbent is that it is easier to balance a long stick on the end of your finger than a two-inch stub.

A short recumbent has advantages here, as a short turning radius can bring the center of gravity more quickly above the support line during maneuvering. Steering geometry—angle of headtube and fork rake— also matter a great deal in this regard. Recumbents tend to have more variety in handling qualities than upright bikes. Some have heavy fork flop, others have a very light touch. Some have a steep headtube and negative fork rake for stability at high speed—at the price of having a strange, very

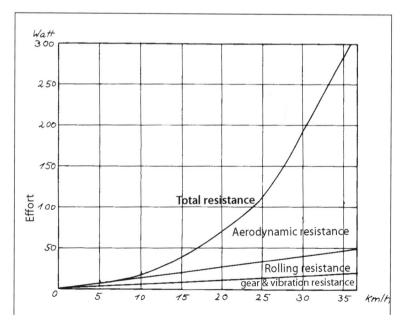

*By reducing the air resistance the power need gets significantly lower. The recumbent offers the best possibilities to reduce the front surface area.*

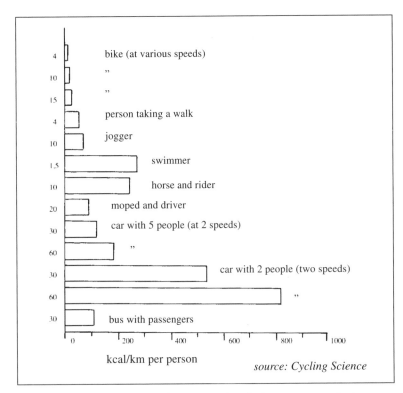

bike (at various speeds)
4

10   ,,

15   ,,

4   person taking a walk

10   jogger

1.5   swimmer

10   horse and rider

20   moped and driver

30   car with 5 people (at 2 speeds)

60   ,,

30   car with 2 people (two speeds)

60   ,,

30   bus with passengers

0   200   400   600   800   1000

kcal/km per person

*source: Cycling Science*

lower speeds. It is constant and the necessary power to overcome it increases proportionally with speed. Air resistance is the most critical factor at higher speeds. The power needed to overcome it rises geometrically in relation to speed—even to the third power. Therefore, for highest speeds, or easiest riding on windy days, we should direct our main attention to reducing air resistance.

Air resistance depends on the coefficient of air resistance (Cw value) and the frontal surface area of the vehicle, as well as vehicle speed and air density.

It should be emphasized that with the coefficient of air resistance alone, you cannot predict the speed potential of a vehicle. Only multiplication by frontal area makes a value that can be compared to other vehicles. This final value is called the effective frontal surface. The strength of air resistance can then be calculated, in newtons, like this:

$$F = \frac{\rho}{2} \cdot v^2 \cdot C_w \cdot A$$

(Rho ($\rho$) is air density, $v$ the streaming speed: ground-speed plus head wind or minus tail wind, $A$ = front surface area.)

If the required power is to be calculated in watts, the following formula is needed:

$$p = \frac{\rho}{2} \cdot v^3 \cdot C_w \cdot A$$

There are several ways to calculate effective frontal surface (Cw x $A$):

• wind tunnel (theoretically precise, but expensive, and of only limited practical application)

• rolling downhill method (cheap and simple, but requires suitable topography; inaccurate due to environmental variances)

• rolling out method (demands an even, horizontal test track, preferably indoors).

heavy steering feel at start-up: a design perhaps best suited for racing. Others are easy to ride at slow speed but twitchy when fast: perhaps more of a citybike set-up. It all depends on your druthers and your goals.

### *Resistances*

After inertia, air resistance is the next major factor in determining the speed and acceleration of a bike. If air resistance is lowered, the improvement can be felt right away. Other resistances determine speed as well. We will look into all of them.

Resistance in cycling can be categorized as three different types:

• air resistance
• rolling resistance
• mechanical friction

Mechanical resistances—such as friction in the drive chain—are relatively small. Rolling resistance is the biggest factor at

## *Aerodynamics in Theory*

In the following section some aerodynamic principles are described using a theoretical ideal. The deviation from this of a fully-faired recumbent is rather small. But when it comes to partly-faired models, style as well as quality of fairing play a major role. As a general rule one can say that any partial aerodynamics are worse than they would be if a similar design was extended into a complete fairing. The unfaired bike has the most disadvantage.

Contrary to the widespread opinion of a drop of water being the ideal aerodynamic form, one has to say that it is only ideal for its qualities and airflow surroundings. The same holds true for the oil drop which is sometimes in the literature thought to be optimal. Neither shape can be used to make an ideal vehicle body. At the most, only an "ideal airflow body" can be seriously considered. (See figure on page 63.)

A streamlined body has to part the airstream at its front then reunite it again in the rear. In theory, air flows without turbu-

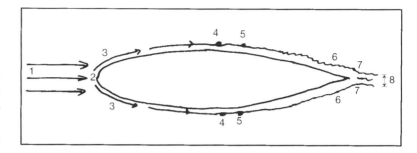

lence directly prior to the front of the machine (1). Pressure builds up right in front of the body (Pressure = force per unit area). Correlative with build-up of pressure is decrease in air speed. This accumulated pressure is not form-dependent, rather it depends only on speed of airflow. At the front part of the form, the speed of the flow will be zero at one point (called the 'accumulation point'), and here the pressure is at its highest (2). Now the air streams around the front part of the body, the accumulated pressure decreases again and the speed increases (3). The form determines the extent of flow dis-

*Streamline-optimized body. (See detailed explanation, starting on this page.)*

*If a fairing is supposed to be really fast, the total surface area and front surface have to be minimized.*

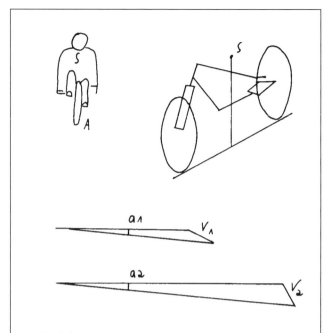

*The left sketch shows the position of the center of gravity "s" in a frontal perspective. The right sketch shows the center of gravity in partial profile. The lower sketch shows why steering a short recumbent is easier. If the center of gravity breaks free at one side, the rider has to catch his HPV until the center of gravity is back on the support line. Due to the shorter wheel base of short recumbents, this can be done easier than on a long recumbent. (source: Pro Velo/Werner Stiffel)*

ruption. A square wooden box has the same pressure accumulation as a streamlined body with the same frontal surface, but turbulence forms immediately at the edges of the box, and smoothness of subsequent airflow is disrupted.

From the second quarter of the body on, surface air layer friction gains influence. These are the layers of air which lay directly on the body. The body air in these surface layers rubs against the body surface and speed is lost. However, one must differentiate between laminar and turbulent border layers. With laminar air flow, the flow is parallel to the surface area. With turbulent flow, the flow is disturbed by cross move-

ments. When the speed is 0, the flow peels off and heads back to the front area (4). Turbulence develops (5). This phenomenon is called surface layer flow disruption. From this moment on, laminar flow turns into turbulent flow. This process is irreversible, but its development can be delayed. The turbulent air flow now follows the outlines of the body in the direction of the main flow (6). In the rear area of the body, the air streams reunite (7). With decreasing speed, however, the pressure from the rear increases again. The pressure behind the body will never equal the pressure in the front, though, because turbulence consumes part of the energy. Due to this incomplete regeneration, pressure resistance comes into play. If the pressure behind the body corresponded to the accumulated pressure in front, the coefficient of air resistance (Cw) would equal 0 (not taking friction into account).

Air flow does not have any chance to follow the outline of a wooden box, neither can it cause a pressure regain in the rear area. A big transfer area comes into existence. The size of the transfer area (surface measures of the rear turbulence) is the measure for the loss of pressure (8).

Beneficial aerodynamics thus keeps the pressure at the body's front and back relatively even. Unfortunately this theoretical ideal cannot be realized in practice. Four factors are responsible for that:

• angled airflow
• design compromise
• surface roughness
• system vibration

*Angled airflow*: In practice, there are no absolute 0-degree-airflow surfaces. In automobile construction, a 5-10 degree angled airflow is usually assumed. This circumstance makes the construction of aerodynamic parts very difficult. Moreover there are few laminar air flows in nature. Ground unevenness, obstacles (trees, houses, bridges, etc.) and moving bodies (cars, humans, etc.) cause permanent turbulence on the ground before vehicles ever even move through that air.

*Design compromise*: Even an unfaired recumbent is a very generous compromise made with the demands of aerodynamics. Given this perspective, it becomes obvious why even the smallest fairing has good effect. Even a small fairing or streamlined form improves the compromise towards better aerodynamics. Fairing design and a detailed analysis of side winds can be found in Chapter 5 on Design in the section on fairings.

*Surface roughness*: The surface roughness of a fully-faired vehicle equals the surface quality of the body paneling. If the bike is not faired at all, the surface roughness is determined by the individually streamlined components and the rider. As the rider represents the biggest surface, smoothing efforts at this place pay off (clothing, shaved

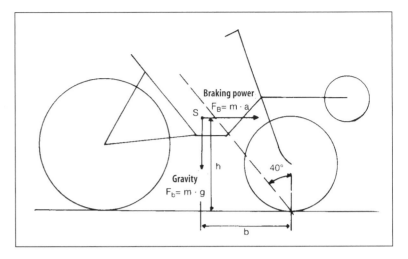

| Cw | Vehicle and position of driver |
|------|-------------------------------|
| 1.1 | BMX dirt-bike, driver upright |
| 1.1 | standard European bicycle, driver upright |
| 1.0 | touring bike, driver with stretched-out arms |
| 1.0 | tandem bicycle |
| 0.88 | racing bike, driver in racing position |
| 0.7 | bike with partial-fairing |
| 0.77 | unfaired recumbent (Easy Racer) |
| 0.5 | an upright bike drafting another |
| 0.11 | Vector—singletrack, world-record fully-faired vehicle |
| 0.05 | theoretically perfect recumbent |

(Cw-values of muscle-driven wheeled vehicles. From: *Spektrum der Wissenschaft* ["Spectrum of Science"] Feb. 1984, pp74ff.)

legs).

*System vibrations*: System vibrations are highly significant to aerodynamics. While suspension is usually only considered for reasons of comfort and improved traction, it is also beneficial to aerodynamics. "Micro bumps"—fine unevennesses on the road—cannot be absorbed even by wide, partially-inflated tires. Micro bumps put the complete system of vehicle and driver into constant vibrations. These vibrations cause the airstream at surface layers to tear off prematurely. This effect, however, is only relevant for fairings. System vibrations also develop as a consequence of asymmetrical pedaling, body movement, or rocking the bike. Good suspension can reduce all these effects. Even a fairing can be "suspended" with dampeners to reduce these losses.

## Braking

When it comes to recumbents, a combination of long wheelbase and low center of gravity increases braking capacity. In studies it turns out that a long recumbent's braking ability was 60 percent better than a normal bike. However, any increased weight will lengthen braking distances.

The process of braking is a combination of braking power, forward movement, gravity and surface friction. Gravity and friction create the practical ability to brake. Because of inertia, however, driver and vehicle tend to keep moving despite braking strength.

The forward-pointing moment of inertia that arises (which is as big as the braking strength) makes up the "flip-over" inertial moment (power x lever arm) above the height of the center of gravity. It always has to be smaller than the standing moment of inertia which is formed by the distance to the front center of gravity and the weight power. In the moment just before a vehicle begins to tip forward, both momentums are equally large and the burden on the front wheel is the biggest. That also means that the biggest deceleration is possible here. This then only depends on the coefficient for friction between tire and ground. This variable is at the most 0.85, which means that at the most 0.85 times the weight power of bike and rider can be used as braking strength. It is not a physical limit—more is just not possible unless you crash into a concrete flower box. Because of this value one can calculate that a rolling vehicle on tires will never flip forward when braking if the center of gravity lies below a line which goes through the front wheel's center of rotation and which runs in a 50-degree gradient away from the ground towards the rear.

> standing inertial moment = $m$ (mass) x $g$ (gravity) x $b$ (distance between front wheel hub and center of gravity)
>
> turn-over inertial moment = $m$ x $a$ (braking strength) x $h$ (height of center of gravity)
>
> braking strength $F_B = m$ x $a$
>
> momentum $F_G = m$ x $g$
>
> $a$ max = 0.85 $g$
>
> $g$ = gravity = 9.81 N/kg

### Cornering

The recumbent bike gives a totally new feeling to riding in curves which is fascinating and can be addicting. There is one main reason for it: While leaning the upper body sideways on a diamond frame in curves is possible and popular, it is usually unfeasible on a recumbent. The upper body and thus the head follow through every curve and experience every banking motion.

Most recumbents have ground-clearance enough for pedaling at speed through any "rideable" corner. This lets you increase speed in many corners. However, there are models with only a small clearance between pedal and front wheel. Thus your foot might hit the tire in tight or slow curves where the wheel has to move a lot to turn the bike. After you get used to it, proper pedal positioning to avoid any foot-strike becomes a reflex. However, you should be careful with such bikes while making tight or slow turns until you have fully internalized the required pedaling style. In high-speed corners, put the power on!

# Recumbent Biomechanics

The recumbent bicycle challenges body and mind differently than a normal bike. (It's interesting how each of the various HPVs challenge us differently, including tandems and trikes of all types.) With a recumbent, the out-of-saddle rocking pedal action is lost, but force against the seat-back is gained. In the beginning months you need to gently and gradually build up new muscles. You won't immediately be comfortable or efficient with the changed strain on the body—including knee joints, ligaments, blood flow to elevated legs, feet and sometimes hands.

Often, when conversation turns to out-of-the-saddle pedaling, it is said that it mobilizes amazing power. The real strength of the rocking pedal action, during which the rider stands in his pedals, however, is to be found somewhere else. Martin Staubach, recumbent rider and builder, comments on this in the following:

"So what is body weight able to do anyway? It only forms the counter power against the power, which the standing cyclist conveys into the pedals. Action equals reaction. What happens on a recumbent? The seat takes over the reaction, the counter power to the pedal power. If the seat wasn't there, the rider would slide back and the pedal wouldn't move. On a racing upright bike a different process takes place. The racing cyclist pushes down so much into the pedals that he pushes himself out of the saddle. The reaction is that body weight is now too small. Thus he accelerates his body upward instead of his pedals downward—this he doesn't really want! So he pulls himself down again at the handle bars. Consequently he strains his muscles and metabolism, but not to go forward. However, when standing while pedaling he uses different muscles which have not yet been overused. That means he's using 'fresh muscles. That is the only real advantage, and not the dubious 'use of body weight.'"

However, gravity does seem to assist the uprighter in another small way: it helps the legs drop through the most powerful phase of the pedal stroke, through the 3-o'clock phase, where the leg is exerting the most force. For recumbenteers, gravity only helps the pedals to fall through the "bottom" of their stroke, where the leg is extended and exerting less force. Still, recumbent riders can learn to take advantage of such help, by letting the legs "fall" in a relaxed way as they go through that part of the stroke, or

by adding downward force there to greatly minimize that infamous dead zone.

But how do these factors fully play out when it comes to the recumbent bike?

Options for out-of-saddle rocking pedal action would be desirable in a recumbent, but are unfeasible at this point, construction-wise. It would require a dramatically convertible frame that switched between upright and recumbent modes, ideally on-the-fly. People are exploring this, though! One almost-stylish model was presented by George Reynolds, another by the ultimate scavenging designer, Joe Kochanowski.

The current situation requires a rather different way of riding for the recumbent cyclist, especially in mountains. Cyclists must be conscious of the fact that they cannot stand up in case of a sudden need for power. Instead they have to determine their sustainable speed at the bottom of a hill and maintain it as best they can to the top. Lower than usual gears help in case of surprises on the way up. If they start off too fast and greatly over-estimate themselves, they have quite a bill to pay on the way up.

Studies have shown that the significance

*Sam Whittingham getting ready for a run in his 81-mph record-holding, ultra-low Varna "Diablo." Note the ventilation tube running from a hole in the nose. (photo: Arne Hodalic)* of the out-of-saddle rocking pedal action can be overrated, especially at low speeds. T. W. Ryschon determined, after testing at the University Texas Human Performance Center, that at a low speed of about 13 mph and a gentle uphill of 4%, the rocking pedal action style demands more power than if you remain seated. Another study at the California State University at Long Beach confirmed other suspicions. A test took place on a surface 3.5 km long with a 150m rise. The test riders (a man and woman) reached 2.7 and 2.4 on the USCF's "dynamometer" effort output scale. Their results showed that it is not the rocking pedal action in itself that is useful, but the combination of switching back and forth between riding seated and standing which is the fastest solution. The improvement in performance is very small anyway. The rocking pedal action alone is about one percent slower than the "back-and-forth" style, while it took 3% longer to ride entirely seated.

If you transfer these findings to the recumbent bike, I would suspect that with the same amount of training on the chosen bike

*The inner-life of the "Cheetah" 68 mph bike reveals an ergonomy that is oriented towards the exploitation of energy. It is not useful for everyday use or long distances. (photo: Team Cheetah)*

a recumbent of equal weight will not be as far behind in the mountains as untrained recumbent bicyclists and critics think. It goes without saying that a recumbent will never measure up to the mountain goats of the Tour de France: 'bents weigh more and that 3% adds up! However, I was touring in the Scottish Highlands with 45 lbs of luggage, and found that I could master the rises quickly. I could overcome even a 20 percent grade at a speed that I did not have to be ashamed of. Practice greatly improves results! Small, steep hills do seem to require sharper effort on a recumbent, but those willing to make such effort find that they can stay at the front of the pack.

Recumbent riders do usually find in moderate terrain that they make up for time lost in the hills by improved speed on the flats and downhills.

Pedaling in the recumbent position demands a special development of certain muscles. Worth mentioning are the lower fringes of the *Vastus laterales*, the *Vastus mediales* and the *Rectus femoris*. The first two are located just above the kneecap, on the right and left sides; the third one runs all the way from the upper leg down to the kneecap.

Before the significance of the kneecap becomes apparent, it is necessary to take a look at the motion sequence in the knee area. Whereas on a normal bike, gravity helps the legs to be sent on their way in the strong phase of pedaling, in "benting" the legs have to be held up. The weight of the legs, feet, pants and shoes pulls them down and demands muscle tension and energy to hold them up (see "Pedals and Shoes" section of Ch. 2; pg. 48). The nature and consequences of this specific strain can be compared with those of a construction crane.

A lifting crane has a base pole (femur) with a joint at its end (knee joint), which is connected to the swing arm (lower leg). Wires run across a steel trestle at the joint.

Here is the focus of highest strain. The more the swing arm approaches a right angle towards the base pole, the bigger the lever gets and the greater the forces are at the joint. There are exact tables for cranes about how much weight is permitted in which swing arm position. There is no such table for the knee. Neither does human sensitivity to pain replace this table—because if humans had nerves in their joints, every step would be painful.

The kneecap's task is similar to the one of the main cable at the joint of the lifting crane. The *Vastus mediales* and *Vastus laterales* hold the kneecap in its groove. The *Rectus femoris* pushes the ligaments up and reduces the forces which work on the kneecap. If this muscle is underdeveloped, the cartilage under the kneecap gets used up more quickly.

During recumbent pedaling, these three muscles are used to a high degree. Hard work with such tension in a horizontally held leg can have painful consequences for a cyclist if he makes the following mistakes:

• pedaling cadence too low
• start too soon with strenuous rides
• not allowing recovery or build-up phases in muscle training

The consequences of these "deadly sins" of recumbent sport are simple. If the pedaling cadence is too low, the need for power rises and so does length of time in each crank position. If frequency is high, strain is reduced enormously. One also needs the already-mentioned muscles for the "holding-up" work of the legs. Not even racing cyclists possess either to a sufficient extent to start with aggressive recumbent riding. Only the long distance runner uses these muscles to a similar degree as the HPV pilot. Those who come from running to riding the recumbent won't have many problems with their knees. Here are some rules that can help the novice:

• start off your training very slowly
• do running as well
• use a high pedaling cadence
• no straining in the first three months
• develop and perfect a "round" spinning style of pedaling
• do not use long crank arms; they make round spinning more difficult; use 170 mm or—if you are over 6' tall—you can try 172.5 mm, 175 mm max

Once a recumbent is bought, some racers think that they have to achieve a personal best on their home course right away. In realizing this goal, they might put a death sentence on their recumbent life. If these small, special muscles are strained, they will need a long time to recuperate. If they are overused again during recuperation, they get inflamed. Then up to half a year may pass before one may think again of cautious training.

If a rider starts with slow, daily workouts of 2 to 3 miles, which might be raised to 10 to 20 miles over 3 months, avoiding steep mountains and racing, the muscles will be built up without problems. At the same time, cadence training has to take place. From the beginning, pedaling cadence should be about 90 rpm, for hillclimbing it should go down to no less than 75 rpm.

In conclusion, riding with a recumbent (especially on uphills) is mostly a matter of adaptation. With a good start and a continuous rise of demand in the training plan, the recumbent bike will not be more harmful to the knee area than a normal bike. There are certainly people with physical abnormalities (e.g. too small kneecaps) who will have disadvantages. They will only become happy on the recumbent with elaborate training. But they wouldn't be any better off on a normal bike.

By the way, the lower the crank is in comparison to seat height, the easier it is to adapt to recreational riding on a 'bent.

*Matt Weaver races this elegant LWB, FWD, indirect-steer custom highracer from Rotator to first place in the unfaired road race at Battle Mountain, Nevada. (photo: Arne Hodalic)*

### *"Round" pedaling and spinning*

Round pedaling is a controversial theme in the world of cyclists. During one rotation of the crank the pedaling leg goes through various positions which have different lever forces. The well-known and feared dead zones in the extended or retracted positions do not produce any lever force from above during simple pedaling. Only when pedal power is applied tangentially is it possible to overcome these weak points quickly.

The more time spent in overcoming dead spots, the more "square" or "edged" one's pedaling becomes. Pedaling should be as round as possible for both physical and bio-mechanical reasons. High pedaling frequency makes it easier to keep the stroke round as the foot spends less time in the weak zones of each rotation.

In contrast to the dead points on an upright racing bike, which occur in the vertical 6- and 12-o'clock positions, they occur in the horizontal 3- and 9-o'clock positions on a recumbent. The advantage here goes to the recumbent: when pedaling down through the 9-o'clock position, the weight of the whole leg helps minimize the dead zone—in fact, a sneaky bit of power can be added using a chopping action, best applied with the help of a longish seat-length.

This gravity-assist attack on the dead zone at full extension can be effective and exciting to use. It is more powerful than its counterpart in upright riding where one pulls through the dead zone in a manner like wiping your foot on a rug, but without gravity helping.

A cyclist who has a smooth spin on an upright will find that he somewhat has to relearn spinning as he adapts to a recumbent. The areas where one must exert to stay smooth and get through dead-zones are shifted back 90 degrees out of phase with gravity. For instance, the fully-retracted dead-zone at 12-o'clock for an uprighter is easy to get through, but for a benter this occurs at 9-o'clock and is where gravity is working most against his stroke.

The seat determines the position of a recumbent rider. Because a chair-type seat allows less room to shift around, the knee constantly works in the same angle, while the angle on a normal bike can be changed easily due to small rocking in the saddle, or shifting from fore to aft, or by raising the torso in going from the drops to the tops of the bars. One should prevent an overly focused burden on the knee area by occasional changes of the leg-length distance or by a soft tension seat, or seat straps which can be tightened or loosened.

With regular pedals or toe-clips, it takes some effort to keep the feet on the pedals, especially for long rides. On bumpy roads, it's easy for the feet to get tossed off the pedals and out of the clips. Working against this increases the burden on the knees. Fortunately there is a marvelous and reliable solution: a clipless pedal binding system. Look, Time, Shimano SPD, Speedplay—all these and many more make great clipless pedals. Only when the shoe can take over the effort of holding up the foot can the knee be eased from this burden. Cleat position for 'benting is sometimes preferred to be more toward the heel to further reduce knee strain.

*The first modern European production recumbent was the Windcheetah from the British Mike Burrows. (photo: Mochet)*

*Moi pris par
"Dagbladet"
18/5 - 35.*

The pre-war streets of Europe were very trying on cyclists. But even on cobblestone roads the recumbent was more comfortable than a normal bike. Recumbents were available with lights and fenders. Thus their advantages were also beneficial in everyday use. (photos: Mochet)

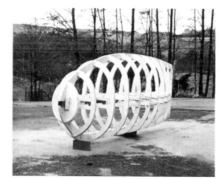

Fairing made by Zillner Design:
– establishing the measurements
  with a "wooden man's" help
– skeleton
– original form
– female mold
– mounted fairing
  (photos: Zillner Design)

The start of the Trondheim-Oslo
long distance race. Recumbents
with or without fairing were
allowed to participate.

(photos above, below: John Cassidy)

Above, Whittingham's Varna "Diablo" streaks by at record speeds at the Battle Mountain Speed Challenge in Nevada.

Below, exhausted racer/builder Thom Ollinger is helped from the "Coslinger Special" after a speed run on the 3-mile course.

Sam Whittingham celebrates his 81-mph world record with Georgi Georgiev, Varna designer. "Virtual Rush" camera bike, below.

(photos: Arne Hodalic)

*(photos above: www.tim.be)*

You can always admire the huge variety of creative constructions at gatherings such as Cycle Vision. Above is one of the rare belly recumbents.

The "Tour Easy" series by Easy Racers is one of the oldest and most successful recumbent lines in the US. It is renowned as the archetype of the "chopper recumbent," but you'd better watch out: it is much faster than it appears to be...

*"Gold Rush" on its way to a record race. Fred Markham was the first person to reach the 65 mph mark in 1986. Gardner Martin, builder of the vehicle (R), and a team member launch "Fast Freddy." (photo: Easy Racer)*

*Before you sew a cloth fairing you should build a test model. Old bed sheets or trash bags will do...*

*The race of the giants starts. The foremost places are often taken by faired vehicles, thus the danger of falling due to traffic congestion at the start gets reduced. (photo: Veloladen)*

*"WYMS" ("With Your Main Squeeze")—front and rear drive.*

Martin Sörensen in a faired HPV on the road between Trondheim and Oslo.

Fast and beautiful: This is a faired HPV supported by the Mavic company. Lack of foot holes and a tiny windshield mean it is strictly a race vehicle, but many racers create faired bikes which are competitive as well as safe on the road.

The decisive moment: "Cutting Edge" passes "Gold Rush."

The "mixed" field during races is colorful and diverse, but not without risk. As the performance ability varies widely among vehicles who are welcomed into HPV events, passing becomes a refined art.

A front fairing improves weather protection and makes the vehicle faster. Neither field of vision nor handling of the bike deteriorate.

A meticulous wind tunnel test of the M5 "Tour" brings it to light: Faired recumbents are the best choice when it comes to aerodynamics. Other ways of testing let you avoid the wind tunnel —which makes people with small wallets happy.

*The popular children's event at the Cycle Vision festival brings out quite a few young riders. (photo: www.tim.be)*

*A front fairing pays off especially in bad weather. It helped the French Francoise and Bernard Magnouloux to deal with cold winter winds at the North Cape. (photos: Francoise and Bernard Magnouloux)*

*HPV sports: distance races...*

*... 200-meter sprints...*

*... and practical-ability tests...*

To ease knee strain in yet another way, many recumbenteers find that adjusting their seats farther back than usual is a good idea for awhile.

After you acquire a base of training and adaptation, and become a fit recumbent cyclist, you'll find yourself developing personalized pedaling tricks to suit your own special needs (such as "the Hammer Chop," described earlier). However, total adaptation for high performance might take a couple years of steady riding, so don't rush it.

Recumbent racers often pull back hard on the bars to add power to their stroke and to reduce the pushing effort needed for big gears or fast sprinting. You can also change leg angles and muscle groups by pulling on the bars as you pedal and leaning forward in your seat. Or you can shove yourself back and roll the hips downward to use new muscles. Also try slouching down in the seat by sliding your hips forward, to hide out of the wind more and to shorten your stroke, raising your knee height. Also push through and pull down with your heels, using the old 'ankling' technique.

Tim Brummer of Lightning fame describes riding one-handed and pushing on your knees with your free hand to add surprising force for hard uphills (alternating hands).

Occasionally changing your seat angle also allows new muscles to be used. It also changes your exposed frontal area—when further reclined one can often ride faster into a headwind. It changes how your weight is supported—more by your back, or more by your butt. It changes the relative open- or closed-ness of pedaling angle—which can help with hillclimbing. Changing seat angle also has the effect of changing leg-length, so you might have to adjust that, too. It's just another factor to vary to suit your style, maybe even changing back and forth on the same ride. (Spring-tensioned seat quick-releases can allow easy 'on the fly' changes).

Recumbent pedaling is limited in some ways (as is any kind of pedaling) but it opens up other options for creatively getting the most from your arsenal of strokes.

### Frame Fit and Size Adjustment

Like any bike, the recumbent has to be custom-tailored to fit the rider.

Handlebar height, width and orientation is almost as critical to the recumbent rider as it is for the upright rider. Bar position for best power leverage, for best handling and cornering, for easy entering and exiting, for ideal breathing, for least strain in holding, and for best aerodynamics will all vary from person to person. Many racers prefer a short bar positioned quite far away from the chest, so that the arms are quite straight, to optimize pulling power. Some prefer a relaxed "chipmunk" position, with arms closer to the chest, usually mounted with a pivoting stem to let you get in and out of the seat easily. Some choose underseat steering, which can range from a very aero narrow bar under the legs to wide and low, right to hand. Test them all for yourself! The results usually aren't critical to health, but they can change your enjoyment of the ride or your results in a race.

In the field of traditional diamond frames

*Production highracers such as the Bacchetta "Aero" are competitive in racing yet offer a smoother ride than lowracers, with better view of traffic for everyday use. "Touching down" from the high seat takes getting used to.*

there are very exact scientific studies about the ideal distance between the saddle topline and the crank. Of all of them only the "Eddie Borysewicz" method is transferable to the recumbent. The saddle, or other leg-length adjustment such as a sliding boom, is first set at a distance which is likely to be too short—as when your heel touches the pedal with outstretched leg. Then, gradually, the length is increased until the pelvis starts moving during easy pedaling. Now it is cautiously shortened again until pelvis movement stops. This is then likely to be a fairly correct leg-length setting for you.

Bernhard Klar found an interesting way to determine ideal bottom bracket distance from seat during his recumbent-ergonomy research. The Klar method involves first unmounting one crank arm and reinstalling it in the same direction as the other crank arm on the bottom bracket, so that the crank forms a 'U.' Then while sitting on the bike, one puts pressure on both pedals and inserts a stout 15 mm disk between each pedal and heel. Adjust seat position so that one is just able to straighten out the heels and still clamp the disk.

From an ergonomic view it is perhaps better to chose a distance somewhat long rather than too short, because a long setting allows for changing strain-angles for ligaments and muscles while a too-short distance concentrates the burden. Pain (mostly in the knees) can be the consequence. Some knee problems can be helped with an extension of this distance. Sometimes early-season weakness can be worked away by riding with a shorter leg-length on short, easy rides, until the initial adaptation to holding one's legs up is made.

Regardless of scientific studies and research, individual specialization is possible, even likely. Everybody should ride with a length adjustment that does not cause him or her pain. I personally ride on my normal bike with a saddle 10 mm higher than science recommends. On the recumbent my seat is 20 mm "higher" than it "should" be.

### Ergonomic efficiency

Chester Kyle has recently done studies on aerodynamics and ergonomics. Although such research is still in toddler's shoes, one can deduce a few coarse generalizations. Taking a racing bike as 100 percent, Kyle found that the degree of efficiency of the recumbent position is 97 and the belly recumbent is third with 96. There was no listing of the ergometers/bikes tested, neither were the riders described, so the conclusions aren't overly solid.

Still, this does hint at what a lot of recumbent fans do not want to admit: the recumbent does not seem to measure up to a traditional bike when it comes to basic ergonomics. Such measurable losses, however, are compensated for in various recumbents by greater comfort, more pleasure when riding, and superior aerodynamics.

*This rider improved the sports ergonomics of a stock Vision R-40 by using a 20" rear wheel (replacing a 26") to lower the seat, and by raising the crank due to reversing the fork! (photo: Jeff Potter)*

# Ch. 5 / Basics of Recumbent Design

## A Showcase of Philosophy in Design

On a formal level, bike design is about measurements, weights, degrees of strength, and angles. However, these are only the culmination of an original guiding philosophy. That is why this chapter does not start with an elaboration on tube lengths and angles. Instead, I'm first going to tell the "big picture" story of several different bike designs, to cast light on the general ideas behind why they were built as they were. Perhaps in this way new recumbent fans can gain insight into which qualities seem to demand which basic construction, before they start their quest.

These profiles, and the detailed feature comparisons that follow, apply equally to those who wish to home-build as to those who want to know what to look for among the many models and options offered by manufacturers.

This basic info plus the ever-important *test riding* of as many models as you can find, will confirm what you really want in a bike. For the detailed specs of available models, look to *RCN*'s "Buyer's Guide" and reviews, as well as BentRiderOnline.com; also explore the many websites in the Appendix.

For illustration here I have chosen neither the popular long recumbents from Easy Racers and RANS, nor the typical short recumbents of Lightning or Bacchetta. My examples are given simply to illustrate conspicuous differences in overall design theory. The selection does not imply any quality comparison.

### Bevo Bike: power due to relaxation

Klaus Beck ("Be-") and Hans.-H. Voss ("-vo") possess years of experience with recumbents. Their goal in making a new bike was to create an everyday model that ensured both active and passive safety plus comfort; permits adjustment to the size of the cyclist and his seating preference; can carry luggage and which itself can be easily carried—all for an inexpensive price.

For safe traffic visibility, the seat was positioned at a 30" height. Thus even if the seat is tilted back very flat, one can still see and be seen.

To keep frame construction simple, to reduce the chances of your pants being splashed with dirt, to avoid a long chain, and to guarantee the smooth working of the rear suspension, Beck and Voss decided in favor of front wheel drive. FWD is still a rather uncommon drive solution, but it offers all those virtues, plus enough maneuverability for driving defensively. If com-

*The luggage rack of the BeVo is ideal. When loaded, the driving behavior changes only slightly. (photo: Voss)*

*The BikeE combined functional design with low weight and a good price.*

*Following the motto "cost what it must," the Lightning R-84 (shown with revised F-40 fairing) stands out: The frame costs over $1000 per pound!*

and the result is astonishing: this bike meets the needs and hopes of mobility for many people who had not even been interested in recumbents before.

### Lightning R-84: $$ doesn't matter!

Tim Brummer, owner and developer at Lightning, discovered the recumbent via the HPV record sprints and his bikes show this original inspiration. He strives to bring the intoxication of riding an Italian race bike to a faster, more comfortable position. The results are also similar to Italian racing bikes in regard to price.

The profile of the R-84 features a low seat (16") and a high crank (8" above the seat)—this bike is fast! Superior mountain-climbing and sprint capability are produced by a relatively upright seat angle. The brash geometry also meets the demands of speedy criterium races. Complete suspension provides for sufficient ground contact, even on rough surfaces. Is anything missing here? Maybe one thing: weight.

Of course, an Italian racing bike pleases the eye, and your eyebrows rise admiringly when you lift it. No difference here: with suspension, hydraulic brakes, 24 gears, fabric seat and top steering, the bike still weighs only 20.2 lbs because of its light carbon frame (3 lbs). The other side of the coin, however, is a price of $3,500 for frame, $6000 for a complete Campy/Ti bike, or $7500 for faired F-90. Price is not a worry for this series. The "only" goal is a fast racing vehicle with great handling qualities in turns and in the mountains.

bined with hub-shifting, FWD is absolutely suitable for everyday use. Beck and Voss defined the best wheelbase to be "somewhere between short and long recumbent." In this way they were able to combine the advantages of both approaches, and they arrived at a bike that is not much longer than a conventional city bike. This is called "compact" or "medium" wheelbase and is popular on increasing numbers of city recumbents. The over-seat steering reduces the time one might need for getting used to a recumbent bike and contributes to better aerodynamics.

It is a great creative challenge to construct a bike for town, country and water (ferries!)

### BikeE: you only get real change when you reach the masses

A small company from Corvallis, Oregon, pursued an entirely different goal. For this co-op, "change" meant transportation for the masses. And the masses can be most easily characterized by a lack of money. Accordingly, a recumbent has to be inexpen-

sive. Furthermore, it has to be easy to make, easy to ride, easy to adjust, look nice, and not use special parts.

Only three (!) welds create their main aluminum frame (for bottom bracket and headset area); the rear end is bolted on. The goal of really simple handling suggested an upright seat, low bottom bracket position, and adjustable top steering. A well-organized production, close tolerances and spiffy details such as quick-release seat, simple frame, and invisible welds flush with the surface all was available in this city bike for under $1000. Plus you got a 3x7 Sachs hub, and weight under 30 lbs, other models offered suspension. This compact or medium wheelbase brand isn't suited for racing or long tours, but it is perfect for shopping trips in the city center since it offers easy on-off, maneuverability, and easy oversight of traffic. However, BikeE's attempt to mass market eventually hit a snag and it declared bankruptcy after years of leadership and popular success. An online fan-club now helps fans of this brand keep their bikes in good shape. Huge companies like Sun and CCM, and small ones like Cycle Genius, are taking up the cause of quality affordable recumbents, and—like pioneer BikeE—are finding the compact to be a popular, market-friendly format.

## Aeroproject Ultratief: flying low to takeoff

In the beginning was the goal: to win the European HPV Master Championship. Only then did the team form: Aeroproject—Guido Mertens and friends. Then the fairing came into existence using 'Whippet,' a copy of the proven Mavic body. Only the bike was missing: thus the 'Aeroproject Ultratief.' ('Ultratief' = 'ultra-low' in German.)

The actualization flowed step by step from the givens. First, measure fairing and driver. The fit between the bodywork and the measurements of the driver formed the

*The "Ultratief" early-era lowracer was originally designed for a fairing, but it looks and rides good "naked" as well.*

basis for constructing the bike. Seat and crank height arose from the limits imposed by the fairing walls. The seat angle was determined according to the shape of the front end. Now the bike should run as smoothly as possible. The idea of suspension was set aside due to the already extremely low-down construction, so the choice was made for a smooth-riding 28-inch rear wheel. It would be stiff at least and have a very good jump for passing. Because the frame was stretched out and quite long, and due to the curves in the design, it was actually quite soft-riding while still being extremely stiff side-to-side for pedaling performance. A comfortable racing sedan thus came into existence. An S-shaped fork increased ride smoothness even more. During testing the bike turned out to ride very nicely without a fairing—so teammate Manfred Harig decided to offer a series of 10 to the public. By the way: they reached their goal and won the European Master title.

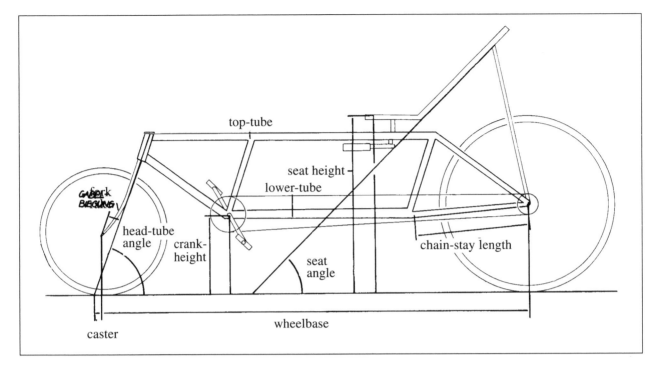

## Basic Design Principles

The basics of any bike are the wheels. Seldom is there a question as to their number; the basic rule being two, as in a classic bike.

The recumbent mode does include the possibility for the sensible use of three wheels—for advantages in stability, especially at low seat heights and low speeds, and for improved handling in slippery conditions. But due to the added complexity and variety of frame design and steering arrangements for the trike concept, this book will only discuss the two-wheeled (single-track) vehicles.

The most common comparative criterion for recumbent bicycles is length. This evaluation is based on the length of the wheelbase and position of the crank. Overall length of vehicle is the result of wheel size and wheelbase.

Variation between models in a category are more a consequence of design and ad-justment to rider height than a desire to change the general handling qualities of the format.

The wheelbase of a long recumbent (often labeled "LWB") results from the position of the seat, the position of the crank and the wheel size. This is because if the seat is high it can be placed well above the wheel-hubs, which can allow for a short wheelbase model (termed "SWB"). If you put the seat low, the seat must be between the wheels and they tend to then be placed farther apart. If you put the crank low, the crank also tends to be positioned between the wheels, again resulting in a long wheelbase, or the crank can go in front of the front wheel, either high or low, thus creating a SWB and/or a Lowracer.

The seat on a long wheelbase is located near the rear wheel. It can be located in front of the rear wheel, like the bikes from Easy Racer and Radius, or over the rear wheel, like those produced by Roulandt. The distance between crank and seat will equal the frame height plus seat post of a normal bike, with reserve space for adjustment. The customer's choice of a thicker seat mat or even different shoes can make the frame-size vary a few centimeters, which should not be neglected when evaluating. However, most makers design their frames to be adjustable for a wide range of rider heights. This is achieved by a sliding seat and/or an extendible crank area. As for the next distance from crank to head tube, an additional 10 cm should be included so the front wheel can easily clear pedals, shoe-tips and fenders. These calculations result in the wheels being spread far enough apart to be called a long recumbent and to give the ride comfort and stability expected of this breed. 65-70" is an average wheelbase for a long recumbent.

The total vehicle length of a short recumbent is calculated by considering the size of the rear wheel, the length of the driver's legs and the position of the seat. The final wheelbase then results from the intended weight distribution—determined by the position of the seat between the two wheels—and from the size of the front wheel.

The compact or medium wheelbase bike is a form of long recumbent. This format puts the crank very close to the headtube, often with some heel overlap of the front wheel, but it gives more stability than a SWB with easier handling than a LWB, and is the design choice of several mass-market oriented models.

Lowracers are a high performance breed of short recumbent. They have an extremely low, reclined seat (4-10" above ground) and high crank (between 5-10" above the seat). If you can stop and easily hold yourself up with your hand, you have a lowracer. They have a short wheelbase because the front wheel needs to be tucked quite far under the rider so the pedals can clear it.

Highracers are another racing variant. They are as high or higher off the ground than a typical SWB, but their seats are greatly reclined and wheels are often large or even equal in size—these features add to speed, comfort and traffic visibility, but hinder easy starts and stops.

### Advantages of long recumbent:

- relaxed upright posture with great view of road
- feet are on the ground quickly
- easy starts and stops
- clear chainline makes all gears usable
- luggage transport very good
- partial fairing easy to mount
- extremely good braking power
- smooth straight-ahead riding and superior comfort even without suspension
- front and rear wheels as crumple-zone

### Disadvantages of long recumbent:

- heavier than short model
- longer turning radius, less responsive
- weight distribution can be too much to the rear so front wheel is prone to sliding out
- often mediocre aerodynamics
- bulky

### Advantages of short recumbent:

- wider variety of positions to select from
- sporty handling
- lightweight
- same length as normal bike
- improved aerodynamics

### Disadvantages of short recumbent:

- slowspeed handling acquired after some practice
- harsher ride, needs more suspension
- sometimes less highspeed stability
- sometimes requires adjustment of riding style

• steeply reclined seats make turning head to see rearwards uncomfortable
• in some models extreme braking can result in tip-over
• only carefully measured geometries and lengths are all-around useful

### Advantages of lowracers:

• small frontal area
• low air resistance
• good standing at traffic lights, since hand can easily be put down
• extreme speeds in corners are possible

### Disadvantages of lowracers:

• limited steering angle
• low height demands great care when riding in traffic
• slowspeed riding only possible after some practice
• mounting and dismounting can be awkward
• harsh ride without suspension

# Wheelbase

Wheelbase is not just a way to describe recumbent categories, it also plays a major role in vehicle riding behavior.

A short recumbent wheelbase is in general 42" or less (but less than 36" is uncommon). This gives us clues as to likely riding behavior.

In general a wheelbase under 42" provides:

• maneuverability at slow speeds
• agile handling in fast turns
• sensitivity to steering input

Longer wheelbase provides:
• rock-steady straight-ahead handling
• safe reliability, including rough surfaces
• stability at high speeds

Any desired handling quality can be realized by a combination of steering-head angle, fork rake, trail, as well as front wheel flop. (The trail, or caster, is the distance between the point where the imaginary line formed by the projection of the steering axis hits the ground, and where the tire hits the ground.) The existence of these four factors would seem to make the previously men-

*Steve Delaire's Rotator line includes the classic high performance "Pursuit" —rare among long wheelbase production models in that it's made for speed as well as comfort, with low seat, high crank, light weight. It is available with front and rear fairings.*

tioned descriptions of ride quality based on wheelbase more vague—and rightly so. But in all cases, only a good mix of all four variables creates good handling qualities. In this regard they behave like punch ingredients: only good proportions result in a good final flavor, with each factor affecting the others. No one attempts to get the best of all worlds by making the same punch both sweet and dry, but specific ingredients go into making tasty varieties of each!

To track down the various phenomena of ride quality, one starts by distinguishing between steering behavior and suspension behavior. Steering behavior is determined by head angle, fork rake, vehicle height and trail. The head angle is the angle between the horizontal line of the wheels' contact area and the head tube. Trail results from the interaction of head angle and fork rake.

It is interesting that knowledge and variety in this area in the field of upright bikes isn't as active and widespread as it once was. 'Knowledgeable' upright cyclists tend to gravitate toward sporty models for the most part, which vary very little. Riders of relaxed-handling bikes are perhaps considered uninterested in anything besides getting to the store or beach.

It seems that recumbent designers and buyers have to know more, across the board, to make wise decisions. They can learn to use the amazingly wide range of available ride qualities and handling features to their great advantage. The field of HPVs really opens up cycling.

# Trail

Generally, the following holds true for the trail of a 20-inch front wheel:

Trail longer than 2":
• stable handling at high speed
• slow response to steering
• steering mistakes are more tolerated
• comfortable, solid handling in curves
• slow riding is easy
  = "great for touring and racing"

Trail shorter than 2":
• light, steering reacts quickly
• agile behavior in bends
  = "good for sporty use"

The handling and steerability of a bike depends on the trail of the front wheel. If you have chosen a very steep headtube angle and you want to change the handling, you will have to change the trail. The practical effect of this is that the longer the trail gets, the greater the tracking firmness becomes. The longer the trail, the safer the bike can be steered at high speed, although it is the other way around when riding slowly. The headtube angle creates the initial trail, the fork bend or angle modifies it.

The steering behavior of a flat steering head angle can partly be compensated by a stronger fork bend. A vertical fork without a bend would have zero trail and would have absolutely direct steering. In unicycling or acrobatic cycling such forks are used, because direct ultrafast steering is a necessity. Child tricycles have steeper steering angles as well.

How would a steep-head, no-trail combination effect a recumbent bike? —On a fast ride down the mountains, a small pebble would be enough to put the front wheel out of track and an accident could not be prevented. But with proper trail a bike just glides over ground unevenness and stones.

What is the explanation for this? A rotating wheel stabilizes itself around its long axis. In physics this quality is called gyroscopic force. The above-mentioned pebble makes the front wheel, tightly connected to the fork, move the fork together with the headset bearing. This wheel diversion gets enhanced by a dropping in vehicle height. A bike moving straight ahead is in its highest position. When handlebars are moved to the left or right, the front end of a bike is lowered. The weight on the front end causes a bike that is slightly tilted to turn even further in the direction it is already going.

Fortunately, reality doesn't work out as drastically as theory would have it. You learn to counter all these forces from the first day you learn to ride a bike—we steer the bike quickly back under itself to prevent the falling action. With increasing speed the influence of these forces on handling and ride quality actually get less important, because gyroscopic force and rolling resistance increase.

Fork and wheel design can all help to counteract the 'falling front end' phenomenon. A lever is added to the stabilizing gyroscopic force of the front wheel. This is done by way of the trail which results from the bend in the fork. The power of gyroscopic force also depends on wheel size and weight. A bigger wheel has greater inertia which makes gyroscopic power stronger. A heavy wheel has a similar effect. Here we can see how small ultralight wheels could have a surprising influence on bike handling.

The weight on the front axle is also significant for handling and ride quality, since rolling resistance rises as weight increases. Additionally, as it becomes heavier, leaning the steering assembly becomes more difficult. Thus driving slowly becomes harder. To sum this up, the following general rules can be deduced:

- heavy front axle burden—make trail small
- long wheelbase—make trail smaller

- large wheel—make trail proportionally bigger
- if you want to improve tracking steadiness—increase trail
- if steering should be quicker—shorten trail

Extreme angles, rake and trail are not advisable, as it requires other unconventional measures to counter-balance them. Your goal should be a smooth-riding geometry.

However, if high speeds are your thing, with a small front wheel it has been found that a steep headtube angle with a straight, or negative-rake, fork makes for very secure handling and steadiness. This set-up creates lots of trail—the front wheel tends to follow the direction of effort very reliably. This is like the set-up used in motor-paced racing on the velodrome at very high speeds behind motorcycle dernies. (In contrast a steep headtube plus strong forward-raking fork can create negative trail and an unrideable bike!)

Fork bend plays a double role in handling and ride quality. On the one hand it has the above-mentioned role in steering, on the other hand it can help a lot in vibration damping, shimmy reduction, and shock absorption. The lever arm (created by the fork bend or angle from crown) is important both for steering and as a lever to control against road unevenness and to help steer against vehicle weight (plus rider), all at the same time. When a rider gets on a bike not only do tires and saddle flex and compress, but also the frame. The sag of the frame when loaded occurs to a significant degree in the flexing of the fork. Even a centimeter of flex is significant. During rides the fork responds to road unevenness to a smaller extent—it functions as a spring. The radius of curvature plays a role here. With enlargement of radius the spring-capability decreases. A small radius, bent directly at the end, produces the most comfortable forks. Fork stiffness is also an important factor.

Ride quality is often referred to in terms of good and bad road shock by way of the fork. The small front wheel of a recumbent brings along a short fork which flexes less than the long fork of a 27-inch normal bike wheel. This makes for correspondingly more road shock. (A long wheelbase, a frame which flexes more in the vertical direction, or suspension can all help here.)

To sum up the aspects of ride quality, one can say it is important to find a compromise between steerability, tracking steadiness, the demands of steering forces, and the suspension effects of the fork. This search is incredibly time consuming and demands that builders have a great fondness for experimenting. Hardly any reliable vehicle geometry has been developed exclusively on paper.

What holds true for the length and diameter of the fork is true for all tubes. The longer a tube is, the more flexible it becomes—in all three directions. Fork elasticity in the vertical plane is desired and beneficial to a comfortable ride. Fork curve and head tube angle help achieve this, while effectively limiting side-flex. This is what is desired at the rear end, too. To reduce sideways flex—which occurs when pedaling, costing energy—seatstays and chainstays are used. Based on their diameters, tapers, and triangulation (and some stays are even curved) they can produce a stiff ride for pedaling yet be comfortable for the rider. This is done without adding much weight and without needing much calculation or complex factors in physics. Stiffening stays can also be found in the front area of a recumbent near the crank, or anywhere else on the frame where light, slender tubing requires extra triangulation for stiffness.

A great significance is connected with the length of the chainstays. With upright bikes their length can be no shorter than the distance from the axle of the rear wheel to the bottom bracket center, minus tube sizes.

*The seat fastening of this bike has been integrated cleverly with the steering. The "headtube" and headset for the indirect steering is merged with the seatpost.*

Longer lengths are preferred for touring models. Since a recumbent hardly ever has its bottom bracket located at the end of the chainstays, you cannot use this measuring method here. Here, one usually only has to consider the distance between the axle of the rear wheel to the beginning of the main frame. A long chain stay often has more beneficial effects on ride quality than just an extension of the wheelbase—longer chainstays provide internal suspension without hardly changing the geometry.

Frame stiffness works differently with recumbents than with uprights. With uprights, pedaling occurs in the same structure as the primary support, so that the problem often occurs where good energy transmission results in a harsh ride. With a recumbent the support plane is entirely separate from the power plane. The pedaling forces from side to side can be easily resisted with stiffness in that direction, while allowing plenty of comfortable flex in the up and down vertical supporting plane.

*A steering transmission via cable takes a lot of time to build and demands a lot of maintenance. Moreover, you need spare parts which are not always available, but it does let you custom-tailor handing traits.*

## Wheel size

Wheel size influences the final bike as much as any other factor. Wheel size affects handling, weight, price, speed, aerodynamics, bike purpose and shape of frame.

As wheels roll over the ground they transmit bumps to the frame in form of pushes. How sensitively the wheel reacts determines how severely any bumps jar the rider.

The rule is that a bigger wheel rolls over stones and bumps much more easily and smoothly than a small one. The angle between obstacle and approaching tire is the reason. The shallower the angle becomes, the less that bumps are passed on to the frame. The wheel absorbs or weakens them and deviates less from its path.

Wide tires, which increase the absorption zone between rim and ground, absorb more pushes and enhance the effect of shallower approach angles to obstacles.

Wheels also affect bike weight. Smaller wheels often weigh less. Their dimensions are smaller so they are also essentially stronger. They can be built with fewer spokes without losing strength. Tubes and tires are lighter as well.

But small wheels have other disadvantages, too. A small wheel has higher rolling resistance, tire wear and tear is higher, and getting spare parts is often more difficult. A BMX-size 20" wheel (406mm) has the most available tires and parts. The road-size 20" nominal tire (451mm) is much more scarce. To "help" you differentiate these two, note that BMX sizes are marked in decimals, like "1.75," while road-size is marked fractionally, like "1 3/4." Parts for 16", 17" and 24" wheels are likewise difficult to obtain around town. However, quality parts and tires for all sizes of wheels are now more available than ever from specialty shops—including 29" wheels now being innovated in the mt-bike scene.

For comfort and everyday practical value, it often makes sense to set up small wheels with big, wide tires and strong parts, since they take harder hits and have to soak up more shock from bumps. This gives comfort and strength for everyday use. Some riders even find that certain brands of bigger, heavier tires roll faster than thin ones on small wheels in typical riding conditions.

Highspeed HPV commuters should use big, stout tires as well, to avoid dangerous blow-outs and to smooth out roadway surprises which even suspension can't always keep up with. Highspeed cornering also leans small tires over farther. The broad traction patch of a wide tire can improve HPV racing speeds in twisty conditions.

For racing on smooth race tracks and roadways, however, one can take advantage of the reduced frontal area of small wheels and tires, as well as all other possible weight savings.

Gearing has to be adjusted to deal with small wheels, which can increase problems and cost. Small wheels don't travel as far per rotation. To make up for this reduced translation, one might choose to use a larger chainring on the front, or smaller cogs on the rear (but such cogs tend to wear out more quickly), or one can go with an intermediate drive, offering step-up gearing between chainring and rear cogs. The better aerodynamics and smaller moment of inertia are still sometimes beneficial enough to compensate for the higher friction of an extensive transmission system.

### Advantages of small wheels:

* lighter
* stronger
* reduced frontal area, thus more aerodynamic
* frame can be somewhat lighter
* easier to build suspension around
* small disk wheels less sensitive to wind

### Disadvantages of small wheels:

* do not run as smoothly
* wear and tear of tires higher
* more jarring in bumps
* more loss of speed due to speed-scrub in bumps
* higher rolling resistance
* transmission adapting necessary
* parts, tires, rims harder to find
* due to lower heights, derailleur, cog and chain get dirtier
* if intermediate drive, then more parts to clean and maintain

### Advantages of big wheels:

* absorbs bumps better
* less rolling resistance
* strong, light construction using standard parts
* easy availability of spare parts
* huge tire selection
* *note*: with unfaired lowracer, which locates a big rear wheel right behind rider, a big wheel improves aerodynamics in comparison to small wheel

### Disadvantages of big wheels:

* heavier
* less aerodynamic
* frame construction is more crowded

It seems obvious that the advantage is rather on the side of big wheels (26-28 inches). It's mostly frame construction which argues against large wheels, as when deciding how to handle the front wheel.

Experts have time and again examined the rolling resistance values of smaller wheels. The British bike designer Sir Alex Moulton demonstrated that his 17-inch high pressure tires had a smaller rolling resistance than a 28-inch wheel. The suspension of his bikes play an important role in his results, of course. But in the real world, clever tire selection often results in the fastest, smoothest ride. There are many factors involved in making a fast tire. Equal-sized tires at the same inflation can vary widely in rolling resistance. Sometimes wider tires seem to roll better, but at highest speeds their bigger frontal area might become a handicap.

Mixed wheel sizes is a very common recumbent situation. Large in rear, small in front seems to work out very well, with the main downside being more spares to carry.

## Steering

There are two locations for steering recumbent bicycles:

1. Over-seat steering (OSS; top)
2. Under-seat steering (USS; beneath legs)

...And there are two modes of steering:

1. Direct steering—which controls the front wheel via a conventional direct assembly of handlebar, stem, headset and fork.

2. Indirect steering—in which the handlebars or control levers have their own set of pivots, and control the fork via push-rod, cable or chain.

Unlike the one way to steer an upright bike, these four factors can be used in every possible combination to create comfortable, reliable steering to suit the needs of a rainbow assortment of recumbent designs.

### *Advantages of top steering:*

- very aerodynamic if combined with narrow handlebar and/or horizontal, outstretched arm position
- easy, familiar handling similar to upright bike and to car or motorcycle steering position
- can be built with ordinary bar and stem components
- pushing the bike by the bars when dismounted is easy
- bar-mounted computer and other accessories easily seen and accessed

### *Disadvantages of top steering:*

- collision with legs and knees possible
- mounting to ride sometimes more difficult (might require pivoting stem)
- during accidents the handlebars might prevent quick, safe dismounting

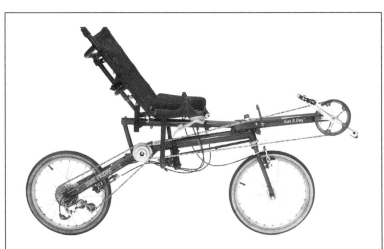

*Bike Friday's "Sat R Day" unique folding recumbent with indirect USS, mid-drive and 16" wheels fits in a suitcase. Bike Friday is a famous maker of a variety of high-end folders. (photo: Bike Friday)*

- longer shifter and brake cables

### *Advantages of under-seat steering:*

- arms at ease in this most relaxing of all positions
- can be aerodynamic with narrow bars mounted a bit forward
- enjoyable, thrilling, refreshing way to ride since nothing obscures forward view and it is so unlike other modes of riding—like a magic carpet!
- hands are in supporting position during a fall
- possible increased security from theft due to intimidating appearance

### *Disadvantages of under-seat steering:*

- can be momentarily intimidating, but one test-ride cures this
- gear and brake levers can be damaged in a fall

### *Advantages of direct steering:*

- lighter weight
- saves time in design and fabrication
- uses standard, available parts
- easy mounting of brake and gear shift levers
- no play in the steering
- no getting-used-to-it necessary
- low risk of mechanical trouble

### *Disadvantages of direct steering:*

- steering mechanism position restricted by frame form
- limited steering range
- length less adjustable (only through the front end or by changing parts)
- creates lots of 'tiller' action in long recumbents, where the bar swings far to the sides

### *Advantages of indirect steering:*

- ergonomically perfectly adjustable
- low risk of injury

- permits any frame design
- turning angle can be widened via stepped-up steering linkage gear
- improved weight distribution on the wheels is easier to realize

### *Disadvantages of indirect steering:*

- heavier
- time-consuming and costly in planning and installing
- more risk of malfunction
- some slop and play in steering
- uses special parts
- needs adjustment, maintenance

In general a limited range of steering is only a problem on slow rides. Leaning over when riding faster is what causes most of the actual turning, rather than turning the bars. Thus racing vehicles usually have limited steering without disadvantage. However, city and touring recumbents need to have a wide range of steering motion.

With short recumbents, a direct steering is generally preferred. A short wheelbase with seat in the middle lets the rider be positioned close enough to the front wheel so that the steering set-up can easily be built with conventional parts. Depending on frame form, seat position and design goals, the steering can be easily located either under or above the frame. Standard parts will keep the damage probability low and spares will be available everywhere, even where the recumbent is not very popular.

The majority of long recumbents have indirect steering. This results from the front wheel being far removed from the seat, and that makes steering via the traditional way of front-end-steering-combination more difficult.

Also in the case of the long recumbents there are over- and under-seat set-ups.

USS steering in general has advantages which are hard to argue with. The work of the shoulder and back muscles is less, as

the arms just hang down, with hands finding their way to the grips naturally. The steering mechanism also is out of your way when you mount the bike.

Indirect steering disadvantages, because it is more complex and vulnerable, tend to outweigh the benefits. One should only consider it if the frame form demands it or an ergonomically sensible assembly is not feasible in another way. If indirect steering is necessary, there are four proven ways of getting it on the road:

- shaft or push-rod steering
- cable steering
- universal-joint steering
- stub axle steering

### *Shaft steering*

The shaft or push-rod mode is the most common and is the simplest of indirect options. Under the seat, there is a bearing pivot (usually a headset) whose race is set into the frame, as well as a tube the size of the headtube to which a stem is mounted. It holds the handlebars which have a pivot point attached to them some distance away from their central pivot from which a shaft

*Lowracers have influenced the design of some everyday recumbents, which can be seen in production models as well as do-it-yourself constructions. Here you see an American low construction with detachable seat, fenders and a diverted and guarded chain.*

*Recumbent formats in a direct comparison: Seat height, bottom bracket-to-seat relationship, and differing steering mechanisms, all strongly influence the frontal surface area and cleanness of presentation to the wind. Low is fast, but also impractical for everyday riding in heavier traffic.*

leads to the fork. A ball joint at the other end of the shaft fits into a socket in a bracket on the fork. This guarantees transmission of steering movements from the handlebars to the front wheel. For alignment, the shaft often has an adjustable length.

The cyclist counters forces that exert on the front wheel by holding the handlebars, but the ball joint also has to absorb all influences. Thus such joints wear out relatively quickly and slop in the steering mechanism increases with use. By shifting the mounting position of the shaft on the handlebars or fork (changing the distances from center axis to outer pivot) you can create handling where the handlebars have greater or lesser effect on the front wheel.

### Cable steering

A transmission for cable steering can be achieved by way of pulleys. Cable steering avoids the wear-prone ball joint. But for perfectly tight steering without slop, the cable has to be absolutely stretch-free. Neither heat, cold, wetness, nor constant tension can be allowed to have any influence. This means that steel cable is your material of choice. Attempts with carbon fiber and simi-

lar material have not been convincing.

This mode demands an uncompromising installation. The axis of the pulleys has to run exactly like the radius of curvature of the fork steerer tube and handlebar bearing. The cable has to wind around each pulley before it is led to the next one. This prevents the cable from slipping. To support this precautionary measure, the cable should be clamped with a washer and screw on the pulley.

To be able to change the tension of the cable and the distance between steering mechanism and front wheel, the cable ends have to be connected to a component that is length-adjustable so that the total length of the cable can be altered.

Note that cable tension burdens the headset bearings and contributes to early wear.

### Universal-joint steering

U-joint steering is more robust and demands fewer securing mechanisms. This type of steering can be found on old recumbents with chopper-style handlebars or on the Velocar from the 1930s. It is only usable for top steering mechanisms which are set up to stay close to the body when moved. They eliminate "tiller" in steering. A three-way turnable joint is mounted to the top of the headtube and sends handlebar input through a sharp change in direction, without alteration, to the front wheel. The handlebar is located in an ergonomic position and the shaft that connects it to the U-joint is supported by framing. A common solution is a tube at the main frame that leads to the steering tube and is attached to it with a hose clamp. Neither clamp nor joint is free from mechanical play, so that this steering mode is usually quite wobbly.

## Stub-axle steering

The stub-axle solution behaves totally differently. It is a high tech device that allows very precise steering motions but it is also very expensive. Much special engineering, special parts, and meticulous work is necessary to enjoy the advantage of this mode of steering which is absolutely free from play.

Adjustments should be made very carefully with all steering variants. The distance from handlebar to body must always be less than the length of the arms. It is advisable to subtract five percent from the arm length. While this adjustment is not as important as the leg adjustment, if the bars are too far away it will cause backaches. The shoulder joints would be forced to bend forward to make up the missing inches. On long distances or multiple rides, related muscles get tense, ligaments are burdened and consequences occur similar to the ones triathletes suffer from when their streamlined handlebars are too narrow.

Use the following rule: the adjustment of steering should be done in a way that your shoulder joints are aligned with your spine. The arms must not be stretched beyond their length, but should form a slight bend, just as the legs do when pedal distance is adjusted properly.

## Handlebars and aerodynamics

The form and position of the handlebar is mostly derived from the ergonomic demands of the bike frame. The position and type of handlebar also influences the exposed frontal area, the bike's air turbulence and thus the aerodynamics.

The aerodynamically ideal form of handlebar for an unfaired recumbent can be easily determined. The smaller the handlebar, the smaller the frontal surface. It is best if the handlebars lay in front of or behind that surface, that is, if the frontal area which already exists is not enlarged by the bars.

Handlebars which position the arms next to the body create up to 10 percent more air resistance than handlebars which hold the arms in front of the body in a straightish position and which locate the hands at no wider than the width of the shoulders. This way the frontal area of handlebars and arms is immersed in the already exposed surface of chest and shoulders. This issue is not rel-

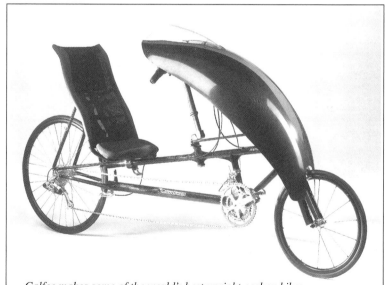

*Calfee makes some of the world's best upright carbon bikes. Now they offer the "Fast Freddy" Markham-designed carbon LWB "Stiletto." It's an elite 24-pound bike, with optimized handling courtesy of indirect steering, and trademark bold, translucent frame colors.*

evant when it comes to handlebars within or behind a fairing. In this case one only needs to watch that the steering mechanism does not increase the frontal area dimensions of the fairing. The handlebars should be set in the most ergonomic position within the extent of the desired fairing values. One also has to allow enough range of steering.

### Handlebars and ergonomics

One has to give the nod to the low steering mechanism with regards to comfort. The hands do not have to do any supporting and the arms do not have to do any lifting since the hands find their way to the grips without effort. If a bike is supposed to be comfortable for long distances, the handlebars under the seat are the logical position.

For the above-seat position, people often find that a relaxing position can be achieved by having a folding-stem that settles the handlebars close to the chest so that the hands are in a "chipmunk" posture.

Racers sometimes find that an above-seat handlebar position that puts the arms in an outstretched position lets the rider pull on the bars and increase power. Some have bars positioned so far forward and low (for maximum sprinting power) that the racer's torso is no longer even reclined back, as with the record-setting Cheetah and Gold Rush streamliners.

Most handlebars are custom-shaped to fit the needs of your position on the bike. Only rarely can they be adapted from bars intended for road, mt-bike or city-bike use. 'Bent bar shapes vary greatly, so be sure you're comfortable with what you pick! If experience proves you wrong, however, manufacturers often sell their bars separately and they often fit into each other's stem assemblies, letting you fully dial in your favorite riding posture.

## Seat and pedal position

The pleasure of riding a recumbent lives or dies on its seat, so to speak. Pain in the behind is, together with the headwind problem and lack of rain protection, the most frequent argument against cycling. Life is simpler on a recumbent. The larger seat contact area and far broader weight distribution are responsible for the fact that chafe, circulation disturbance and bruising belong to the past. But quality of seat is still highly important. An uncomfortable recumbent seat has the same effects on behind and well-being as any bad upright saddle.

There are two basic types of recumbent seats: shell seats (also called rigid seats), and tube-seats with mesh covers.

The first ones are made from fiberglass, metal, carbon, wood, or plastic and are most comfortable with fitted camping-type closed- or open-cell foam rubber padding.

The second type of seat consists of a tubing framework which is covered with a tight hammock of mesh nylon fabric or other strong material or webbing.

*Although the low construction variant reduces the overview in traffic, such recumbents can be built for everyday use, equipped with weather protection and suspension (rear, in this case).*

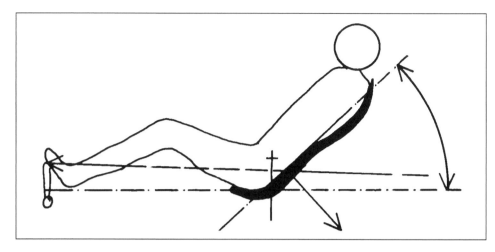

*Ideal angle between seat back and legs is generally 120°.*

Bike manufacturers create a very wide variety of seats based on these two formats and it's likely that you'll enjoy one the most. Hopefully it comes on a bike you prefer! If not, makers often sell their seats separately and they can occasionally be interchanged with little difficulty. Getting the right seat will be worth any effort involved. Seat suitability is critical and probably hovers around being the fourth most important factor behind riding purpose, wheelbase and rider position.

### Advantages of shell seats:

- lighter
- replacement and installation is easier
- more compact
- construction of seat can merge into frame
- by changing padding, degree and zones of firmness can be custom adjusted
- almost no flex
- excellent power transmission

### Disadvantages of shell seats:

- sweat-enhancing since they don't breathe
- adjustable only by pads
- depends on material which is not very environmental
- ergonomically almost not adjustable

### Advantages of mesh seats:

- air-conditioning effects
- material can be replaced
- covering firmness can be altered
- construction of seat-tubes can merge into frame
- more comfortable
- easily adjusts to any rider

### Disadvantages of mesh seats:

- heavier
- prone to malfunction
- larger, wider
- mounting can be complicated
- bad power transmission—push absorbed by flexible mesh
- rearward anatomy more exposed in cold or wet riding

A shell seat allows for impressively light weight, if material and construction are selected carefully. This holds true especially for artificial fibers. Fiberglass and carbon fiber are common materials in shell seat construction. Light construction is possible when using plastic, as the seat can be built easily in the 'hollow profile technique.' Using this method, the needed stiffness is not achieved by the accumulation of mass, but by the creation of three dimensional integrity. The seat can be made from a mold that perfectly matches the rider's posterior.

It is the opposite with un-molded rigid seats. They gain their stability via the mechanical values of the materials. The form is then only influenced by finishing techniques, ergonomic needs and construction method. With either molded or straight-built shell seats, design plays the major role.

The shell seat can be a complete construction in itself, compact and without heavy or bulky supports. Fastenings are reduced to a few screws and big support points where power comes to bear. Thus mounting or changing such a seat can be quite simple. Tilt and position can also be adjustable, given telescoping seatstays and/or sliding bottom attachments.

Wood, metal and plastics are rugged materials which deform only slightly under the power of pedaling. Power flow is efficient—better than a webbed seat or regular bike saddle. Shell seats can be very comfortable, but they are rarely very flexible. The downside is that the rider feels 100% of the bumps in the road. You can prevent this with padding, to whatever thickness is needed to soften the ride. Closed-cell camping pads work fine: cut to fit and fasten or glue in place. Open-cell pads can absorb water and sweat—approach with caution. Make sure the forward edge of the seat doesn't cut into the legs and allows free room for the legs to work with a variety of seat-tilt angles.

Mesh seats are built entirely differently. The seating area consists of fabric stretched over a frame. The seat frame is mounted separately to the bike frame (with most recumbents) and its angle and position are often highly adjustable. One can thus often adjust 'frame length' to fit leg-length just by sliding the seat. The traditional seatstays of the frame are spread as wide as they have to be to support the tubing that holds the fabric, so you do not need additional tubing.

There are two subgroups of mesh seats. Some have lacing that wraps behind the seat-tubing, others have a tensioning device integrated into the seat-frame.

Depending on type of mesh, you can get good "air-conditioning" with this style of seat. Plastic mesh webbing is, for instance, very breathable compared with leather. Leather can be a good supplemental covering for heavy wear areas, if limited to a few straps where there is less moisture buildup.

A mesh seat is only adjustable to rider ergonomy by type and tension of the fabric. That is why the seat frame itself should be formed to an anatomic curve and shape. Some mesh seats have separate bottom areas from the back, which can also be adjusted separately. Some even use a wide bicycle seat for a base! Some also have a 'horn' under the mesh at the front between the legs to prevent sliding forward.

These types of mesh cloth are appropriate:
- leather (warm, natural, expensive)
- plastic (airy, expensive, light)
- nylon webbing (cheaper than cloth by the yard)
- seat belt strapping (cheap, car graveyard)

*Most long wheelbase models avoid low, reclined seats and high bottom brackets. The RANS V2, or "Velocity Squared," steps out of type —for more performance—and comes with a stock front fairing.*

Cotton and other natural types of cloth are not really appropriate because they stretch when they come into contact with water or sweat. Producers like Lightning or Ross show that a mesh seat does not have to weigh much more than a good plastic seat. The form of the seat should correlate to the double-S-form of the spine, because this is the only position in which the spine can rest. Such a position can be achieved easily if the lumbar region is given support. A slight convexity in the seat is sufficient. The tension on the mesh fabric should be significantly harder in this area. Lumbar support also helps support of the pelvis. With such support, you get something better to push against; that is, the sliding back and forth in the seat, comparable to standing up a little on the pedals, is reduced. If the pelvis cannot be supported in the seat, the spine is fatigued and compressed disks can be a consequence. Small wedges of wood or foam plastic have proven to be good support for the pelvis, but they need to be fitted exactly.

The lumbar support also determines the position of the pelvis. If the pelvis is positioned too flatly, the burden on the spine increases. If it is positioned rolled too far back under, the spine has less contact with the seat and stretching the legs will be hard. Too much lumbar support also tends to cause a hollow back, rolling the pelvis too far under. An inappropriately tilted seat-bottom area can also be responsible for that. Tilting this portion backwards can help.

One should avoid seats with a concavity in the back. Such a bend rounds out the spine which positions the pelvis flat and compresses the heart and other organs.

## Relation of bottom bracket height to seat height and angle

The interplay between bottom bracket height and seat angle is one of the most important factors for power transmission. Here is the simplified relation: the higher the bottom bracket (in relation to the seat), the more reclined the seat should be. And the lower the bottom bracket, the steeper and more upright the seat should be. (It is interesting that with recumbents a bottom bracket is usually nowhere near the 'bottom' of anything. The German translation "crank bearing" is perhaps more appropriate.)

A high bottom bracket improves aerodynamics, but it demands a well-formed seat since you ride with far more weight on your back than if you had a steeper seat angle. The lumbar support of a reclined seat must be more pronounced as the back tends to slide around more when pedaling.

The weight of the body is almost always sufficient to keep skin and clothing firmly in contact with the seat. The sliding hap-

*The "Spirit" compact from HP Velotechnik is a well thought out urban stylist with efficient, sporty crank-height. (photo: HP Velotechnik)*

*Close up view of the cassette shifter set up as an intermediate gear. It is light, cheap and lasts forever.*

of about 120 degrees to the line of the legs. Angles that are much smaller fold the body together, limiting breathing, organs and leg movement. Bigger angles cause sliding and power loss despite lumbar support. One can choose an angle which quite closely replicates the power feel of an upright bike of whatever performance level or style you like, from city bike to touring to racing. Some recumbent angles, however, seem so open that the big quadriceps muscles can't apply full power, or require more adapting than usual to do so. For a sports design, one should have the bottom bracket high enough that the quad muscles can work the most, but low enough so that the gluteal and hamstring muscles get a full range of play as well.

A seat which is too reclined can require more neck work, as one then has to hold one's head up to see down the road ahead. It results in a similar but opposite strain to the fatigue of holding the head up while riding a regular diamond frame bike. Too much recline can also impede vision, and should only be considered for a very limited-use race bike, such as on a velodrome in solo events.

Too upright of a position results in too much weight being put on the seat bottom—and *your* bottom—and not enough spread along the length of the back. An upright seat tends to make for an effectively lower seat height and easier starts and stops—great for a city bike. But too much weight on your rear can cause the dreaded 'recumbent butt.' With most recumbent seats, your weight would then be on the very muscles you have to use—unlike regular bike saddles where the weight is supported by pelvic bones, leaving the butt muscles free to work. Too much weight on the butt can result in a compaction of these well-used muscles and early fatigue, pain or cramping.

It seems as though a commonly ideal weight distribution is along the lines of 50-

pens 'under the skin,' so to speak. The back's connective tissue between skin and bones serves as a spring and gets used and tired. This phenomenon occurs sometimes during hard riding and on bikes with a very flat seat (less than 33 degrees up from the horizontal). Again, this can be helped by a lumbar support and/or by a concavity in the shoulder area which would also reduce the work of the neck muscles in holding up the head.

The line of the back should have an angle

50 butt vs. back, but special design considerations can change this quite a bit and still have good results.

### Distance bottom bracket to front wheel hub

Unfortunately there have been few studies in this field.

### Advantages small distance:

- good braking behavior
- long wheelbase and compact-length designs are possible

### Disadvantages:

- heels, thighs and crank-arms could touch front wheel
- needs getting use to for slow riding, to avoid footstrike

### Advantages big distance:

- freedom of the heels
- no slow-speed riding change necessary

### Disadvantages:

- worse braking behavior
- bottom bracket outrigger boom is longer (more flex)
- design usually limited to short wheelbase

## Center of gravity

The position of the center of gravity is decisive for recumbent riding and handling qualities and for type of use. The clue for the center of gravity's position is your navel. If the position of this center of gravity is the same on the recumbent as it is on a normal bike, it is equally easy to ride, and handles similarly, because the bike's reaction to weight shift and braking happen in a way one is already used to. Only the horizontal position then demands some adaptation.

A low center of gravity usually comes along with a relatively low air resistance, because drivetrain and luggage is carried low and does not produce any additional frontal area.

The highwheeler pilots often went head-over-teakettle on their monstrosities. Two things were responsible for this: First, the center of gravity was very high, and second, the center of gravity lever arm was short, because the center of gravity was so close to the effective brake center. This design asked for a flip-over. On the other hand, a low recumbent with a low center of gravity is absolutely protected against such spills.

### Advantages of a high center of gravity:

- good view in traffic
- handling is similar to a normal bike
- bike wobbles only a little during startup

*A lowracer recumbent to be used with a fairing. Notice the front wheel drive (FWD). The intermediate gear is located right at the steering head pipe, from which a chain leads to the hub. If you turn the steering mechanism, the chain crosses over itself—a pure racing vehicle that is not so useful to go pick up some coffee in the morning.*

*The pivoting front drive of a Flevo Bike connects the entire drive unit with the front fork. The frame and mechanism swing together to steer —a feeling that takes a lot of getting used to. (photo: Pichler)*

### Disadvantages:

- danger of flipping over forwards
- worse aerodynamics (even for highracers)
- bad consequences in case of an accident

### Advantages low center of gravity:

- small risk of braking flip-over
- good aerodynamics
- mild consequences in case of an accident
- extreme cornering possible
- frequent direct eye contact in traffic

### Disadvantages:

- smaller overview of traffic
- needs more adapting to ride easily
- bike tends to wobble at slow speed; more difficult startups

### Advantages of short center of gravity lever arm:

- front wheel has good weight on it for traction

### Disadvantages:

- higher risk of turn-over
- rear wheel often under-weighted
- vehicle will be longer
- heavier

### Advantages of further-removed centers of gravity:

- no risk of turning over
- lighter
- rear wheel well-weighted

### Disadvantage:

- not enough weight on front wheel

In relation to the distribution of weight the center of gravity is decisive. On an upright bike a distribution of about 40% in the front and 60% on the rear wheel is relatively balanced. Thus it is guaranteed that the driving rear wheel has enough traction that it won't slip under strong pedaling, nor will the front wheel slip in cornering or braking under normal circumstances.

A similarly beneficial distribution should be accomplished on the recumbent. As the recumbent's center of gravity height is mostly more beneficial, the distance to the effective braking center is negligible. The coordination of the center of gravity's position should be done above all things under consideration of the wheel-weight ratio and the envisaged use.

### Determining Front/Rear Weight Distribution

A simple method to establish the relative division of weight on the axles requires only two bathroom scales and a carpenter's spirit level. The two scales are slid underneath the wheels and the level is used to make sure the bike is horizontal. Then, one sits on the bike in a supported manner and a helper reads the scales. The figures can be transformed to percentages. The axle weight can be corrected by shifting the center of gravity of the design. Figuring out and optimizing this ratio is vital when it comes to the construction and fine-tuning of any suspension. A highly adjustable seat and/or crank boom can also help in this regard.

# Chain routing and power transmission

The chain transfers the power you generate from the crankset to the cogs of the rear wheel. During pedaling, the upper chain is pulled through under tension, while the lower chain is returned passively back to the cogs.

In contrast to an upright bike, the recumbent has more options for guiding the chain from the crank to the distant cogwheel. But every intermediate cog or pulley costs power. Thus, a chain, in general, should be bent only when it must be. When planning a frame, the chain line should be planned so that it runs freely. If you cannot avoid a change of direction, there are two feasible options:

- change direction via a pulley
- use a dual set of gears, or an intermediate cog.

An idler wheel pulley can be used on either the part of the chain under tension or the passive part. An unguided, freely-swinging passive chain can interfere with steering and makes noise and scratches on the frame, and splashes dirt on your clothing and luggage. For these reasons, a change of direction to tame or put tension on the passive chain makes sense. It is different with the drive chain: since it is under tension when pedaling, it searches for the most direct way from cog to crank. Any re-direction means increased friction in the case of the powerside, because of the rubbing of the chain components and pulley bearings against each other. Estimations assume a 3% loss per pulley in the powerside drive chain.

For lower chain diversion (the passive part of the chain which returns from crank back to the hub), many builders use a pulley off of a rear derailleur and put a little cage around it to keep the chain from jumping off. A bigger pulley—such as one made from an inline-skate or skateboard wheel, or furniture caster—reduces friction and noise considerably. Using a pulley with a center ridge so that it works like one from a rear derailleur, makes sense, so the chain does not run on the link-plates, but on the small axles in between. That reduces resistance.

These 2-3" pulleys or caster-wheels are mounted to a support axle stud so they can both roll and slide a bit, so they can move to follow the angled line of the chain according to the gear. The profile of a powerside chain mills itself into these pulleys after only a few hundred meters. This demonstrates the enormous forces which are generated here. Because of this reason an adequately sized axle is necessary (at least 3/8", radius M8 or M10).

*Seat adjustment by a built-in seatpost socket (see p. 115), which creates an unusual but effective seat support.*

It is occasionally possible to avoid using low-side pulleys altogether if one opts to use a chaintube. A chaintube is a tough, flexible plastic hose that the chain is routed through. You can control the direction, noise and cleanliness of your low-side chain with such a tube in many cases. Some people use tubing which runs the whole length of the low-side chain, other times shorter lengths pinned in strategic locations give the needed control.

An elegant solution involves an intermediate drive such as used on tandems. A tandem crank powers a chain on the left which goes to a chainring under the seat which drives another chainring on the right back to the rear cogset.

Unfortunately, tandems (and many uprights in general) have a handicap worth mentioning: due to the closeness of the intermediate drive to the rear cogset not all gears can be used—the chainline would be distorted too much. 'Dead gears' develop. Only when the intermediate bearing is far enough away from the cogset does this disadvantage not kick in, because then the chain has enough room to flex. 20" can be seen as the limiting distance. If the intermediate bearing or powerside pulley is at least 20" away from the cogwheel, all gears can be used without problem.

This version can be made from a conventional (expensive) tandem set. The unused crank-arm forged to the 'spider' of the rear crankset has to be sawed off, of course.

A left-side synchronization chain is not kept under steady tension like the right-side chain on a normal bike. Thus it has to be tensioned artificially. An eccentric camming bottom bracket, as used with tandems, is very useful, but costs more. On the recumbent, however, it should be mounted at the intermediate bearing. If it gets mounted to the actual bottom bracket, the position of the cam-action bearing changes the distance to the seat, and that creates a shift in saddle support.

At the intermediate bearing the two chain wheels cover the access to the bearing. Only when one of them has been removed can one adjust the chain tension of the synchronization chain via the eccentric bearing. The producer of Flux bikes solves this tensioning problem more primitively, but equally effectively. He adds a small pulley to the left side of his bikes, which is height-adjustable and located in a metal holder. This small pulley pushes the chain up and thus puts pressure on it.

The only disadvantage of this easy, cheap and uncomplicated variant is a slight power loss. Strong forces attack the driving chain when under power which causes a slight hanging through of the lagging chain.

How much energy an intermediate bearing set-up wastes is still in dispute. There are no unequivocal statistics. The supporters as well as the doubters, however, agree that increased friction is only acceptable if it brings enough advantages elsewhere.

You can also add a shifter and full cogset

*Chain protection is required for most races. It is safe and takes a little bit of the racing bike's aggressive looks away.*

to an intermediate drive. Due to such doubling, you can use a wide range of front chainrings and avoid expensive big chainrings. If you select components cleverly you can also reduce weight a great deal.

Inexpensive tandems have a right-sided chain leading from the front crank to the inner chainring of the rear crank. If the rear is a triple crankset, its two outer rings are available to the secondary drive for transmission changes. This reduces the gears to 16, but it is cheaper than a 'right-left' combination.

The 'Z-2' by Martin Staubach is worth mentioning in this context. He mounts a Shimano-cassette as his intermediate drive. Four cogs with spacers are mounted on the cassette body. One holds the chain which drives the rear wheel, and there are three which can be driven by the crank in front. A standard derailleur shifts the front chain among these latter three. In this way he creates a light, inexpensive construction with a fully-functioning 21-gear shifter.

The cassette body is mounted to the hub, heated (to neutralize hardness) and turned from the inside to mount to a stub on the frame. Then Staubach presses in industrial strength bearings and screws the cassette to the frame.

If both chainlines are equipped with freewheel and shifter, more than 50 gears can be realized without any problem.

All intermediate drives are helpful for designs using rear suspension. They help minimize loss of power because the chain line moves less when different gears are selected, so the position to the suspension-pivot differs less. They also simplify the accompanying greater needs of chain management.

## Advantages of...

*...a direct chain routing:*
- lightweight
- no loss of energy
- inexpensive

*The "Quetzal SE" is a stylish, affordable semi-recumbent city-bike from the large Canadian parent company, CCM.*

- standard parts
- no problems with chain tension, because the rear mech provides it
- can use all gears

*...controlled return chainline:*
- light
- inexpensive
- standard parts
- can use all gears

*...tandem left intermediate:*
- elegant
- flutter free; the chain won't move and "boogie" while you ride

*...tandem right intermediate:*
- lighter than left
- standard parts

*...cassette drive:*
- the lightest tandem version
- 21 gears and more possible
- cheaper than left
- standard parts
- fast shifting in the front, since Hyperglide equipment can be used

*Derk Thys getting an all-body workout on his innovative and smooth-functioning Rowingbike, in the bright sunlight. This is the general sport model; he also offers a lowracer.*

## Disadvantages of...

*...a direct chainline:*
• lower chain vibrates
• limited transmission modifications

*...diverted chain:*
• loss of energy (small)
• pulley is source of potential malfunction

*...tandem left:*
• energy loss
• expensive standard parts necessary
• crank arm has to be removed
• heaviest tandem variant
• difficult to get spare parts
• problems with chain tension
• cannot use all gears

*...tandem right:*
• energy loss
• crank arm has to be removed
• hard to implement
• expensive, as additional parts are needed
• problems with chain tension
• cannot use all gears

*...cassette:*
• special brazing necessary
• energy losses
• heavy
• cannot use all gears
• not all gears can be shifted with just a front shifter mech

### Front Wheel Drive

The front drive is an alternative to rear drive. In practice, usually recumbents with a short or medium wheelbase use this type of drive. The design of the front wheel drive can be divided into two kinds:
• pivoting drive
• flex-chain drive

The unit of a pivoting (or swinging) drive is constructed into the fork, with the crankset boom being mounted to the fork as well. When you steer, your legs turn, too. Thus the legs can contribute to the steering work and riding no-handed becomes simpler. This, however, depends on how well you adapt to the new driving behavior of such a drive. The biggest advantage of such a construction is a compact and efficient drive. The chain is short and directly routed, with no diversions. The power supports can all be easily triangulated with short, light pieces. The pivoting headset for this mode can be handled normally. It can even be located quite rearward of the fork so that 'lean-steer' qualities of handling can be built in. The fork is then made rigid with the front part of the frame, which pivots altogether. A well-known representative of lean-steer is the Dutch Flevo-Bike.

The flex-chain (or rigid) FWD presents a mechanically 'unclean' solution. The chain is re-directed in the area of the headtube and is led by pulleys to the cogset at the front wheel hub. There are variants with an intermediate drive located at the headtube. All these modes involve chain twist when turning, which creates considerable friction losses. But then, one is usually not riding under heavy power or requiring great speed when turning the handlebars a lot—except on steep uphill corners and switchbacks. (...Then we all need all the help we can get!) Flex-chain FWD can often be the choice of racers, since they don't turn their bars much.

In both types of FWD, one should load the front wheel with more than usual (55-60%) body weight, otherwise the front wheel is likely to spin-out on an upgrade.

### *Advantages front drive:*

- light
- short chain
- rear suspension can be easily constructed
- carrying luggage below seat is now easy

### *Disadvantages:*

- cannot use all gears
- traction problems when starting

*...rigid drive:*
- chain might kink or lock when steering
- limited steering angle range
- mechanically 'unclean' losses due to chain-twist

*...swinging drive:*
- needs a lot of careful design

### *Alternative drive options*

Since a recumbent has a long, complex and rather money-consuming chain and drivetrain, vehicles with novel drive systems not using a conventional chain regularly appear in the field of HPV's to attempt to achieve improvements.

The belt drive is usually ruled out for two reasons: It only allows for a simple 3-, 5-, 7-speed hub shift, which barely meets everyday demands. Furthermore, it is relatively expensive because the market only offers few usable materials. Thus when homebuilding much time-consuming indi-

vidual initiative is necessary. (Creating your own bike takes a lot of time as it is! Innovating your own drivetrain adds to your duties enormously!) Otherwise, it has a lot of virtues: maintenance-free, light, clean (no oil).

Some builders have tried smaller chain sizes to lower the size and weight of the drive unit. A loss of reliability usually goes hand in hand with the reduction of overall mass. The parts are not strong enough for the stress. They break or get bent. Further problems open up with a small chain's lack of compatibility: neither shifter, crank, or gears can be used without modification.

Only Derk Thijs, a Dutchman, has so far been able to make a name for himself with an individualized drive. He developed an arm-and-leg rowing drive for his "Rowingbike" model. The motion sequence greatly resembles that of a sliding-seat oarsman. The legs slide next to each other in parallel and the arms pull a lever at the same time. The lever for the arms is actually the steering handlebar and is installed on a pivoting joint at the headset. This enables the use of the rowing lever also during turning as well as when fine regulation of direction

*A pack of Thys Rowingbikes (R) alongside a pack of lowracers in a Cycle Vision race. Notice that the lead Rowingbike is a lowracer model. (photo: www.tim.be)*

is needed at high speeds. Clipless pedals for the leg-drive are located on a slider which glides on metal rails on the main tube of the bike frame. The combined pulling power straightens a steel cable connected to an amazing patented "Snek" mechanism that creates an efficient, wide-ratio, stepless gear range. Derk has won significant marathon races with this drive, in competition with upright racers and other HPVs. Rowingbikes now have their own race series.

Handcycling is a growing aspect of the HPV scene, with several high-end models now offered and world records now established in various classes.

In the field of motorcycles, the Cardan shaft drive is highly praised. On a bike, however, it is too heavy and complicated and thus rarely seen.

As authors Whitt/Wilson have stated in *Cycling Science*, the chain has an ideal efficiency of 98.5%. And even after half a year of use the degree of efficiency of a typical chain is still at 95%. On the other hand, you lose 7-17% with a Cardan shaft drive.

### Chain protection

Chain protection can be understood in two different ways:
- protection of the chain from dirt

*The ATP chain protection for their "Vision" protects your pants and legs from dirt. This chainguard is pretty now, but will itself likely become dirty and scratched in short order.*

- protection of the rider from the chain

It makes sense to protect the chain from dirt, especially with everyday bikes. A clean chain needs less oil, which again slows the accumulation of dirt and thus greatly extends the effectiveness and life span of the chain. A complete enclosure in a capsule is difficult to achieve, and only barely doable, but represents the best solution. The 'Revive DX' from Giant has done good work here. This deluxe version of their compact semi-recumbent bike has an enclosed drivetrain and rear suspension and is still quite affordable.

It is simpler to lead as much chain as you can through plastic tubing. Such tubing has to be interrupted at any pulleys and has to be built in a way that the chain can run freely.

Clothing, legs, and passers-by have to be protected from the chain as well. A dirty chain leaves ugly stains on clothes and body. A plastic tube serves well in this case, too. A chainguard of metal or even stretched fabric can be helpful.

It is also important to guard the chainrings of short recumbents and lowracers. The prominent chainrings are a danger during any collision with others and they can cause lasting injuries. Chain protection guards of the mountain bike style, chain boxes or bent metal profiles are good solutions.

# Frame adjustment

An adjustable frame lets you match your bike exactly to your leg length and body size. A major function of the frame with the diamond bike mode is simply to support the saddle. Two different areas of adjustment are common in recumbents: Adjust the frame and/or slide the seat. A frame 'boom' adjustment can be found on most short mono-tube recumbents. Their design is very simple.

The main tube of the frame does not end with a bottom bracket, but as a hollow tube. The bottom bracket itself is built onto a tube that in its outer circumference equals the inner circumference of the main frame tube. Thus the bottom bracket assembly can slide into the main frame. Two clamps fix this crank boom in place. A more elegant solution is a slot with bolt-clamp at the main frame tube, like a seatpost clamp on an upright bike.

You should be careful though. To ensure strength, the length of the section sliding into the boom has to exceed its radius by at least one-and-a-half fold. Otherwise there will be a danger of torquing the crank assembly out of the frame when pedaling vigorously.

Seat adjustment is more complicated. Here, I will only explain two different designs. First, there is the option of sliding the seat in a slotted bracket on the frame. Second, the position of the seat can be altered with clips on the frame or position-holes drilled through it. Here, the seat can move on firm holding devices so that it has a free-standing but stable construction, as it only finds support at two points of the frame. Seats made of steel tubing are appropriate here, because their stability is sufficient. The frame has at its main tube two slits of about 2-3" length which can be used for seat bolts. The seat gets a second support at shoulder height to resist pushing strain.

Mertens, the racing cyclist and bike producer, came up with a clever solution for his frames. They use a conventional seatstay lug brazed to the seatstays and a seat tube at the rear. The free lug opening for the top tube is used for the seat support by sticking an aluminum tube through it that connects to the seat. Because of the seatpost clamp a rider can alter his seat up to 3". In other words, you can move the seat up to 3" on the tube by way of slotted braze-ons that fix the seat-base on the main frame.

More complicated and heavier are seat ad-

justments which work on the basis of clamps. The clamps circle the main tube and clamp to an assembly on the lower part of the seat. In the back area two stays support the seat. They are length- and angle-adjustable to follow the preconditions of the lower seat fastening. These stays, their integration, and the big clamping block on the main frame create a lot of production work and weight, but they let you mount a comfortable mesh seat.

### Advantages of sliding boom:
- light
- stable and firm mounting
- easily made
- adjustment is millimeter exact
- distance between handlebars and seat remains constant
- seat can be integrated into frame

*...seat adjustment at the frame:*
- light
- stable
- easy construction
- chain length does not change
- combines easily with adjustable seat-back

*Handcycles are part of the mix at HPV events, and have their own records and innovation—with fields of a dozen or so riders reaching speeds of 30 mph in sprints. (photo: www.tim.be)*

*The Sun EZ Tandem was designed by Easy Racers.*
*It's a solid, easy-to-use, affordable tandem. (photo: Easy Racers)*

*...seat adjustment with clamps:*
• seat angle adjustable
• installment of a mesh seat is easier
• chain length does not change

### *Disadvantages of sliding boom:*
• chain length changes
• exact vertical alignment of the crank can
  be difficult (many bikes have guide stud
  on boom that rides in slot in main tube)
• tubes tend to rust together
• bolts and clamp can fail, allowing slip

*...seat adjustment at the frame:*
• heavier
• higher production cost/effort
• seat can be stressed (less frame support)
• alters angle between seat and handlebar

*...seat adjustment with clamps:*
• heaviest variant
• high production effort
• seat can be stressed
• alters angle between seat and handlebar
• center of gravity can change

# Storing luggage and cargo

The recumbent is especially popular and appreciated as a travel bike. Tours to the North Cape, in China and across Africa have been made. The comfort, range, noticeably faster average speed and the nicer view combined with beneficial aerodynamics, as well as luggage capacity, have all made recumbents attractive to tourists.

The variety of designs opens up a multitude of stowage possibilities for luggage.

A backpack can't be used en route, of course—although I bring one on every recumbent tour. On the one hand, a backpack is good for trips on foot in the evenings, and on the other hand groceries or unexpected luggage volumes can be transported for short distances on your belly! (And it can sometimes be mounted on the seat back.)

An external transport option is a trailer. It rolls easily right behind, in your draft.

If you use standard parts, only a rear luggage rack and regular panniers can be used. Amidst the seat supports, two or three bags can be strapped and clipped onto a luggage rack. Only a few brave pilots of long recumbents trust themselves and their head tube to install a lowrider pannier rack or luggage carrier to the front wheel fork.

Some producers offer brazed fittings in the rear triangle area under the seat which let you mount panniers in this unusual triangular opening left by the seat. The carrier is mounted to the seatstay, so it rides in front of the bags of a rear luggage rack. Bolts on the chainstays create a stable hold. These bags replace the function of bags at the handlebars since they can be opened and closed while under way. Such bags 'hide' in the lee of the seat and direct the wind to the rear bags.

More recumbent companies are offering racks and panniers to fit their bikes and models similar to them. These let bikes keep their good looks, function and aerodynamics. Accessory makers are popping up as well to offer luggage tailored to recumbents. However, if you are willing to modify conventional parts or to build a carrier system yourself, then the storage space on most any recumbent can be greatly enlarged. The simplest and most practical tinkering comes in building a bag holder behind the seat. Often one only needs to bolt the mass-produced fastening of a handlebar bag to the seat to mount a large one there. For bags which mount with a simple hook to a rack, it is sufficient to attach a tube of the radius of a luggage rack across the seatback.

Lowrider bags can often be set up to fasten under the seat at the main frame. They have to be attached to the frame with sufficient spacing to avoid having the rightside bag collide with the chain.

The bike producer Patria offers a luggage rack of CroMo steel tubing. He also sells this tubing to interested homebuilders. It is greatly suitable for building a carrier. If all details are planned carefully, it is possible to build a luggage rack which is superior for your bike to models available on the market.

Aerodynamic rear tailboxes with a lot of space are very useful. Form, space and price vary. Not every tailbox fits every bike.

Other fairings can also sometimes be fitted with interior cargo bays.

# Tandems

It is often much more fun to ride with two on one bike than two on two! This is not much different when it comes to recumbents.

Now, the significant things about a conventional tandem are quite clearcut. They can vary in frame height, since sometimes the stoker is in a "lady's size," but otherwise they are straightforward. The recumbent tandem scene is entirely different. Here, nothing is simple; it's just the opposite: the variety of recumbent options rises geometrically in the field of tandems.

In principal, the type and position of seats has to be determined before moving to other steps of planning. The following are typically options:

- recumbent seat in front/normal bike position in back
- upright-position recumbent in front/upright recumbent in the rear (usually with lower crank positions, with rear crank under front seat)
- reclined recumbent in front/reclined recumbent in back (longer, due to high crank heights)
- 'back to back': regular in front/reversed seat in back
- side by side (called a 'sociable')

The combination of recumbent and 'Normalo' is very interesting. A lot of small construction and detail solutions are possible here. A clever model presented by the American producer Bilenky is the "Viewpoint" (formerly the Counterpoint "Opus"). Stoker and captain have switched seats, so that the rear steers and front provides only power. The rear 'captain' has a good overview of traffic above the front rider. Their two heads are also closer together, for easy

*Elegant, fast...and pricey: The Dutch M5 tandem. (photo: M5)*

*A unique design: the Bilenky "Viewpoint" mixed-position tandem.*
*Front stoker reclines; captain steers, pedals upright from the rear.*
*A fairing boosts speed. Adapts to child sizing or handcycling.*
*(Previously this bike was made by Counterpoint.) (photo: Counterpoint)*

As a consequence synchronization problems do not occur and practice rides and adaptation are less necessary.

Several makers, such as Rans, Vision and MicWic, have perfected their own fully independent transmissions, or dual-wheel drives, so that either rider can choose any cadence they like.

Suspension for a recumbent tandem gains new meaning because the mass to be handled is doubled.

The homebuilding of a recumbent tandem might be tempting, but you should remember that costs and time input are likely to more than double.

# Recumbents and the auxiliary engine

A lot of HPV fans, muscle power buffs, and motor-phobes in cycling loathe the idea of equipping a recumbent with an auxiliary engine. However, there are occasional experiments and products put forward in this direction.

Paul Rinkowski equipped some of his recumbents with Mokick engines as early as 1958. The bikes had a 50 cc engine and zipped along at 35 mph across the peaks of old East Germany. And they still got 250 mpg! The reason for this was the great aerodynamics which got even better now that the legs did not have to move.

Options, today, include the ZAP Power System and Chronos Hammer—add-on electric motors that assist the pedaling effort, each for about $500.

The concept in principal is not very farfetched, especially not for fans who use the recumbent as an everyday vehicle and who want to improve their use, speed, range and options, combined with an effective relief from pedaling.

If you carry around the thought of building such a recumbent, you should remem-

speaking. The accessory options are extensive. As usual, there is space for rear racks. And there is a small front fairing for the front person which can be extended with a stretchy Lycra "bodystocking," as the producer calls their cloth fairing. The aerodynamics of this bike are superior to an upright tandem.

A tandem recumbent's chainline can become very complicated. I recommend a conventional tandem crank set-up located near the rear as a starting point. It carries the chain to the cogset on the right side and takes in chain on the left. Bottom bracket locations must be fine-tuned according to the different seat positions and angles. The Viewpoint Mixte tandem surprises here with a clever technical trick: the recumbent cyclist has his own shifter and can choose between seven gears, even though he's still somewhat dependent on the captain's gear selection. Thus a racing upright cyclist could increase his cadence while the recumbent pilot can pedal according to his own style.

ber that stresses on frame and materials are higher due to the extra weight and power applied and have to be constructed accordingly.

By refusing to use combustion engines and electricity out of the socket, the most environmentally conscious of cyclists do tend to limit their practical range, of course. In the future, auxiliary engines and fairings in combination with user-friendly recumbents could be a successful relief for over-crowded cities. One can get excited just thinking about the prospect. I am primarily thinking of the combination of small combustion engine, pedal power and fairing in an integrated module.

# Turning a homebuilt frame into a finished bike...

Once the frame work is finished, it should be equipped with braze-on attachment points which eliminate the use of hoseclamps. Hoseclamps are a source of errors, cannot be used everywhere on the frame and get rusty. However, they are easily exchangeable if defective. Brazed attachments are the aesthetic choice for fastenings to the frame.

### *Advantages hoseclamp:*
- can be used exactly where needed
- cheap, available, easily exchangeable

*...brazed attachments*
- elegant
- simple
- light
- can be installed almost anywhere

### *Disadvantages hoseclamp:*
- ugly
- limited use
- trickier mounting process

*...brazed attachments:*
- not quickly exchangeable
- difficult to repair if defective
- initial mounting laborious

Pretty braze-ons, bosses and other attachment points built into a bike (or glued or molded in with a carbon frame) when sensibly arranged, make a frame appear very clean and stylish. The advantage is obviously on the side of such features. Moreover sometimes you cannot forgo some of the little parts needed to complete a frame, such as cantilever brake bosses.

Braze-ons serve as good fastenings for:
- brake bosses on seatstays
- mounts for chain-pulley axles
- brake bosses for cantilever brakes
- cable guides
- cable stopper
- bottle holders
- levers
- M6-nuts for fairings or luggage racks
- outer cable and chain guides
- pump holders
- chain hooks
- fenders
- luggage racks

*The popular, high-quality RANS "Screamer" offers independent cadence for both riders.*

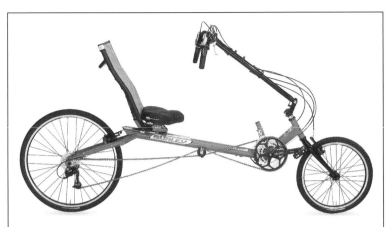

*Burley's "Jett Creek" makes a strong stand for an affordable, high quality LWB, including a pivoting handlebar for easy stepover. Burley is a large trailer maker who now offers a full line of quality bikes.*

- front gearing mech
- chain-holder for removing rear wheel
- brake bridge fastening
- stiffening struts
- pulley guides
- front lamp
- back light
- dynamo
- computer
- kickstand
- reflectors
- race number fastening
- fairing fastening
- bag fastening
- chain protection
- gear shift protection

Furthermore, many metal parts can be used for other purposes than those for which they are intended. A bolt, for instance, can be part of an elegant fastener for a lighting dynamo at the frame. Mounting a dynamo with a clamp would be difficult and would look improvised.

This should not be the end of the striving for creativity. What you braze on should be made with regard to all later uses. Once the frame is painted, it is too late for correction. Thus it is very important to evaluate the exact position of the braze-on and to check the mounting several times. Nothing is more frustrating than a cable stopper that got soldered the wrong way on a frame that was meticulously painted for $100 in supplies.

The mounting of braze-ons for shifting and brake cables demands great care and planning. Modern, super-precise shifters are unforgiving. The cause of every bend of an outer cable casing are the braze-ons for shift levers and their works. Every bend causes tension in the outer case and friction for the inner surface. So smooth functioning of shifters depends on the positioning of the guides. Guides must not force cable into extremely small radii. It is advisable to let the cable run along the frame as often and as long as possible without outer guides. The same is valid for the brakes: any bend or any unnecessary inch of cable eats up braking power.

Test the furthest range of steering on both sides while measuring cable. That saves you unpleasant surprises, like during braking in steep corners. If the handlebar is supposed to be adjustable, all cables have to run in all positions in an ideal line. Cable guides from mountain bikes are good objects to study for these aspects. Similar guidelines hold true for lighting and computer cables. A lighting wire only costs 50¢, whereas a torn computer cable will eat a $20 hole in your wallet.

When the frame is equipped with the necessary brazed attachment points and painted, it is time to consider and put together the rest of the bike. Basic things like wheel size, bottom bracket threading, fork steerer tube size and brakes have been predetermined by the frame construction and the brazed attachments. Their final selection and detailing, however, demands attention and is not as easy as it looks. Whether you leave it up to the manufacturer or assemble it all yourself, it pays to know the pro's and con's of these components.

## Wheels

### Front wheel...

A recumbent's front wheel undergoes more and heavier strains because you do not leave your saddle, or lift up with the handlebars to ease the impact of obstacles. To lower the risk of failure, high pressure tires have to be used. There is a broad choice in the field of 20-inch tires: from 20 x 1 1/8 inch 1o0 psi high pressure tires with racing profile to the 20 x 1.75 inch version with all-terrain profile to the same size with a thick, slick profile. Watch out, because there are various 20-inch sizes which cannot be combined:

20 x 1 1/8 inch = 451 mm dia ('Road')
20 x 1 3/8 inch = 440 mm dia (rare)
20 x 1.75 inch = 406 mm dia ('BMX')

The tire size with the decimal point ("1.75") is called the BMX size. While fractional notation indicates a tire called "20-inch Road," because it used to have the highest quality options.

Since the summer of '96 there have been narrow, race-worthy tires for the 406 cm size. Overall today, you still find the biggest selection in the 406 range.

Hubs for small wheels should be of high quality because of the high rpm's. At the same time maintenance can be minimized by using sealed bearings, as they have been used by the French company Mavic for years. These hubs run smoothly and are maintenance-free.

Purpose and style of riding determine the number and crossings of spokes. I would prefer a 3-cross 36-spoke set-up for a touring recumbent. If it is a racing set-up is needed, which will be used for everyday riding as well, 28 radially laced spokes should suffice. They should be, like the rims, of high quality. Spokes by Biel DT or Prym made of stainless steel last the longest, do not rust and do not stretch significantly. I can recommend the rims by Alesa, Araya, but most of all by Sun Mistral from the U.S..

### Rear Wheel...

The strains on a recumbent rear wheel are also of a different order than those on a normal bike. The influences of the rocking pedal action or of extreme acceleration are nonexistent. On the other hand, shocks from bumps are much stronger, which can be traced back to the lack of the normal "springs" of the pilot. The natural bodily suspension systems are limited by the benter's reclined riding position. A racing or everyday bike is well-equipped with 32 spokes and 3-cross. 36 or even 40 spokes with 4-cross can be used for touring.

Hub choice is unfortunately tied to your choice of cogset. Get the best that works with the cogs you desire. For rims, what works on the front will work for the rear. Choice of tires is a question of experience and riding style. Whether it's an 18-mm high-pressure slick or a 47-mm touring tire—depending on your desired purpose and frame-width clearances, all tires can be used for recumbents.

*Varna of Canada doesn't only make record-setting HPVs. They make the "U-Bike," a semi-recumbent utility/city bike. Both feet can rest on the ground when seated. Getting on and off is a breeze.*

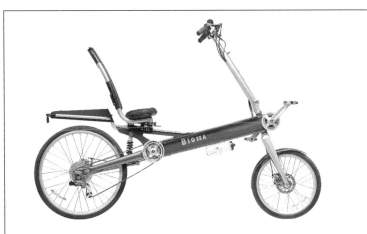

*BigHA is Apache for "because." Former BikeE people produce this feature-packed, luxury CLWB. A handlebar console includes lights, turn signals, speedo, heart rate monitor, wind direction, horn. They emphasize high-tech direct ordering via a deluxe website.*

In general, highspeed commuting and open-road riding done in race-quality fully-faired HPVs should be done with the protection of wider, stronger tires to avoid dangerous blow-outs and time-consuming repairs, and to absorb more shock.

Bikes with suspension can sometimes use lighter wheels (on the suspended wheel only) as impact-stresses on them are much less.

### Cockpit and steering instruments

Grip-shift, thumb or bar-end levers all work fine on recumbents. Design your set-up so that together with brake levers, the handlebars form one steering unit which always allows quick reactions to traffic or race conditions. Individual anatomy, steering mechanism radius and weight can all be criteria for the choice of shifters and brake levers. (Dia Compe levers are very light, inexpensive and have good leverage ratios.)

The integrated brake-lever-shifters which work by pivoting the brake lever seem to be harder to use on recumbents, since the typical recumbent has more of a mountain-bike style handlebar. Those levers seem to require a strongly curved bar and parallel mounting for proper function and wrist-activation. Above-seat-steering usually doesn't allow for parallel installment or easy pivoting wrist-action, and under-seat-steering usually isn't conducive to a strongly curved bar. So, those new levers see only limited custom use. Regularly curved roadstyle handlebars just don't see much use on recumbents.

A computer finds its place wherever you can see it and push its buttons—at the main frame, the handlebar or the front derailleur 'sprout'—to provide you with all the information you could want. Computers seem especially important for faired vehicles since one often has less direct sensation of speed and how it is being affected by wind or discomfort. Headwinds are often harder to locate and judge, and 30 mph can seem to be a gentle speed. The numbers can help! The steering center is finally complete when you add a bell.

### Derailleurs, shifters, gearing and brakes

In the case of rear shifting components, it is advisable to match the model of your shift levers, otherwise today's index systems will likely suffer loss in precision, or simply not be usable. High tech gears are too precise and too complicated nowadays. No more "combining as you please" allowed. The longer cable housings of many recumbents cause some imprecision anyway, similar to an upright tandem, which should not be made worse with a mix of components. When in doubt, check with your local pro shop. Cables with Gore-Tex or Trac-Pearls-lining (as Zabel and Ulrich use at the Tour de France) are fine, but about $150 in cables for brakes and gearing is a lot.

Sometimes, though, when homebuilding a fully-faired vehicle, as long as you can get the gear you want and have it work, this is enough! You have bigger problems to worry about...and you make far greater gains in other areas, so that your main concern with shifting might be to just keep it simple. Even older parts are sometimes employed to good effect.

So we have now reached the problematic question of what transmissions work best for the special needs and diversity of recumbents. The transmission has to have a wider gear range to make up for the loss of stand-up pedaling and the loss of out-of-saddle sprinting capability. It might have to cover anything from perhaps a mountain climb to a 40-50 mph top speed attempt on a flat race course, to a 60 mph mountain descent, and it also has to do justice to the distinctive cadence needs of the recumbent (see Physics chapter).

The over-long chain of most recumbents has an obvious advantage: the 'dead' gears of upright bikes do not have to exist on HPVs. Thanks to the long distance between bottom bracket and cogwheel the chain never runs too obliquely. The complete spectrum of the cogwheel can be used fully with each chainring. Thus the transmission can be planned differently. The useless gear overlappings of an upright bike regain their lost value. However, if a recumbent is equipped with an intermediate drive, or FWD, dead gears can reappear.

If the distance between rear wheel hub and intermediate bearing approximately equals the length of the chainstay, the shifting follows normal bike criteria. The further the transmission is away from the rear hub, the less the chain is slanted, and 'dead' gears get new life. Triples are very popular. A small chainring suffices for big hills, mountain rides and slow sections. The middle one covers city traffic. Steep descents and races demand the Big Ring. Each range then uses the entire rear cogset.

Mostly, the choice is made for an 18-24-speed transmission. It is not smart to fall into boasting about riding up a mountain in racing gears. The consequences for your joints and muscles are not negligible. It is no shame to drive with a 1:1 ratio, especially when you live in the mountains. I personally use a transmission of 32/42/54 in the front with a Dura-Ace cassette of 12/13/14/15/17/19/21/24 in the rear. The 32- and 42-tooth rings help me to manage everything up to a 10% grade. The close cog gradations in the rear enable me to shift smoothly and harmoniously, especially in the mountains, and you can quickly jump up 5 kmh by spinning in contrast to stomping, grinding or hammering. A nice mountain cog-range might be: 12/14/16/19/24/30. In the end you reach the top sooner without using more energy.

Someone's custom transmission might look weird at first, but it is usually the product of years of experience.

The right transmission can only be developed if you know your cadence preferences, shifting style, speed range, bike type and typical riding conditions.

Remember that small rear wheels require bigger gears. MTB downhill racing companies, with their CNC computer aided milling machines, seem to be the best source for big rings of 60-70 teeth. Rear cogs of only 10 teeth are also available via special order.

The best solution for those who are undecided is the French company Specialite T.A. They offer crank lengths from 150-185 mm and chainrings from 26-68 in one-tooth increments. They can make custom rings with up to 146 teeth! The real attraction, however, is their abundance of combination options. They have a basic hole circle for their outer chainring from which all their other chainrings get made. Either one or two other chainrings of the inner hole circle can then be mounted to the outer chainring. The one-, two- and three-ring mounts are built all on the same crank-arm. You decide the

*A classic elastomer rear suspension. This construction is quite simple. The aluminum cross-tube in the picture is a fairing fastening mounted through the frame.*

individually and have them in good availability. In Europe, the European products (Mavic/Edco/Campagnolo) have the advantage of better access, usually.

SRAM (was Fichtel & Sachs) has created an interesting alternative to the triple: the 3x7-speed internal hub gear system hub. These days this hub is being used in many configurations by manufacturers and homebuilders alike. It is often used in combination with a derailleur and cogset to give huge gear-ranges!

The same holds true for the amazing new Mountain Drive transmission by Florian Schlumpf. By pressing on a button mounted on the crank-arm with your ankle, as you pedal (easier than it sounds) you can get two gear ranges without altering your shifter or cogset. The gear mechanism is built entirely into the bottom bracket axle. Some record attempt HPVs are using this device. And of course one should not ignore the Rohloff Speedhub with its 14 gears, but take care: if you have a rear wheel smaller than 24" you will need a big ring on the front to keep the hub working fine when reaching higher speeds!

All kinds of brakes work with recumbents. However, a concern arises with the higher speeds of faired bikes and/or heavier bikes in general. Braking has to be more powerful, also heat buildup can become a problem. Today's disk brakes, as a result, are becoming popular with fast recumbents and HPVs. Strong V-brakes have also been helpful. Yet older brakes and BMX brakes also play a role with wide tires or a need for offside cable routing, with older brakes offering more variety. Again, less beautiful solutions might be acceptable inside a faired homebuilt HPV, with whatever works with everything else being sufficient. Aluminum heat-sinks have been crafted to reduce brake overheating for very fast faired HPVs in mountainous areas.

number of chainrings simply by how many mounting bolts you buy. Tinkerers have built quadruple cranks from T.A. parts. For this latter change you need only more screws and chainrings. This pleasure is not cheap, of course.

Most recumbents use a long chain—typically two upright chains pinned together—which has to be kept under tension in a way that saves power and weight by the rear shifter pulley tension spring. Because of this strain most shifters do not last longer than two or three years, or 10-20,000 miles. Preventionwise, it is advisable to buy a shifter whose producer sells tension springs

### Lighting

This point is similar to a normal bike: in cycling, so far, the world of lighting has dramatic flaws. Neither the reliability nor the power of available light units is satisfactory. We have become used to sub-par performance.

In the darkness, the size of and posture of your vehicle is not really important. Only the strength and size of lights matter. The recumbent does not suffer any disadvantage if it is equipped with good lights. There are many models available today with bright high-beams, multiple fields, generators and rechargeable battery packs. Small firms have done their best with the problem. One can now ride in cold or rainy darkness for a few hours before needing a recharge. Dynamos light up quite nicely once under way.

Highspeed HPVs with full-fairings need more powerful lights to give longer and wider illumination. One needs a lot of lighting to ride safely at 35 mph in an urban environment, to see and be seen. Things happen much faster at such speeds!

I ride my unfaired recumbent with a Union dynamo, halogen front lights and Seutec rear lights. Additionally, I switch on the truly perfect Vistalite. Its flickering bright red light grabs the eye even at long distances and makes you safe. The new small, bright, long-lasting LCD lights are also very useful.

### Pennant

A pennant is not only great for kids' bikes, it helps protect low-riding recumbent bikes and their pilots from inattentive car drivers. This is an incredible safety device. Normally, an HPV pilot can make eye contact with car drivers, but this doesn't always work with dangerous trucks and buses. Tall flags are a safety benefit to all cyclists in this regard.

### Rear-view mirror

From a laid-back position it is difficult to turn around and see alongside or behind oneself. To avoid pulling out in front of a motor vehicle when making turns, and just to keep tabs on what's happening around you, it is advisable to use a rearview mirror. Rhode Gear and others specialize in creative and useful accessories, including many versions of rear mirrors. Their models use a distorted mirror that shows a larger area behind the rider than is normally visible. Three models mount to brake levers, two go on helmets and one has its place on your glasses. Two mirrors are often a rule in HPV racing.

## Ultralight racing designs

The system of driver and vehicle is together the point of attack for inertia and gravity. If an HPV driver reduces the total unit weight he will gain advantages in the mountains, in sprints, in starts and stops and everywhere else.

Although many cyclists live contrary to such a concept, it is obvious that personal

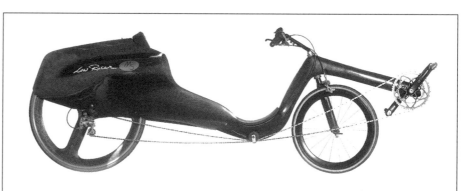

*M5 Carbon Racer is the world's lightest and fastest production recumbent, at 9.5 kg with tailfin. M5 holds seven world records. Stunning craftsmanship. (photo: M5)*

*A suspension, where the suspension elements are pushed away from each other. The advantage is the easy adaptability to the weight of the system (driver plus vehicle). If the bike is heavily loaded, you just add additional elastomers, if the weight is less, you take some away.*

body weight should be kept to an optimal level as well. This does not mean that you should weigh as little as possible but you should strive for the ideal compromise between highest possible achievement and lowest possible body weight. As the tuning of a bike demands less self control than the tuning of your own body mass, the first is much more common. It only costs dollars! —But common sense is greatly involved as well.

A typical recumbent is, because of its construction (mainly in the seat) heavier than a comparable upright bike. I should also remind us here of the 2.5-times as much chain often used.

Mainly, though, this heaviness coincides with a lack of industrial interest in recumbents. Intense research and development success has made weight reduction in the typical bike sector commonplace, but recumbent frame tubes were left out. The reason is the small demand...so far. The required orders from renowned tubing produc-

ers are too large for small HPV-producers. Such a giant adjusts machinery to a customer's wish only for orders of 500 meters of tubing, or one ton, or more. With the second or third kilometer of purchased tubing, the price gets reduced by half per meter—but these are economies that small producers cannot take advantage of.

Thus savvy tinkerers can only keep the weight of their machines low by smart construction and clever component selection. Often this means they pay a premium in both time and money. The door to their workshop offers the answers. They can also invest in light, useful and even affordable parts such as those the mountain bike fashion has brought forth. As a result, the successes of individual lightweight constructions are nothing less than amazing.

'Self-baked' carbon chainrings, light-gauge alloy brakes, and thin-wall fairings on the quality level of a fine forge or injection-molding plant can be found in the form of many high-end bikes, which please the eye and the scale.

Only personal initiative makes successful lightweight building possible. The Frenchman Rodolphe Brichet, for example, presented a 30-lb fully-faired complete short recumbent HPV in 1990. The bike consisted of an aluminum honeycomb frame covered with carbon fiber, with a fairing made completely of carbon fiber. A non-indexed 8-gear-shift and no second brake saved a few more grams. One should be excited by what new designs and processes will spring forth from the backyard labs in the near future.

Some are already working on the fully-faired 22-lb bike. There is an unfaired 15-lb bike and the Lightning R-84 is commercially available at 20 lbs.

People are sharing plans by way of videos and the Internet for relatively easy to build lightweight fairings from thin-wall Coroplast corrugated plastic panel. They are sharing information on building vacuum facilities with hair-dryers, heat guns and such for shaping lightweight plastics. They are collaborating on concrete and styrofoam ovens for curing and molding. Shortcuts and tricks are shared far and wide for working with high-tech materials, glues, and CAD software. (An easy weight-saving tip for fiberglass: squeegee out all excess resin!) Carbon fiber also seems promising for even the small team shop. Suspension is even acquiring some established protocols so that each builder is not reinventing the spring, so to speak.

Mysteries in each area are giving way to this global volunteer effort, without any help from regular bicycle manufacturers. Some high-tech materials producers, though, have seemed happy to help create new markets where the regular bike makers have sat idle. They give excess materials and scraps to HPV clubs and wait for their test reports to see what can be done. To find answers for your own club project, just look around, ask around and get in touch with other clubs by way of the larger, national and international HPV associations and the Internet.

# Suspension

"The shopping cart and the bike are the last two vehicles in the civilized world which have no suspension," says Werner Stiffel, bike builder. Full-suspension bikes came from the mountain bike sector. Their systems are not necessarily appropriate for everyday use and are expensive. However, these innovations have rapidly trickled down into commuters and even road racing bikes. Today about half of commercial recumbents offer forms of suspension. Note that long wheelbase models seem to need suspension the least of any type, something to remember as complication from complexity rears its head!

Suspension is vital for daily riders on the bad roads of urban areas or on the hardly-speedy bike paths. Studies from the University of Oldenburg, Germany, reveal that long miles on bike paths on an unsuspended bike can lead to health problems.

Due to your position on a recumbent, the bodily suspension mechanisms of knees, spine, shoulders and elbow joints cannot be used, so external suspension is more important than on an ordinary bike.

There are a few ways to suspend a bike: by way of tires, seat, frame or fork. A suspension confronts the frame with special demands. The design has to leave enough space for the suspension and has to avoid any collisions between components and moving frame parts.

Tire suspension is without doubt the

*Suspension in the steering head tube demands proper mounting and careful planning. It is only feasible for those with good technical abilities.*

cheapest, easiest and lightest option. Reducing air pressure raises the level of comfort. However, a general rule for all tire sizes and profiles, is that if you decrease pressure then rolling resistance and likelihood of flats increases, moreover tire sidewalls become brittle due to flexing. Thus you should not ride below the pressure marked on the tire. It is best to determine tire width and pressure in the planning stage, according to your needs.

Seat and frame suspension can be based

*Effective, but complicated front wheel suspension.*

on tension or pressure. Rubber and PU blocks as well as coil or fluid/air springs can also be used for pressure-oriented suspension. A criterion for the suspension element is the spring number. The number tells you by how many newtons the suspension power rises per centimeter of compression.

When two springs get installed next to each other using the same lever, the spring number adds together and the needed power doubles. A spring twice as hard is the consequence. For the other way around, the powers get divided by half if two springs are mounted in line. Spring travel is twice as long as any given strain on the springs.

Spring forces are usually transmitted with the help of a lever to keep the size of the suspension mechanism small. That means that the spring lies closer to the pivot than the wheel. If the rear axle is 20" from the swinging axis and the spring is 10" from it, you arrive at a 1:2 ratio.

The selection of the suspension element should be done with regard to the work capacity. This term signifies the maximum strain capability of an element which should not be reached or surmounted for safety reasons. Based on experience I recommend a 2-2.8-fold statistical burden. If the suspension is fine-tuned according to the lever relationship, then the suspension will never reach its maximum point, and you can expect it to be comfortable. The work capacity can be deducted from the maximum extension and its power thereby in a formula:

$$E = 0.5 \, P \times s$$
$E$ = work capacity
$s$ = maximum extension
$P$ = apparent power

For example, imagine mounting a suspension system directly to the rear wheel which is supposed to resist a statistical strain of 720 Newton. You arrive at a maximum impact of 1800 Newton. If you desire a total suspension travel (which includes the weight of the statistical strain) of 18 cm, it demands

$E = 0.5 \times 1800 \times 18$

$E = 900 \times 18$

$E = 16.200$ Newton/centimeter $= 162$ Nm

The decision could be made in favor of four rubber blocks with a work capacity of 40 Newton-meters each.

Then there is the question of the positioning of the rubber blocks. The lever relation at the pivot plays an important role. If you position the blocks in parallel, with a lever ratio of 1:2, you will gain the same effect as if you had positioned them in line and made the ratio 1:1. If all four blocks are switched to a lever ratio of 1:1, the statistical strain on each block would be marginal. It would be about 50 percent less than in example 1 or 2. However, you'd get a suspension as hard as a board because of the doubled spring number. If you leave it at two rubber blocks and one lever arm of 1:2, the suspension would be all right but the blocks would be overburdened.

Strain on springs can be calculated very well on paper, but it is more complicated with a frame to be built laying in pieces in front of you. It is even more complicated to determine the assumptions about the strain which form the calculation basis.

If the individual dampening frequency is about 200 cycles, it causes a noticeable reduction in frame strain but no comfort. A desirable comfort starts with about 150 cycles. The dream-like feeling of gliding over pavement as if on a sofa kicks in at about 120 cycles a minute or less.

Suspension critics often point to energy loss. They believe that suspension costs energy. Stiffel, an expert in the field of recumbent suspension, holds a different view. He contributed a calculation for the correct position of the pivot point:

"Even a badly constructed suspension that seesaws during pedaling only consumes the

*Various items can be used to create suspension. Here, somebody used the pistons from a car trunk lid.*

energy of the friction in the suspension parts. However, the pedaling suffers and becomes inefficient. This can be avoided by choosing the proper pivot point. The calculation is not so easy, though. Let me only say this: You must not only consider the rhythmically changing chain pull power which kicks in at the tire resistance point and which works horizontally. There's also the acceleration power, which includes a pulsation, as well as a residual burden. These three powers have to be summed up with vectors. The optimum pivot point is located on the resulting vector. The conventional long recumbent has a turning point at about 12" below the powerside chain. Bikes which are constructed like this have already proven their suitability in competition."

The overall energy equation tells the final story. Are the suspension's power losses and distortions smaller than the power that would be lost otherwise due to ground unevenness? If a suspended rider can pedal with disregard to ground conditions, he will crank more efficiently than without suspension, and will save energy that would've

*"Nilgo III" design by Raymond Brichet of France is hardly taller than a kneeling human. It only weighs 30 lbs and is reminiscent of a spaceship.*

been lost to bumps and vibration.

Kickback, or pogoing, as it is called in the mountain bike scene, plays an important role in the suspension of the driving wheel. Avoiding it is critical for the drive's efficiency, and its three individual effects influence pedaling smoothness greatly. If you are aiming for mutual independence of drive and suspension you have to avoid any kind of pogoing.

Pogoing (or kickback) means:
• planetary movement
• shifting movement
• extension/shortening of the part of the chain which is under tension when you are pedaling.

These effects, their significance, and the design possibilities to influence them are very complex. A detailed description cannot be given here, but look into literature on motorcycle design for the best data available on this presently. Special and irreplaceable information about specific suspension problems (and more importantly, their solutions) are summed up in Werner Stiffel's

small manual *Suspension*.

The terms attenuation, damping and 'stiction' are often used in context with suspension. They refer to kinds of friction in suspension; for instance bearing friction, inner material friction in PV-blocks, or fluid friction in hydraulic absorbers.

A suspension without attenuation would never stop oscillating if it was once touched by a ground unevenness. If a second push follows, it turns into a very unpleasant vibration. Thus it is necessary to attenuate the suspension, e.g. to destroy the vibration energy.

Martin Staubach says that "An attenuation is ideal if it damps during compression lightly and more strongly during expansion, to prevent over-vibration. Hydraulic damping elements show this behavior. Friction attenuation is a simpler type. A tightly fastened pivot bearing is representative of friction—it's simply hard to move. The general reaction of this system, however, deteriorates, and even when it's working fine unevennesses are not absorbed very well. A good compromise between elaborate hydraulics and friction damping are the suspension elements made from polyurethane. They possess a large amount of self-attenuation."

A gas and coil suspension with additional hydraulic dampers would be ideal. Progressive suspension elements are useful. A suspension is called progressive when it reacts to soft nudges without losing the capability to counter harsh bumps. This principle is standard with automobiles. With growing compression, the suspension becomes harder.

A simple suspension is usually not enough, it should be adjustable to the level of likely strains. On Monday you ride to work with your luggage and on Tuesday a relaxed tour in the evening is what you want. It is very practical, almost indispensable, to have an adjustable suspension.

It can be easily done with an adjustment

screw for the fasteners of the rubber blocks. If you have a suspension with rings, the number of rings will determine the results. If the suspension is cleverly constructed, you can change the lever ratio with a few turns of the hand, which is very efficient. Suspension with leaf springs can be changed by adjusting length as it relates to the strength-number of the leaf spring raised to the fourth power.

### Suspension at the front wheel

Long recumbents rarely have suspended front wheels, because only 23-35% of the weight rides on it and the long lever arm makes bumps less noticeable anyway. However, it is exactly this lighter axle load that can make a front suspension helpful for safety reasons, because it improves the tire's contact with the pavement considerably. Without suspension, the front wheel could bounce off little rocks which could lead to loss of traction and accidents, especially in corners. It is a totally different situation on a short bike—here the weight distribution can be 50-50%, so that a suspension noticeably improves both comfort and handling.

I will not talk about the front wheel suspension in great detail for the following reasons: the market offers many suspension systems for the front wheel. With the wave of mountain bikes, producers for suspension forks and suspension systems are flourishing, so that the purchase of inexpensive systems from the Far East is altogether cheaper than if you build your own.

You can simply shorten and change a Manitou suspension fork, for instance, so that it is suitable for a 20-inch wheel—but only when using disk brakes or a Magura oil pressure cantilever brake (whose bosses are mounted the other way around). Furthermore, 20-inch suspension forks are available from BMX producers for about $200. All problems about insurance, purse, and construction are thus neatly solved.

However, none of the available suspension forks are optimized out of the box for use on a long recumbent. They are too firm for the relatively small load. (They are designed for greater weight on the wheel.) So you have to go to any of the renowned producers who offer custom tuning kits which can offer you a big playground for fine-tuning.

Rear shock units are also available, but a homebuilder will have to take care of the pivot and mounts.

As more recumbent makers offer standard suspension options for front and rear, the availability of parts to homebuilders will greatly increase for special sizes and uses.

## Clothing on the recumbent

While it is quite easy to equip a recumbent bike with conventional bike parts, it's harder to satisfy a recumbent *rider* with regular bike clothing. They are only usable in a limited way for recumbent-specific needs. The ergonomic position and the resulting changes in where the wind hits you are responsible for that.

*Volae offers a high-quality line of touring and performance high-seat SWB bikes. Volae president Rolf Garthus is shown here enjoying a winter ride. It's easy to do with the right clothing. Garments with double layers on shins, under thighs and on butt, plus under arms, are ideal for recumbent riding in the cold.*

### The wind takes a new approach...

Tight biker's pants with leather chamois are not a necessary accessory on the recumbent. Nonetheless, I'd advise you to wear them. They prevent abrasions and smooth out air flow and offer good ventilation. Moreover, I heard from a recumbent cyclist that a bee once lost her way in his flapping casual shorts—certainly not a desirable travel companion. Some recumbent shorts are now offered without chamois.

The wind blows through any bottom holes in your bike shoe soles and can cool off the feet very quickly. Thus you should plug the holes in your racing shoes with beeswax (*Rivendell!*) and possibly use a second, insulating insole for winter.

All bike pants for cold weather are made for protecting vertically positioned legs. So there are extra warm layers in the upper thigh area, shins and knee caps. On a recumbent, insulation is needed more in the whole under-thigh area, rather than at the upper thigh. I also recommend extra layers for groin, crotch and butt. These parts all now directly face the wind, which can lead to colds and bladder infections. Your pants should have tight cuffs. Loose pants easily become 'wind pants' which cool off the legs and annoy. It is especially important to get good coverage for the whole lower legs, on

*Example of a sensible synthesis of ergonomy and strict shape limits: the "Bean" by Kingcycle. (Drawing based on art by Miles and John Kingsbury.)*

down from the calves—they are what lead into the wind. You will see that not many regular bike clothes fit these needs and you may have to look for special recumbent outfits or make your own.

A high crank height plays an important role in this context, by the way. Low crank recumbents (most of the long recumbents) have advantages here, because the air flow more closely resembles the normal bike. Racing machines with a high bottom bracket (10" above the seat) change the wind profile of the legs completely so that the phenomena described above gets even more pronounced. The same holds true for the position of the hands. Steering under the seat resembles the arm position on a diamond bike. Above-seat steering with straight arms, or arms bent upwards, creates conditions solved similarly to the high bottom bracket—tight cuffs, warm gloves, extra insulation along the undersides of the arms and complete coverage of the leading lower arms.

### Leaning back instead of bending over

Seen from an ergonomic viewpoint, the position on a recumbent demands special attention to clothing. The helmet has to be adjusted to the new use otherwise it slides into the back of your neck or it chokes you with the strap digging into your throat as you tip your head forward instead of back as it was designed for. The more reclined the angle of the seat is, the stronger is this negative effect. Unfortunately the market does not offer helmets with enough adjustment possibilities. But wear one anyway: available helmets might be awkward and ugly...but fractured skulls are uglier.

In the case of jackets and jerseys, the usual extended back is useless. Front-buttoning raincoats and short front waistlines can leak due to puddles in the belly area. Back pockets of jerseys can only be used with narrow seats. 'Benters need pockets on the front and

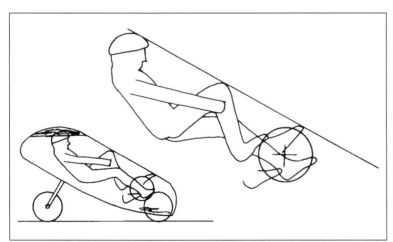

raincoats with a side-zip. Some recumbent producers, such as Lightning, are starting to offer suitable clothing.

# Fairings and Fairing Plans

Every recumbent rider seems to dream of a streamlined fairing that allows high speeds in winds and bad weather. However, what seems good and simple in theory, often becomes an almost unsolvable problem in practice.

It has less to do with the weather conditions or the best possible aerodynamics, but more with the combination of these demands with everyday appropriateness.

Vehicles during high speed sprints show what is possible and feasible in the pure field of aerodynamics. Gardner Martin's Gold Rush, with an effective front area of 0.46 qm and a Cw-value of 0.09, and the personal effort he put into it, rivals the quality of automobile prototypes which cost millions. The result stands on its own: 65 mph for a 200 meter sprint.

In the world of everyday riding, we have to put a big emphasis on convenience, access, reliability, cargo-capacity, weather-proofing and crosswind stability. These are areas that the record-setters don't have to worry about!

(Don't you wonder why more upright cyclists, with their aerobars and tri-spoke wheels, don't also fantasize about adding a fairing to integrate with the aerobar or to streamline behind the saddle and perhaps offer cargo space? We rarely hear them mention such reasonable projects, yet they spend as much time and money on improving airflow as most recumbenteers!)

The simplest forms of fairing starts with a cowling "nosecone" mounted in front of the bottom bracket which hides the rotating legs from the air stream. These fairings can be built easily and quickly from fiberglass (see construction section). A similar cowl-

*"The Bean II" is the successor model of "The Bean," which held the Hour world record in 1990. Muscle-powered vehicles have to be slim, light and as aerodynamic as possible to achieve highest speeds.*

ing at the rear, called a tailbox or shark fin, helps the off-streaming air re-acquire a clean line to prevent rear turbulence. The rear fairing can be readily configured as a trunk and tail-light-holder. These are the simplest forms of fairings.

Fairings give another opportunity for recumbents. They can be made in a huge variety of shapes, then finished with a wide-open range of graphic design—in a way that other aspects of cycling don't allow. Advertising on fairings is a possibility as well.

Fairings also offer significant crash protection. Sam Whittingham crashed at 80 mph in his Varna—without injury. Obviously, everyday riders can also benefit.

When built for speed, a fairing is above all characterized by a very small frontal area. Based on the measured height and breadth at the heels, feet, shoulders, steering mechanism, hands, head, seat, and rear wheel, a plan can be made. To find out the best fairing form, you connect the individual points that you have measured so that they surround the driver and the vehicle in the desired form. This edgy outline turns into a

*"Kingcycle": The compact British flier was sold with optional rear fin, a front nosecone and a cloth fairing.*

drawing's borders. The same is valid for the frontal view, though it is a little more complicated because of the distance of the feet from the rear wall. To see whether the dimensions are all correct you can use a camera. Take pictures with a long focal length and a tripod, so that all aspects are in sharp focus. The next step is to build a model.

In principle, there are three fairing types:
- cloth fairing
- foam rubber fairing
- hard shell plastic fairing

### Advantages cloth fairing:

- light
- foldable
- inexpensive
- easily constructed
- easy on, easy off
- can be used otherwise, as rain parka, tent, etc.
- easily repaired
- adjusts to bike and cyclist
- quiet

### Disadvantages:

- not very waterproof
- more sensitive to crosswinds
- less aerodynamic

### Advantages foam rubber fairing:

- light
- can be constructed in separate parts
- easy to give 3D curved shape
- can be used alternatively, as sleeping mat, tent
- simple to adjust
- quiet

### Disadvantages:

- restricted form giving
- mediocre look
- rough surface
- cannot always be painted

smooth, stream-lined form when you connect the contour points in an elegant way, and becomes similar to the form of a water drop, gliding bird, swimming fish or airplane wing. It is helpful to take a look at the design and aerodynamics studies of the auto industry. Many designers there have tried to put into practice the results they gather from expensive experiments in wind tunnels.

You can buy manufactured fairings from several suppliers. For simple, clear, effective windshields and partial nosecones that quickly mount to a variety of popular bikes, your best bet is a Zzipper or Mueller Windwrap. However, if you want something faster and more extensive, your options quickly narrow until you're left with building your own.

So, once the basic form is put on paper you should carefully test the developed body before building. To double-check, you draw the contours of the fairing with chalk on a wall, put the bike in front of it and sit on it. Another person checks whether your simulated movements stretch out past the

### *Advantages hard plastic fairing:*

- very aerodynamic
- holds shape well in strong winds
- construction can fulfill additional tasks (integrate with frame or cargo bays)
- easily waterproof
- less sensitive to crosswinds
- protection in accidents

### *Disadvantages:*

- often uses toxic materials that pollute the environment and are harmful to work with
- time-consuming construction and mounting
- each fall causes damage
- big resonance inside: noisy
- expensive

## Cloth fairings

To create a cloth fairing some kind of "form-giver" is required, because cloth does not have power to hold its own shape. The simplest way to make a form is to stretch the cloth over a scaffold-like frame. This method has been used to great success with big airships like blimps and zeppelins. A scaffold made of tubing which starts in front of the bottom bracket and the rotating radius of the legs, and which surrounds the body of the driver and ends behind the rear wheel, results in the same 'fish-form' or torpedo shape as an airship.

Hollow fiberglass rods can be connected like tent poles with sockets or cabling to form a frame that can be mounted and dismounted quickly. Tent poles can even be recruited for this purpose! (And then converted back to tent-use for camping at night on tour!) Then all you need is a cloth covering tailored to fit. Parachute silk and sailcloth are very light, UV-resistant and water-proof, tear-safe, inexpensive and easy to sew. These materials are usually better than Lycra or Spandex since they don't stretch: stretch-cloth sags in the wind and should only be used in areas where strategic 'give' is needed. (Stretchy 'body socks' are less aerodynamic than other cloth fairings, but still find their place.) Your first pattern should be tailored from bed sheets and fastened with needles to find and solve design errors. It is important to remember to include a good exit and to make sure that you can get your feet on the ground quickly. Otherwise the fairing could become a riding stuffsack...or coffin!

The steering range of the front wheel has to be able to work unrestrictedly, as well as all the shifters and chain pulleys, when setting up a cloth fairing. You should also have good access to water bottles, lighting dynamo, and shift and brake levers. To insure good aerodynamics, one also has to have as few seams or flat spots in the front area as possible.

When the cloth pattern is finished, you have to determine the position of the zipper, Velcro or snaps for the exit and mountings. A piece of sewn-in stretch cloth

*This is a fairing that leaves the head out and that has big openings for the feet as well. Perfectly appropriate for use in traffic.*

brings the necessary tension into the overall fairing. It is very practical and time-saving to sew in the stretch piece at a place in the fairing where many seams come together to create the shape. Often this is at the nose of the fairing. Although the stretch piece produces somewhat more turbulence than sailcloth, it is negligible in such a small area. Next, the pattern is cut, and in as few pieces as possible. (Attention: Do not forget to add a few centimeters for seams.) If the parts are tailored with the original cloth, they 'only' have to be sewn together and be equipped with fasteners and reflectors, and you're done.

Scaffolding can also be made to integrate your head profile into the fairing. The scaffold can be made higher and broader in the head area and a transparent plastic piece sewn in. Transparent plastic such as that used in windsurfing sails is very suitable. It can be treated with a product like Rain-X so that the water runs off and the sight is not obstructed by reflections. (Keep the windshield small and close to the face.)

As a cloth fairing can be taken off completely, it can also be used for other purposes. Some HPV buffs in the Netherlands have made a design that can be used as a one person tent. This is very practical on tours as the same item fulfills two purposes and a large amount of weight can be saved.

Apart from the light framework option, there is also the option to stretch the cloth fairing over a solid nosecone. The partial-fairing can then be used alone, such as on a sight-seeing city trip, with the cloth portion stowed away.

The nosecone, in this case, has to be constructed specially for this purpose, as it determines the shape of the rest of the cloth fairing. The dimensions of the rotating knees and heels have to be considered in the height and breadth measures of a partial-fairing. Another part of the nosecone supports a frame above the shoulders, the cloth then adjusts itself to the driver's size and the luggage in the back.

A rod at the bike's rear serves as a holder for the end of the cloth fairing. Instead of this light and simple solution, you can also use a rear fin over which, similar to the front cone, a fairing 'sock' is stretched. As cloth always stretches tangentially between points of contact, this fairing type acquires more sharp 'edges,' which reduces the aerodynamic qualities. The variability of the cloth produces concavities in the sides during strong crosswinds and high speeds. These will cause aerodynamic problems and increase sidewind sensitivity. Basically, you get blown around more, which is not always safe or relaxing. Lastly, cloth can be used in partial-fairing applications of its own: stretchy doors and 'bomb-bay' floors can be made to close off openings in hard-shell fairings.

*Foam fairings combine advantages of both cloth and fiberglass fairings.*

# Foam rubber fairings

The German Harald Winkler is a pioneer in the field of foam rubber fairings for recumbent bikes. At the beginning he laughed about fairings made of foam rubber, but since then it has for him become a fully-acceptable alternative to the two traditional fairing types. More environmentally-friendly and less process-sensitive than a plastic fairing, more stable and safer than the cloth fairing, and clearly very light— the foam rubber fairing is a goose that lays golden eggs with fairings.

Winkler, the "Meufl Man," works with closed-cell, elastic PE-foam which can be bent spherically by shortening the edges. This bend creates an amazingly stable and stream-lined form. All you need to work with the material is glue and a pair of scissors. The mats are simply cut and glued. Thanks to this method and material it is also easy to integrate zippers. Thus the fairing can be taken apart and transported in a bag. The main problem is creating the right form. In creating a cutting pattern for the fairing, you can forget about computer or even pencil. The pattern cannot be calculated, only experimenting will lead you to your goal. A first model is conceived, is cut, and material is added or cut off where it is too short or too big. Thus you use up about 10-20 yards of material before you find the ideal pattern for a removable body.

# Hard plastic fairings

Plastic fairings are the fastest. They also have the advantage of built-in structural stability. They keep their form nicely if the material used is sufficient and if the stresses aren't too great. Only in strong winds or at high speeds do they give in slightly. These types offer less air resistance and less sensitivity to sidewinds. Their sides can easily present a curved and flowing 'view' to cross-

*A compact "command and control" center in a fairing.*

winds, letting wind slip over easily without taking hold. (Lowering any higher portions of a fairing is also a good way to reduce sidewind bothers. A tall tailfin or windshield will result in a bike being pushed around greatly. Lower is better!)

Due to material qualities, plastic does not need a skeletal, tangential construction. This category includes epoxied fiberglass, carbon fiber, Kevlar, etc. The shape can be perfectly designed to purpose and vehicle. Neither stress-related problems nor vehicle layout need obstruct the realization of your plans.

Wood and metal are ruled out when it comes to building a light, stable and safe fairing. Wood is not stable enough and metal is usually too heavy. Although there are useful tin variants, they offer more weather protection than speed gain.

Coroplast corrugated plastic board is a great new addition to hard-shell fairing material options. It's best available in the U.S., where it is quite cheap, only about $10-15 per 4'x8' sheet of 1/4" panel. It's not actually very hard. It cuts easily with a box-cutter and can be fastened with zipties (matching color duct tape makes a nice finish

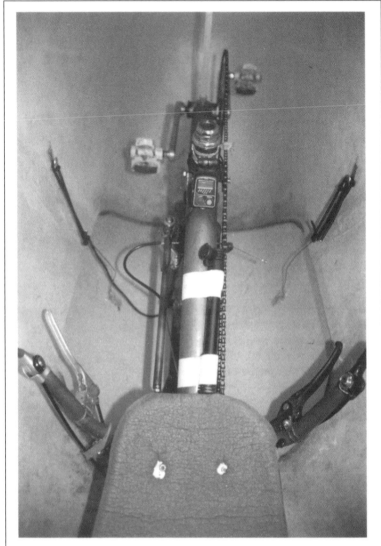

*Cockpit view of "Antigone" by Martin Sörensen. You can see the rubber straps with hooks used to control the "bomb bay" foot flaps.*

terial for fast shapes—and for beginners with a small wallet. The combination of fiberglass cloth and synthetic resin can be shaped into any form and demands less experience and talent than working with the expensive hi-tech resins and fibers of the car racing field, the airplane industry or sailing yacht construction.

Fiberglass is available in two kinds of mat: fleece and webbed. Webbed consists of, as the name suggests, woven fiber threads. Fleece is unwoven, unstructured fiber matting. Mat strength is measured in grams per square meter. If you use epoxy resin, add the weight of resin to the weight of the mat. Synthetic resin and matching hardener is necessary to give a rigid form to the mats. There are two basic products on the market: polyester resin and epoxy resin. Polyester resin smells bad (it is poisonous) and hardens quickly. There's not much time to distribute the resin cleanly on the prepared mats.

Epoxy resin, on the contrary, gives you an hour for shaping, correcting and connecting.

It can be used to easily improve your end result. Epoxy resin intertwines with the fibers better than polyester resin, so it is more flexible than polyester and thus more resistant against breaking. The neutral smell of it while you're working is also convenient. However, do not be fooled: this resin as well might damage your health. Please pay absolute attention to the instructions of the materials you work with!

There is also Kevlar and carbon fiber which can be used as a basis for fairings. These miraculous materials of research make fairings even safer. They are more abrasion-resistant during falls and are less likely to come apart than fiberglass.

If you want to make the lightest and safest construction, you can't avoid epoxy resin or even carbon fiber/Kevlar. Unfortunately, working with these improved products is more complicated and demands more care

seam). It bends easily in one plan only, however. It allows a light, simple fairing to be made, with simple curves, for good speed gain and utility. It's rugged, brightly colored for visibility, and even offers fair crash protection. Several plans are available free online.

Fiberglass is a great fully-moldable ma-

and routine, and is disproportionately expensive.

Once you have answered the question of material, you have to determine the type of construction. Three basic variants are in the range of possibilities:
- layer construction
- rib construction
- sandwich method

## Layer construction

With this method, a large, arbitrary number of layers are laminated one on top of the other. Fairing stability is accomplished by material accumulation. It is obvious that this method tends to be heavy. It is suitable for smaller items like a nosecone or tail fin. Also, it's easy for beginners. To get a enough stability to counter the forces coming from all directions, layers have to be put down in alternating fiber direction.

Only by using quite a lot of material do you end up with a product that is stiff enough. If you decide to build a full fairing with this type of construction, it will become quite heavy. If you use an average number of supports, they'll have to be able to securely hold about 20 lbs each with such fairings, unless you use an extra quantity of mountings.

## Rib construction

In principle this is built the same as layer construction, but you reduce the layers to two and insert ribs along the stress line between the woven layers. Ribs are fiber mat strips which are laminated on a prepared profile form so that they acquire tube form and thus acquire tube qualities. Styrofoam or other light materials are also good. In this way you can greatly reduce the weight of a fairing. If you create a clever design and work professionally the body can finish up under 15 lbs. But, in contrast to the sandwich method, the ribs method offers less protection in falls or accidents.

## Sandwich method

Except for its structure and name, this method does not have much in common with fast food snacks: two thin, hard layers enclose a thick, slightly soft, but very light layer.

Fiberglass, carbon fiber or Kevlar are used for the outer layer. The selected material should be able to take a lot of point pressure, but it is thin enough that it would tend to sag or weaken if used by itself over a large area. Thanks to a light, but thick intermediate layer, this weakness is prevented, giving an effect that resembles the work of ribs in the layer construction. The inner layer is like the outer, only can be more thrifty.

The fairing that results is light, can be strained enormously at all areas, and is totally self-supporting; e.g. only a minimum attachments are needed, giving you plenty of room to ride. Support is not needed for stiffening.

In practice, this means, if all is done

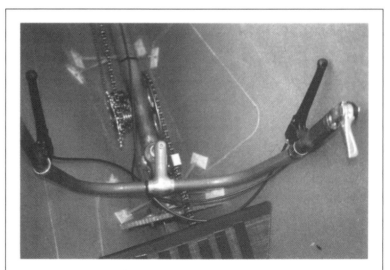

*Inside view of "Bean II." The gear deserves special attention: A left-sided cogwheel for the primary chain is run via an altered gear shift! To save every millimeter, the handlebar is bent to be as narrow as possible. If you look closely, you can see the thick, but very light honeycomb material of the wall.*

*Even getting out has to be practiced.*

The use of spray foam filling confronts you with the problem that the intermediate layer has to be sprayed very evenly onto the inner layer to acquire an equal strength at every place when you sandpaper it later. Each wave or drip in the foam will be mirrored in the outer layer of the fairing.

A fill-in mat does not have that problem. The flexible fill-in mat adjusts itself to the big forms of the fairing and creates a constant distance between the two webbed fiberglass layers.

The sealed honeycomb construction prevents that material from being soaked in resin and tends to weigh less. The first layer of the small hollow spaces in the honeycomb can be soaked, which is also necessary to guarantee the connection of the individual elements. A small amount of perforating of the outer layer of honeycomb can allow enough soak-in for good bonding. Special attention should be dedicated to the producer's instructions with regard to the resin intake capacity and the resulting weight of the product, otherwise you might be unpleasantly surprised. You need some absorption capacity, but not too much.

You'll need a releasing agent for all construction variants which will release the negative from the original mold form and later the positive from the negative. If you have accomplished a smooth surface after days of polishing, a release-agent will suffice. Using wax for this purpose would again cause unwanted unevenness. On rough surfaces, however, wax can be used to fill in small unevennesses and can thus improve quality. When you think of picking a color, you should also consider using color pigments which can be stirred into the resin instead of conventional paints.

cleanly and constructed realistically, that the 'cigar' does not lose form under the pressure of air resistance and even after falls on stony roads there won't be any holes or dents in the fairing (or minor ones at worst).

However, working up these three layers properly is only feasible with a careful hand and a lot of concentration. Moreover, the filling material between the two outer layers is expensive and demands meticulous measuring.

The current technical status quo presents three different materials and methods of sandwich construction:
- web fiber/spray foam/web fiber
- web fiber/fleece mat/web fiber
- web fiber/honeycomb fill/web fiber

# Qualities of the fairing

The following criteria are important for the creation of a fairing for everyday use:

- quick and easy entering and exiting (possible use of 'landing gear')
- big, safe foot-flaps (bomb-bay doors)
- integrated light and signaling system
- integrated rear mirror
- sufficient interior space
- luggage compartment
- good access to all bike parts
- ventilation and rain and fogging control
- splash protection inside the fairing
- waterproof
- small windshield, close to the eyes
- unobstructed steering angles
- good crosswinds Cw value (smallest possible, curved side area)
- option to signal with your hands

Unobstructed entering and exiting, and adequate foot flaps, are vital for safety, as are mirror and lighting. An entrance that will be safe and practical has to be carefully designed, or it will be a source of risk, as well as annoyance and will tend to result in the HPV being used less! A side entrance with removable panel, for instance, is easy to make, but hardly suitable for everyday use. In case of an accident you have to be able to get out of the fairing quickly. In traffic, it is easily a matter of great safety concern, and even life or death. This is partly why HPVers should consider always wearing bright clothing. It draws more attention to their exiting if they happen to fall into the road and have to scramble further out to escape. The consequences of falling onto the only entrance side, or against a limited access, are equal to your worst imagination. Hoods which can be easily taken off or tilted upwards so that they uncover the whole area between seat and feet are desirable. Little aluminum hooks or latches in the main fairing and a bungie cord create a noise-free connection.

The extent to which your fairing stands out strikingly accounts for a high degree of passive safety. A bright color is your only option. Strong contrasting colors with at least one very light color also help: the combination of white and bright red are very effective, for example. White is visible very well in everyday life and in darker conditions. If the white disappears in the color chaos of traffic, the bright red will be there to catch everybody's attention.

Everyday usage involves different clothes, luggage and riding in every kind of weather. To meet these demands a luggage compartment becomes necessary, as well as plenty of interior space, adjustable ventilation, and full fenders. The luggage compartment has its most practical place behind the seat. The room behind the seat is dead space, caused by the broadest place of the fairing (usually the shoulders). Either the seat is installed in a way that it can be folded forward for access to the trunk, or the fairing gets a trunk opening, or the form behind the head is made in a way that allows access right above the seat or behind it. The side-

*Detail view of a rear air channel for the "Carnard" fairing.*

area curving required to defeat the pernicious crosswind leaning, bobbling and dangers, might also leave enough extra room in its hollows to build in small pouches or compartments without interference.

Small windows built close to the face are extremely important for full fairings. Big windows that are far removed from the eye are expensive to buy and to replace. It is also very difficult to see through dirt, haze or running water drops if the window is far from the eyes. Drops and dirt cause reflections of sun rays, lights of cars and street illumination at night, and make it hard to see through. Windows close to the eyes are as uncomplicated as the face shields of motorcycle helmets. The eyes focus right through them. The faster you go the more important is good visibility. A little windshield can also improve your ability to hear traffic and other sounds by cutting down on wind noise, which at higher speeds can be deafening if the head has no shelter.

*This team of Optima lowracers uses carbon rear fairings all pulled from one mold, greatly economizing on time, labor and costs—and giving the team a stylish, unified look. (photo: www.tim.be)*

# Racing fairings

A racing fairing has to embrace the pilot as closely as possible. It should be light, low and narrow. The form should be aimed at a small front surface and the best possible aerodynamics. The breadth, height and other measurements, are determined only by the unrestricted pedaling and steering of the driver. In spite of aerodynamic needs the fairing has to allow the driver the best possible power transmission. This is an especially important consideration in long distance races, which put a premium on comfort and breathing room.

# Form and mold planning

A fairing's form determines its Cw-value and thus the amount of energy lost to air resistance.

The decisive starting points for the conception of a fairing are the 'extreme points' for vehicle and driver. They have to be written down and have to be made into a sketch which also depicts the bike. The sketch is structured in a front view, side view and rear view.

The following 'extreme points' are important:
- head width and height position
- shoulder width and height position
- foot tip rotation circle during pedaling
- heel rotation circle during pedaling
- diameter of the rotation circle
- steering mechanism height and breadth in normal position and at both turning extremes
- hip height and width
- vehicle dimensions, if they have not been captured with body measurements

Apart from the full fairing, there are many forms of partial-fairings:
- head out
- knees out

• heels out
• wheels out
• only front wheel out
• front fairing
• back fairing
• full fairing with side areas cut away

The format must be decided before you plan. The full fairing is the fastest and offers the best weather protection, but it's also the most difficult one to construct and a small error might make it unusable. The 'head-out' variant relieves the driver from the feeling of being trapped, but it is less aerodynamic and weather-friendly.

If you're racing in a league, and your results mean anything to you, it is important to consider the various class regulations. For instance, a front panel that extends past the hipline puts you in a different category in some clubs. In the HPRA in the U.S., for instance, a fully-faired HPV is allowed into the Superstock class as long as no parts are moved for entering and exiting. The Stock class means no fairings, however in Europe the unfaired class allows tailboxes. However, these rules can change. A good thing about most HPV racing, though, is that the racers can often be involved in the regulating, so if you're active, you may have some say in affairs. It's still a small-world scene, after all.

If heels or knees are not faired, air resistance and weather protection gets worse. However, you can saw holes into the fairing and cover them with cloth. Then the fairing is closed, small and relatively rainproof. In a fairing which only covers the pilot's body, the wheels can be seen as usual. The steering angle is kept free, and foot flaps are not needed for the most part. If you integrate the rear wheel into the fairing, you should again consider foot flaps. The whirling air does not get caught in the rear wheel of such a set-up.

If you plan an everyday bike or a touring bike, the calculation of the construction val-

*The WISIL club builders of the "Missile," a prize-winning club racer, saved a lot of time by building the upper and lower halves of their fairing from the same mold. This fully-suspended bike has 50+ mph top speed, 30+ miles for the Hour, and is street-safe with sliding side windows for signaling, trunk for cargo. (photo: WISIL)*

ues need only be accurate to within an inch (in terms of over-sizing), since the fairing's measures have to be kept as spacious as possible anyway. Your analysis has to be absolutely correct, though, when you construct a racing version.

Once the measurements are taken, you have to form a smooth body from the sharp-edged initial design. This is a difficult job. The greatest source of your working power comes from frontal air resistance. You should dedicate your strongest efforts to minimizing it. Starting at the extreme point, the effective front surface has to face the wind smoothly. A ball which equals the breadth of the front surface in its diameter is a good model for comparison. Even if the final form is supposed to be squarish, its streamlined form should be rounded, oriented towards a center point.

All transitions between zones should be blended harmoniously, without sharp angles or bends. Once you get the theoretical form of the front part defined, you have to deal with fairing the rear part and the section in between.

An ending that resembles a fin or wing would seem to have the least impact on frontal air resistance. Unfortunately it is not like that. Such a bike might easily be blown around too much by crosswinds. Airstreams other than those purely from the front should always influence your final solution. Understand that a form which optimizes the Cw-value from the side will conflict somewhat with optimal frontal Cw-value, so you'll need to compromise.

When it comes to record attempt sprint vehicles, crosswinds are negligible and only the frontal air resistance is minimized. If the sidewind is too strong, there's no point in starting. It is different with vehicles for road-racing, all-rounder or league racing—they have to be able to safely (and swiftly) ride in any wind just like any other bike. This is especially true for long distance and every-day models.

The nosecone area usually doesn't present much of a problem in crosswinds. But a perfectly aerodynamic rear fin can create an awful lot of turbulence in crosswinds. That is why it usually has to be most altered to conform to a better side Cw-value (called CS-value). In general, your fairing should have no FLAT areas for any reason—this hugely increases sensitivity to crosswinds.

The 'pressure point' of a fairing plays a major role. The pressure point can be thought of as the point on the fairing where all effective forces are united. The position of the pressure point is strongly dependent on the wind angle. Further factors are the fairing shape and size, speed and vehicle position on the ground, which in the real world involves tilting and rocking, fore and aft, and side to side. It is very complicated and involves lengthy calculations to develop this pressure point. I would direct you to a report by Andreas Fuchs from Switzerland, available via some HPV clubs. If you want to calculate the pressure point and center of gravity exactly, you should look into the Andreas Fuchs article. Just to give you an orientation: the pressure point for small wind angles (0-15 degrees) is located at the first third of the fairing, close to the front wheel. What consequences does the pressure point have on handling in 90-degree crosswinds?

For a simplified answer, you can imagine a weathervane on a church steeple. The mounting rod is the vertical axis. If the surface of the rear part is bigger than the surface of the front part, the weathervane turns into the wind. This resembles what happens when the pressure point is behind the center of gravity of an HPV system (pilot plus vehicle and cargo). The same goes the other way: if the pressure point is located in the front area of the fairing—in front of the center of gravity—then the nose tends to veer out of the wind and to the downwind direction.

The weathervane's rod resembles the vertical axis of the recumbent. Surprisingly, this is only true with multi-track machines. It is different with a single-track bike, because the bike that runs on two wheels can lean to offset some of these forces and offer more resistance to turning around the vertical axis.

If the pressure point is located in front of the center of gravity, the tip of the vehicle tends to turn downwind. To go straight, one has to lean into the wind and counter-steer.

Matt Weaver tried to take advantage of this when constructing his record attempt

*This Barcroft "Virginia" sport bike is set up with a Mueller Windwrap production windshield fairing. Note the two simple attachment points for the fairing.*

vehicle, Cutting Edge. He extended the fairing's front part until the pressure point was located in the direct area of the front wheel. At the same time he put enough weight on it. In practice he produced the phenomenon which resembled the way cyclists swerve in bends. Racing cyclists sometimes swerve to the left before sharp lean to the right, or at least put extra-strong pressure in the bars toward the left to initiate a rightward lean. In this way a bike drops more easily into a righthand power turn. So Weaver's Cutting Edge tends to turn its nose downwind in crosswinds, thus automatically leaning into the wind and keeping the bike going straight.

During unexpected gusts, especially when they blow more from the side, lift—as with an airplane wing—can occur. In combination with vehicle vibration from road roughness this can cause both wheels to lose traction easily. This explains why full suspension is a great advantage for a fully-faired HPV. Suspension makes even more sense at high speeds where all bumps and roughness is amplified and more frequently. Material fatigue also results, with a greater likelihood of frame and parts failures.

The vibration caused by constant ground contact make the use of so-called micro-rough surfaces superfluous. They are supposed to generate a flat air turbulence layer as a cushion between the surface and the airstream and thus they are supposed to reduce the air friction resistance. But it does not seem to be realistic, since a fairing is being vibrated constantly already.

However, this is an area where Matt Weaver claims progress. He says that his new bikes achieve enough attached flow to result in a new level of speed potential, of up to 100 mph. His perfectionism discovers that even a disturbance the thickness of Scotch tape can cause airflow to 'trip' and snowball into much larger drag. Note that attached flow is not the same as laminar flow

but it's still very fast!

Some general fairing tips in conclusion:
- as few openings and sharp edges as possible
- avoid edges and openings especially in the ground area
- flatten the ground side of the body
- when in doubt keep the body too long rather than too short
- a fairing close to the ground has less problem with headwinds and cross-winds
- a fairing close to the ground vibrates more (with risk of airstream breakup)
- the widest part of the fairing should be between the end of the first third and the middle
- all edges, seams, openings, stickers and flaps disturb boundary layer streamlining.

*The Swiss Birk "Comet" full-fairing is a fast, gorgeous, production fairing that fits their lovely lowracer. They also offer a stylish tailfairing. Such high levels of professional polish give the interesting potential of selling ad space on your bike. (photo: www.tim.be)*

# Trondheim–Oslo:
# 540 kilometers nonstop on a recumbent

*Peeeceeeeep*—time starts running—the first turn of the crank carries me the first meter—539,999 are still to follow ...

My pulse is racing, and I transfer this energy to movement. Then I pass the most famous sign in Trondheim. All riders quickly glance at the magic number on it: 539 kilometers to Oslo (335 miles). Somehow I had never questioned the fact that I would arrive in Oslo in all the months of getting into shape. All preparations of mind and body had only been undertaken for this sole purpose. In the undertow of my fellow riders who look at me and shake their heads, I reach the first stop after about two hours. Until then, the racing cyclists had been looking down at me. They barely accepted me in their groups so that I felt sort of out of place. Quickly I tucked away bananas, juice, water, bread and muesli bars. Pushed by the helpers' stares, I start riding again. I avoid long breaks so that I do not cool off too much. What follows is a lonely passage of more than 200 kms. Well, not all alone, because enthusiastic Norwegians at the roadside try to motivate me with "Heya, heya, heya" shouting. This "heya" moves me so much that I almost cry. Then I finally find my inner peace. My seat position enables me to enjoy the scenery, the people, simply everything. A remarkable passage to Dombas leads me to a 90 km leg to the next stop in Lillehammer. Experts say quite rightly that the real race only begins here. The last 180 km consists of little hills which pull the last reserves from legs which have already managed 360 km. Fortunately, some riders form a paceline with me, and in such a group it is easier to cope with the hills even as one is not less conscious of them. The "Belgium Gyroscope" runs as if well-oiled, and we simply pace along the asphalt. We all rotate together, which means overtaking is done on the right and at the left front you move into front position for a while. The overtaking phases get longer and longer as we acquire riders and the group gets bigger and bigger. Without this community, I wouldn't have reached the last 180 km in 16:54:24 hours. I finish in 17th place out of 320 in my age group and 240th overall out of 5282 people who participated. Moreover, I finish in one hour under my personal goal. This was a very special experience: fighting against the distance, against your own body, but most of all against your mind. It was a challenge that every cyclist should take—but watch out: the danger of addiction is very high!

*—Axel Fehlau*

# Ch. 6 / Building Your Own Recumbents and Fairings

There are not yet (!) many recumbent producers—only about 150 worldwide—so the incentive to build one yourself is tempting. Construction in general is fun, gives you experience, and boosts your self-confidence and appreciation from others. However, in our case, doing it yourself has only three things going for it, otherwise I recommend that you to buy a recumbent.

One understandable reason is the handwork itself. If you want to use your leisure time to be productive, to realize an urge to be creative which is not satisfied at your job, or to relax—or all three at the same time—all these motives are heard often. The result of this approach—the recumbent bike—is only secondary, since the path is really the goal. In this case, only few tears are shed if your attempt fails or doesn't quite meet expectations, because the primary goal was the tinkering. If it doesn't work out, the enthusiastic builder just tries again, or turns to a new project.

The second acceptable reason is the market not offering the right bike for you. You have already owned a recumbent and now have an idea of what you really want. But in your case, even the good bike shops do not offer such a bike, at least not in the configuration you demand, or only at astronomical prices. If this reason is the decisive one, you should be careful to set out to create a realistic bike. Make sure you're not overlooking any essential compromises that the market has already made, but which you, too, might wish you had made after you build your dream bike. Building, for you, is a means to an end. So make sure you are realistic about that end. If at all possible test ride another homebuilt bike which is very close to what you plan to build. If you attend large HPV events and never see such a

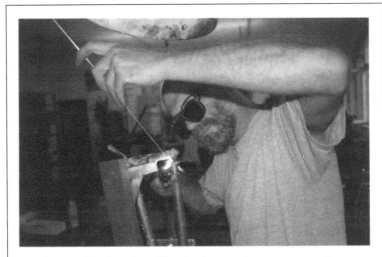

*Good material in experienced hands: the recumbent constructor Kurt Pichler brazing.*

bike, perhaps this should give you pause! Feel free to discuss your plans with your friendly club members who have already built bikes. They can often shed light on design issues.

The last acceptable argument for using the file yourself is of a simpler nature. You already know how to use a file or can guide a torch, maybe even expertly. Perhaps you work with bicycle-like materials in your day job. Thus the market prices frustrate you and you make the experienced appraisal that you can build a dream bike tailored for your needs on your own cheaper, faster and just as good.

Otherwise the facts speak against doing it on your own:

• It takes a lot of time: if the time you spend is only worth, let's say, $6/hr, you can quickly reach the costs of a very good bike. And if you compare results, the quality of a purchased bike is often much better. It is

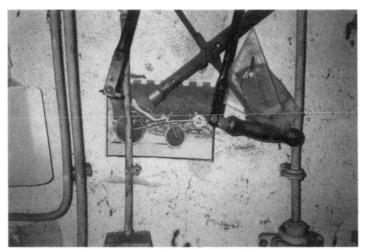

*The ideal always in front of your eyes: Self-motivation during cold nights in the garage.*

likely more economical to be a waitress than to build a bike frame in your garage.

• For the most part, your workshop is not equipped well enough or is set up in a wrong way. Thus your project of constructing a good bike provokes further effort and costs.

• It is difficult even for experts to make a sketch of exact bicycle geometry on paper and then execute it correctly. Trial and error is the usual result. Most production bikes result from a large series of test bikes, which no hobbyist could repeat.

The problem of insurance also speaks in favor of a purchase. Many producers offer a warranty period, and thus perhaps you are insured against a bike just not working out for you. In severe cases you have the option to get your money back.

You are also better off with a bought bike if you get into an accident with severe injuries because of mistakes in material or workmanship. Your own insurer might not want to cooperate with you because you built the frame yourself without adequate qualification. This could be the beginning of a lawsuit.

It's a big challenge to make the right assumptions and to calculate actual stresses in a specific case. The phenomena involved with cycling are difficult to transfer into theory and back out again as suitable bikes. A lot of experience and intuition are necessary. The recumbent bike does not have much history in this aspect. Thus it is even more impressive that people do not just approach the subject practically, but also theoretically, says Manfred Harig.

If you make your decision in favor of the do-it-yourself method, despite all warnings, your success is greatly dependent on planning. Mistakes on paper get transferred to the real project. They are then difficult to isolate and remove. During construction all doors are wide open for the usual mistakes anyway, but those are easier to spot and solve, when a good plan can be used to compare and control.

One thing that might give you comfort is that in some ways recumbent building is easier than upright bike building. The parts are less critically dependent on each other. Most parts of an upright frame, for instance, affect steering in some way. If one aspect is crooked, the rest is thrown off. And because speed is so dependent on weight with uprights, you use very lightweight materials, which are less tolerant. The independence of various functions and the emphasis on aerodynamics before micro-grams makes recumbent building somewhat easier. This also applies to making and modifying accessories and fairings for a storebought bike. Of course professional polish is still difficult to achieve.

The first phase of planning requires an exact analysis of the desired qualities and capabilities of the bike as well as the capacity of your home garage, and your ability, time and finances. But most important of all you should have an exact mental picture of the bike. Pictures, reports, talks and test rides are all helpful. Is the bike supposed to be used every day? Does it have to be carried into the basement or up to the third floor? Is it supposed to be foldable? How is the geometry supposed to act?—Sporty, lazy, agile or touring-like? Is the size, weight or look important? How comfortable is it supposed to be—with suspension in the front, back, both, or just use cushier tires?

Once you clarify these questions, think through your construction options and connect the dots for which set of features will deliver what you want, including any compromises that must be made. Only when you've detailed all your parameters, is it time to start drawing.

# Materials

The frame is the heart of a bike. The affects of various design traits are described in the chapter 'Basics of Design,' so I will only elaborate on materials and building techniques in this chapter.

## *Steel*

Experts use the term 'steel' when they want to describe metal that differs from cast iron because of the addition of carbon. Steel is the most common material in bike frame production. It is also the best: it can be welded, brazed, riveted, glued and screwed.

The common Cro-Mo is an alloy of steel which was refined by adding chrome and molybdenum so that it is strong in tube form even with a very thin wall. Adding chrome and molybdenum to steel improves tensile strength without reducing toughness. These qualities make Cro-Mo the most common for bike frames.

Furthermore, the amount of a steel's carbon is of great importance, it gives hints as to the quality of the material to be welded. The higher the amount of carbon, the lower is the steel's melting point. As the amount of carbon rises, the ease with which you can work with the steel decreases.

Thus CroMo steels which have a high amount of carbon, and which allow a drastic weight reduction because of its combination and treatment, require experienced hands. If such a type of steel gets too hot during work, the chemical combination, having been carefully configured, dissolves, and the steel is ruined, losing stability.

Simple steel, like ST 37 construction steel, which supports the Empire State building and huge bridges, is very good for your first attempts as it can be worked easily and is very stable.

Alloyed steel, like the well-known Mannesmann 25CroMo4, has a high quality and enables weight reduction without influencing stability. Such steel demands more cleverness during brazing and welding so that such brands can only be used by experienced tinkerers.

All in all, steel is the best choice for beginners and experienced builders alike, especially because it is available in all tube sizes typical for bikes, in European and American standards. It is easy to get (scrapyard) and easy to work with in un-alloyed form.

## *Aluminum*

Aluminum behaves totally differently from steel. The various combinations of alloy and heat treatment result in more than 300 available types of aluminum. It is almost impossible for non-experts to differentiate between them and it's easy to make mistakes. This makes it impossible to re-use old, nameless aluminum. Buying it 'freshness dated' (labeled by type) is your only option. Then you decide which of the many varieties is right for you and determine whether it is available in the desired tube or plate form.

Aluminum is characterized by low weight, corrosion protection, temperature resistance and weather (rust) insensitivity. These desirable qualities are accompanied by problems in workability. Aluminum neither creates sparks, nor does it turn red when heated, but it melts almost without warning. This makes it very complicated to judge temperature and to weld. Only experts in procedure and ingenuity can work this metal, and with an expensive welder—which is nothing for beginners to attempt, particularly because worthwhile weight reduction is only achieved with expensive and difficult aluminum alloys.

### Plastics/Laminates

Ever since bike engineers discovered carbon-fiber, Kevlar and other plastics, the recumbent cyclist is confronted with the question whether he or she should try to build a new bike with such miracle materials. The main justification for such an attempt is the incredibly low weight and the creative variety of shapes which become possible. But only the most clever are really able to build a frame that has curves at the desired locations and which is bubble-free at stress

*Without a single horsepower !!!*

points, because this is the starting point for a stable light-weight construction.

Therefore only an extraordinary frame form argues for such material, e.g. a frame shape which makes the use of normal tubes difficult or impossible to find, or you are simply unable to use other materials. There is a lot of information and tricks in the areas of boat-building, modeling and surfboard construction, and plenty of how-to books. They give expert insight into building with "miracle plastics." The section on do-it-yourself fairings that comes later in this chapter gives another look at the effort and costs of dealing with these materials.

# Processing techniques

### Welding

Welding of simple (un-alloyed) steel types is neither critical nor expensive. The common inert gas shielded arc welding machine is very suitable for welding an inexpensive, stout, stable steel frame. The connections need only a few preparation steps, in contrast to brazing. A gap of 1 mm is acceptable. The difficulty of treatment grows with the quality of the steel. That it why it is advisable to gain some practice experience with cheap steel left-overs before you start working with high quality material.

A welded seam is not as elastic as a soldered one and can be corrected only so much by re-working. Thanks to TIG-welding it is now possible to weld really thin tubes reliably. Unfortunately, the required welder is very expensive. But commercial bike frames are made this way: the result is light and stiff.

### Brazing and Soldering

Brazing, or soldering, is done by means of a flame of acetylene, butane, propane gas and oxygen. One weld causes the connection. When brazing the question is: with lugs or without?

Lugs are not used in most cases today, because their production takes up a lot of time and money. Furthermore, there is only a decent selection of lugs in traditional bike tube sizes and angles. Even for common and modern over-size tubes, lugs are very difficult to organize.

Brazing demands, regardless of whether you use lugs or not, a lot of care and preparation. The connections have to be exact to within three-tenths of a millimeter for brass brazing and to one tenth millimeter for silver brazing. Tolerances must be closer yet for quality lugless work, which is sometimes called 'fillet brazing.'

The connection has to be clamped absolutely tension-free, and oil- and grit-free in order to be properly brazed. The use of flux is indispensable. This chemical enhances the penetration of the brazing and cleans the metal of dirt and oil particles which cannot be removed during polishing and other work steps. The use of flux gives the brazing the greatest stability, assuming that the mitered joint has been fitted together accurately.

During brazing you should be careful because the heating of the tubes by a flame can destroy the material's structure. It takes away strength from the tubes and thus has to be reduced to a minimum. A low melting silver solder gives you the best chance to braze a high quality tube with the least possible loss of strength. Silver, however, brings about a higher penetration which demands even smaller tolerances in joint gaps. Secondly, it is softer, which reduces its use to only a few places on the frame.

Using lugs means also using silver since the stability of the lugs in combination with the solder's penetration burdens the tube the least during the process and makes for the stiffest resulting frame. It definitely speaks for the process of brazing that the joint can be corrected by a heating it up over again

*Only leave tiny gaps between tubes and lugs or fittings. You have to make clamp devices which make the connection without tension. The "Lötblock" by Manfred Harig even holds the solder.*

(reduces strength though) and that brazing is much more flexible than welding. Thus the effort and higher expense should be acceptable.

If you just want to make a quicky frame to test geometry, you can just take a welder and fry the pieces quickly together without having to feel guilty. Make a real frame later.

# First steps in frame-building...

Regardless of whether you decide to braze or to weld a frame, you should take into account the following suggestions to build a good frame under home workshop conditions.

First, keep a picture in mind through the whole construction phase of the end result: a rideable recumbent bike frame. Otherwise the frame is in danger of becoming a victim of time pressure, frustration and improvisation.

Always build with full awareness and

*The famous "Sweet Surprise" home-built faired racing HPV (52 mph) hides a bike of similar low-budget construction. The top steering geometry and upright position gives a chopper feeling. (photo: Veloladen)*

quickly and cleanly.

The crown of all processing techniques is a drill-press that drills holes with variable diameters. Being mounted on a drill in a swingable drill-press, every mitered joint will be perfect and can be tailored for every measure and angle. But unfortunately (like so often) such a tool is sinfully expensive.

Such a drill-press enables you to extend the radius of pre-drilled holes. Its size can be changed in 1/10th mm increments, which helps you to create tricky but round miters in very little time.

Inaccuracies do not only sneak in at the joints but also in lengths and alignment. This might sound banal, because that's where mistakes are always found. Measurements should always be taken with a caliper and a good, accurate measuring tape. We should prefer to measure twice—or four times!— than one time too few. To add material with a saw is impossible.

For beginners the biggest problem is alignment accuracy. It is often also called 'center accuracy.' The center is a theoretical line through the center point of a tube or profile. Center accuracy means the relation of the individual centers within the tube towards each other. In geometrical frame sketches for instance the measures are given from center to center. The frame height as well is given from the middle of the upper tube to the middle of the crank bearing, e.g. from the center of the crank bearing to the center of the upper tube. This method has developed from experience and has proven to be very practical. This way you can draw a frame independent of tube dimensions, as only the centers get marked which do not change if you ever change materials and opt, say, for an oversize-construction. This makes construction and comparison as well as planning much easier.

A little negative aspect of frustration comes with the problem of tubes which are butted and/or ovalized, like chainstays. Here

care, if you do not want to endanger the project, whether the task at hand be simple hole-drilling or a tricky solution. This also holds true when a problem comes up. It's better to think about it for two days instead of going into your garage for the brazing torch and then have to admit later on that the product is not exactly what you wanted. Good things take their time. Using this mindset, along with careful preparation and a good plan, is the best way to success.

Before you start the brazing/welding the dull tube ends have to be fitted together. For beginners, a file will likely be what you have to use. (Only buy high quality files; cheapies won't do you any good.) With a good file you can create a "mitered joint," as the raw connection between tube and profile is called, with an accuracy of 3-8/100th millimeters, even without a lot of practice.

When it comes to big curves or holes you can save a lot of work if you pre-drill. If you have an assortment of miter saws in your basement, or if you can ask your neighbor to borrow it, you'll reach your goal it is a little more difficult to find out the center position to use for assembly.

Every project will likely let you make adjustments for minor mistakes, but you should be especially careful with the alignment of the wheels and the crankset. Nowhere else is a mistake as bad as at these places.

Wheels can be out of alignment in three different ways. The wheels can have a 'dogleg'—rolling on different tracks. Or it is possible that they are not in alignment in line of the running direction. And last but not least the wheels can get out of alignment horizontally.

If the wheels have a 'dogleg,' then the centers of the individual wheels (the theoretical line between the two wheel-rims and the center of the hubs) lie parallel to each other instead of being on one and the same straight line.

If the wheels have left the line of direction they are supposed to run in, then the rear wheel hub is on the same line as the front wheel, but the rim of the rear wheel lies outside of this line. In practice, this has only marginal consequences, because the steering of the front wheel counteracts the existing bend, but this then also causes 'dogleg.' Additionally, you can correct alignment by shifting the rear wheel at the dropout. Here, the vertical dropout is a disadvantage because they demand much more precision during construction, as after the brazing has been done corrections are impossible.

The horizontal alignment of the wheels comes about when the center point of front wheel hub lies on one straight line with the one of the rear wheel hub. According to this, the upper rim and the bottom rim also have to lie on one straight line. In order to gain alignment accuracy that promotes a good driving behavior, it is necessary to set them parallel to each other and exactly parallel to the driving direction. Otherwise the bike would not run in a way that you have planned on paper, but the driving behavior would listen to the laws of chance—you cannot base your next plan on such results, because there was a huge difference between plan and reality.

Of course, all these influences of the driving behavior can be compensated by counteracting with steering, or just by getting used to it. Nonetheless, the aspects of a higher tire wear and tear, and the unpredictability of the vehicle in extreme situations persists.

A misaligned crank bearing will definitely impact driving behavior. But the consequences show up in the area of biomechanics. The crank bearing center has to coincide with your pelvis bone centerpoint. If this is not the case, your legs have to distort their alignment all the time during pedaling. This has unpleasant consequences similar to having a bent, wobbly crankset.

Constructing a frame with alignment accuracy of all theoretical lines that determine handling behavior and correct angles for all tube intersections is the crown of the frame building art. It should now be apparent that building a frame is anything but simple, cheap and fast.

The basis of construction is the plan which in turn is based on an exact analysis of desired traits. After all technical data which are relevant for the frame are measured, then you must think about the steering mechanism and seat form as well as components. Martin Staubach says: "Regardless of how clever one is, the first frame will always become trash."

*Infamous homebuilder Joe Kochanowski has built dozens of fast, scavenged velomobiles to suit the "urban assault vehicle" lifestyles he and his friends enjoy. He also participates strongly in regional racing. His large, robust vehicles thrive on rough, rainy roads against heavy traffic. He wears heavy gloves, elbow pads, large visor, customized mirror-goggles and camo jacket for protection and because it all works as needed. (photo: Dustin Wood)*

## Do-it-yourself fairings

As we have seen, the planning of an aerodynamically optimized fairing is complicated and time-consuming. The practical realization takes up even more time and effort!

However, there is also a whole area of HPV hobbywork full of cyclists making quicky fairings of any suitable material they can find. These aren't usually very robust, very efficient, or attractive and as a result they often don't stay on bikes for very long. But it is a ripe area for experimenting. A rough'n'tumble fairing is still often beneficial to speed and yields other benefits we get from fairings, such as warmth, weather, cargo and safety. Tailboxes are a very popular area for this type of work. A common easy-to-use material is Coroplast plastic board sheet which comes in various colors and thickness and is easily worked in two-dimensions. Fabric and even cardboard can be used. Sometimes experience with quicky fairings will finally inspire a builder to make a 'real' fairing from a mold so that he can get the best results he deserves. We'll focus most attention here on molded fairings since

they work the best.

The following steps are necessary for the production of a molded hard shell fairing:

- production of master body (prototype mold, from which copies are made)
- production of negative form
- production of the desired positives

The mold is as critical to a fairing as a plan is for a frame. Moreover, the construction of a fairing is 5-10 times as complicated as for a frame. And the end result is greatly dependent on the quality of the mold. Only the quality of processing can change the result after molding, and usually for the worse....

To build a proper fairing, the amount of work you have to invest is more than what you invest into building a frame. Costs are higher, too. Acquiring the basic tools, then all materials, can cost over $1000, not to mention the hundreds of hours you may well put into it. Thus I would advise you to cooperate with friends, like-minded hobbyists or maybe even potential customers. The work for the mold prototype, the basis of any fairing, is the same for one positive as it is for 3 or 20 of them. The more fairings that spring from a mold, the smaller are the construction prices per unit.

When constructing the mold, you should proceed only after you apply a lot of specific knowledge, care and awareness. You need a material that is easy to work with. Polystyrene foams or lightweight artificial rock are appropriate. Working the mold is easier when using these materials. You will then only sweat because of concentration or when you have discovered a mistake. No need to have your materials cause you extra work!

It is relatively difficult to carve out a fairing shape from a big block (which often consists of many blocks glued together). It is much easier to create the mold from many different layers to start with.

Similar to slicing bread, you 'cut' the fairing's drawing with a pencil into many slices. The thickness of the slices should always be the same and within the area of one slice there should not be much change in shape. Now calculate the full-size measurements of the slices, buy them in the form of insulation foam boards in sufficient quantity, and put two relatively big gaps in the middle. This enables the precise 'cutting' of the slices.

Before that, number them with a pen. According to the numbers in the plan, the sections are now drawn in real size! Afterwards, the contour drawings are cut out (including a small .25-.5"-thick frame) and the shapes glued together in order. The styrofoam body now has the edgy and rough outline of the future fairing. Now you construct a simple but effective tool: Glue a fitted strip of rough sand paper on a long board—this will serve as an overdimensional file. Very soon the mold will gain soft curves. Your garage, however, will look like it has had a snow storm.

If you plan a fairing with a hinging or detachable canopy or hood, it has to be sandpapered separately, but following the same principle, and at the hood joint at the main fairing you have to file in a little support. This one will later support the hood. Finish all with only medium-rough sand paper.

Caution! Grinding and sanding brings out fine dust from the materials which can burden the lungs. Thus you should only work with a dust mask and in a place with good ventilation.

Coats of paint seal the smooth styrofoam block form for the next work steps. You should definitely use emulsion paint. Other types can react to the polystyrol foam and ruin your work.

Normally, several layers of paint are necessary until all the little holes in the base body are filled. White is great—it lets shadows and highlights from roughnesses stand out prominently.

A layer of fiberglass protects this easily deformable, easily dented mold from "wave" bumps. You should not skip the fiberglass—it saves you frustration, time and protects your nerves. It gives you a feeling of safety to work with a strong mold.

After protecting the mold with one or two layers of fiberglass you start the most difficult and important work step: The 'glassed' form has to be covered with polyester filler and polished. At this point of time all (!) unevenesses, waves and weaknesses must be removed. What has not been corrected will inevitably destroy the look and aerodynamics of the future fairing.

So...

- fill-grind-spackle-sand
- fill-grind-spackle-sand

...until you have achieved a 100 percent properly smooth form. Corrections are only possible down the road at the price of much more effort.

The endless cycle of sanding and filling can be simplified and shortened with a little trick: when it seems as if you reached your goal, polish the sanded construction form and spray it with white glossy paint—now

*A team fleet of homebuilt racer/commuters featuring thrifty, easy-to-work-with Coroplast fairings combined with clear plastic nosecones.*

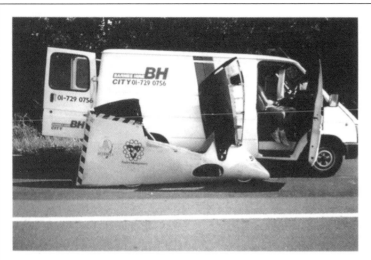

*Mounting and exiting the bike is easier if the hood is installed firmly on the vehicle, with convenient hinging...and so that it cannot fall off.*

unevenesses become apparent in shadows and reflections of the light. The threatening bumps and waves which deteriorate Cw-value now show themselves when the light changes. Some work-intensive weeks will pass until you'll accomplish the desired result.

If you only want to have one fairing to build, then the production of a negative mold is superfluous. Instead, you laminate a fairing over it, after a few steps in between, grind and sand it smooth, and then you either destroy the mold in it or pull it out. However, since it has taken you so much work to make a mold, you might think of a little series of fairings for your friends and acquaintances. Otherwise, the price for a single full fairing can add up to $3000 (if you had to buy everything you need), and for that sum of money you could buy the highly developed models that the market offers.

Now it is time to prepare for separating the mold later. For each separation you have to make a stencil template. Separation is actually the wrong word. It is more appro-

priate to call it 'phase laminating of the negative form.' Separating in the sense of sawing something apart does not occur. You rather laminate the negative form in its individual units and then you combine them.

First, the separate parts should be symmetrical, to make your work easier. You can use the cross-section of the basic form to make simple stencils, e.g. from the front and side view as well as the breadth as seen from above. This way you get parts that are easy to assemble. The theoretical separation is realized by stencils. On a big wooden board you draw the exact fairing's cross-section of the separation line and then you saw it out. The board with the hole can now only find one joint at the mold, because it is everywhere too big (or too small) otherwise.

Later you do not only laminate the fairing-part area of the mold negative, but also a 3"-high flanged rim on the wooden board—it serves as contact surface for the adjacent pieces. Similar to the production of the negative parts the contact surfaces to the adjacent negative pieces have to be done precisely. The surfaces serve as the point of contact for the individual parts and as points to attach clamps or screws during the laminating of the negative.

The contact surfaces should be absolutely parallel to each other, so that the parts do not slide against each other and that they do not put ridges into the fairing's smooth surface. After separation, each piece is covered with release-agent and polished (*careful*: do not apply too thickly). The type and brand of release-agent depend on the type of negative material you have used. Ask ahead about the necessary chemicals for this stage of the game. If one isn't careful one can run into large expenses in trying to keep up with the latest products and the ancillary chemicals they require.

The individual sections get laminated one after the other, e.g. one part gets laminated, hardened and taken off, before the next one gets treated. Material you use here should be cheap. Only the first layer which will later determine the finish quality of the outer side of the negative needs to be of the highest grade.

*Step 1*: surface resin (provides a smooth, hard surface)

*Step 2*: binding layer of resin and aluminum powder (between Steps 1 & 3)

*Step 3*: fiberglass pieces with resin

*Step 4*: two or three layers of rough fabric can follow for the finish.

At all times, do your best to avoid bubbles, gaps and air spaces between layers.

After a piece has hardened, it can be removed from the mold easily by sliding a thin, flexible piece of plastic between the form and the negative. The mold will jump out with a "plop!" From this point on, the negative form must not change its shape (!) later on, not even a tenth of a millimeter. If the negative form still flexes or is unstable and does not hold its shape by itself after Step 4, you have to follow up with additional fiberglass layers.

If you build metal framing or wood laminates into your negative form, you can save weight and money and simplify the later body production. Moreover you can build in thread and screw holes into the contact flanges, so you don't have to fuss with clamps and clips.

To cut weight from the final fairing, you might consider the wet-in-wet construction, e.g. combining the individual pieces during the process of hardening. The fairing also ends up stiffer and more stable. The edges of the individual pieces fit to each other and harden together to become one piece. That makes them stronger than parts which are put together after hardening. A later lamination will never acquire the firmness of a wet-in-wet connection. Additionally, a wet-in-wet fairing can be warmed up from the inside with a heat-gun during the hardening process, which makes the final stability even greater (a process called tempering).

To do wet-in-wet construction you have to add screw holes and flat surfaces for screw clamps at the outside to the various negative form parts. An exact, parallel, final fairing form is indispensable if you want to take advantage of this construction type.

The temperature during wet-in-wet processing should be about 68°F. If it is colder, the resin is difficult to work with; if it is warmer, it hardens too fast. When all treatment steps are done, you wait on the edge of your seat for the final construction of your first fairing. With this method you 'only' have to laminate the individual parts, laminate the complete connection, heat it up and after the hardening let it plop out—and your fairing is done!

However, your fairing body at this point does not have openings for your feet, lights, wheels or ventilation. These various holes have to be sawn out carefully now. First you saw the holes for mounting the fairing onto and around your recumbent. If they fit, you position and hold the fairing to your bike. If you have built a self-supporting, stable fairing, you only need two horizontal anchors and two vertical. These will provide an absolutely sufficient combination against the influences of pedaling power, air resistance and ground unevenness. Practically, the vertical fastenings should be located in the front and the horizontal ones at the rear, so that the fastenings do not collide with either wheels or feet.

Large-diameter aluminum tubes or square channels as a connection between bike and fairing are light, stable and unproblematic. They can be easily mounted to the frame (stuck in the boom end, or screwed to a socket, or embraced in one of the additional braze-on fastening elements). Thanks to being oversize they have great stiffness and

*Matt Weaver stays on the "Virtual Edge" with this camera bike with suction-preventing sealed wheels, ridden here "on the half-shell" for a demonstration. He predicts 100+ mph sprints are possible with such an ultra-smooth, seam-minimized vehicle. He designs on computer and makes much of his equipment in his own shop.*

strength along with very light weight. The fastenings at the fairing have to be flat and secure. Silicone glue, used for building fish tanks, is great as a buffer sandwiched in the connections between rattling bike and secure fairing. It can also be used on its own as a floating connection which harms neither frame nor fairing. It is very stable; it dampens many oscillations and makes the fairing significantly more quiet.

Depending on planned use, here are some breaks and openings you might want in a fairing:
- hood for exit
- side doors for exit
- lights in front and rear
- heel movement radius
- air circulation in front of head and legs
- access to shifters, gears and derailleurs
- access to trunk
- access to brakes, lighting
- access to wheels and tire-valves
- windshield-holes in hood
- ports for hand signals
- cooling holes for brakes, possibly

In spite of the many openings only four closing mechanisms have become common:
- hinge
- velcro
- tension hook
- tape

A hinge gets laminated or is glued at the inside of the fairing with silicone glue (again, from the aquarium shop). Definitely avoid rivets or screws, because holes in the fairing result in cracks when you fall. Screws have another disadvantage: a screw head or point inside the fairing can cause injuries when you get in or out or fall. A hinge creates a bombproof connection which is especially suitable for openings which are used often, like luggage compartment or canopy.

Velcro is fastened with hot or silicone glue and it is more appropriate for less often used openings like the access to components, brakes and lights.

If the openings are to be reachable while cycling, then you can also use a rubber bungie cord with an aluminum hook. Cut a .5-1.5" piece out of flat aluminum tin, file the edges dull and bend it to a 'U' with one longer end. You laminate this to the fairing. A bungie cord finds its counter part with the means of a wire, rivet, glue or a screw. This connection is light, reliable and cheap. The tension hook option is also fine for hood or doors.

If you want to eliminate noise completely, your fairing must have a buffer which can isolate the fairing from vibration. Either you work one into the mold or you laminate it in later.

Every fairing needs openings for the feet, but you should ask yourself whether these should be open during your rides or closed with a bomb-bay door. Such a flap improves aerodynamics and weather protection. Installing these doors is relatively simple: you need a hinge and a few inches of rubber cord for each door. The hinge gets glued to door and fairing with silicone glue. The rubber cord has to be fastened about 5" above the closure inside the fairing. Now the door can easily be opened, and a light pull at the rubber cord closes it again. A small damper here also prevents noise.

Last but not least there is the duct tape option. I suppose I do not need to explain how to apply tape: oil-free surface, smooth and without tension at a position which does not break. Except for an opening that hardly ever gets opened or for racing machines which fight for the 1000th of a second, these poisonous tapes do not have a justification of existence—avoid them for the sake of your environment.

The visor or windscreen of the hood should be incrementally openable for regulation of ventilation. Screws or rivets can fasten windshields fabulously.

Now your fairing is ready to be taken for a ride. Of course, you will probably change innumerable details. A lot of things can be added, and you can also pick your personal look in painting it. There are no limits to what can be done.

### The tape method for aerodynamic checking

Here's a final tip in the form of a simple but effective method to double-check your aerodynamics. In this way you only test a vehicle once, and never twice under the same conditions, but it nonetheless helps you to find rough mistakes or to visualize the difference between open or closed foot flaps and the like.

The mounted fairing gets covered with taped-on 1" strips of old cassette or VCR tape. Tape them on every 6". Then use scissors to trim any tape sticking out ahead of the adhesive tape and cut the strips down to .5" left flapping freely. The 'fringey bike' then gets driven down a long, empty road and is accompanied by two people in a car. They take pictures or video of the bike during the drive. You will see on the images

later where the fairing has weak points. Side wind properties are especially easy to evaluate in this way.

Wherever the 'fuzzy thread skin' has aerodynamically bad spots, the tape threads do not fly horizontally in the air, but seem to flap around undecided. Caution: rough pavement can distort the result. The ride has one advantage though: It awakens the wish for a better fairing—and now the whole process can start all over again...!

### Stethoscope testing?

Matt Weaver uses another method worth noting. He uses a stethoscope with just the rubber hose-end. (He removes the metal end-piece.) The stethoscope lets him detect places where a fairing loses laminar flow and breaks into turbulence. He puts the 'scope on his ears, then rides and moves the open rubber end along the inside of his fairing. (Sometimes taping it, in tricky places.) Places where air flow breaks down are a lot noisier and easy to detect using such a gadget!

*This bike is used under a fairing as well. The frame is distinctive because it uses so many tubes (for rigidity) and has a seat made of old seat belts.*

# My favorite recumbent experiences ...

...when I started riding it for the first time...

...when it got painted a fresh red...

...when I finally reached more than 30 mph on level ground...

...when my thighs stopped feeling like balloons after every little effort...

...when I beat Greg Lemond (OK, that was just a dream)...

...when my steering mechanism broke off in the middle of Canada without any reason...

...when we arrived in Boston after a 200 km night ride without being tired (no dream)...

...when an old granny in a similarly relaxed position in a wheel-chair waved at me...

...when somebody asked me whether I belonged to the on-tour group of a senior's home...

...every time I meet people who share my interest...

...to be one among many at the European HPV Championships and not be constantly stared at...

...every time I have gone uphill and my blood starts to flow back into my legs...

...all those "*Oohs*" and "*Aahs*" and "Hey, look at that!" as long as I'm not in a bad mood...

...after I rode a regular bike after having driven a recumbent for half a year and not knowing after 30 minutes if I could keep seated any longer...

...when it rains...

...when I found out that my brother could not use it because his legs were shorter than mine...

...that since I've been driving one so many other people have felt obliged to do the same...

...when my grandma saw my vehicle she was very surprised and when she said goodbye, exclaimed: "Oh boy, good night!"

...when the truck who attempted to overtake me on a highway FINALLY passed me...

—*Juergen Reimann*

# Recumbent Resources

## At Long Last...

The relationship between the number of existing recumbents and their quality is misleading. Few other bikes offer the unique advantages that recumbents possess in models currently available.

Partly the bike racing associations are to be held responsible for this situation because they still (!) ban recumbents from races. Also to blame are traffic planners and the laws which produce a traffic situation that makes the use of recumbents (and bikes in general) highly desirable but very difficult. And lastly, there are the cyclists themselves. They don't want to spend the comparatively high sum of money on such a bike. (Although they seem happy to spend it on any other type of bike.) Still, the kilogram price of a recumbent can seem to equal the kilogram price of a fighter plane. Thankfully, some affordable bikes are available.

Even so, if you prefer a mass-production bike from Taiwan to a small shop recumbent that has been manufactured meticulously by hand, you make David fight against Goliath...!

If you decide that an HPV is worth it despite the higher cost, you'll hardly regret it. The advantages of a recumbent are soon realized, and you'll learn to use and appreciate them—that is what makes driving with a recumbent incomparable to anything else—for humans (fast and comfortable), for traffic (takes up less space, one car less in a traffic jam), and for the environment....

This book has accompanied recumbents all along their development and through the centuries, it has given you experiences and facts and has dared to look into the future (with hopes and wishes).

The normal bike loses its right to lead in so many fields given all the information and encouragement you've now seen.

Are you interested in these rare but fascinating, practical as well as fast, beautiful and bizarre vehicles? Then just set up a test ride with a dealer close to you and buy one, or go into your garage and unpack your tools! Visiting an HPV event is also a good opportunity to get infected with the virus.

So, while lying down, take a ride over the countryside!

—*Gunnar Fehlau*

*Cycle Vision 2003 racer flying along "in" a stylish Swiss Birk "Comet." (photo: www.tim.be)*

### Note about Directories

Lists of producers are outdated as soon as they are printed. This holds true especially for the recumbent market. New producers enter the market yearly, others disappear. The recumbent bike is not homogenous in its form and never will be. Producers and tinkerers test new constructions which may result in promising developments or a miscarriage. Many companies change their models several times a year. Probably the Internet is the best place to search for specific info at this point, with BentRiderOnline.com offering the most info and reviews in one place online. For print info, *RCN: Recumbent Cyclist News*, with its annual "Buyer's Guide" is the best resource ($8 sample; RCN, PO Box 2048 Port Townsend, WA 98368).

# A World of Manufacturers

### USA

ActionBent Recumbents
17930 NE 127th St.
Redmond, Wa, 98052
Tel: +1 425 881 3696
http://www.actionbent.com

Aerolope
Bob Dillard
Refugio
Texas
Tel: +1 361 526 2977
http://www.aerolope.com/

Angletech
318 N. Highway 67

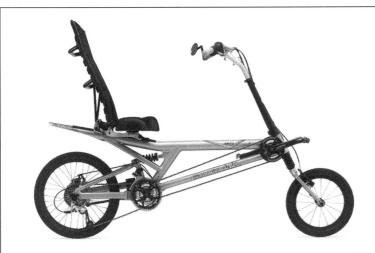

*Cannondale's full-suspension CWB is a well-built, American-made entry to the recumbent market by this large company.*

P.O. Box 1893
Woodland Park, CO 80866-1893
Tel: +1 719 687 7475
http://www.angletechcycles.com

Backsafer
11400 N Kendall Dr. #100
Miami, FL 33176
Tel: 800 815 BACK (2225)
http://www.Backsafer.com/home.asp

Barcroft Cycles
Falls Church, VA
Tel: +1 703 750 1945
http://www.barcroftcycles.com

Big Cat Human Powered Vehicles
826 North John Street Suite#107
Orlando, FL 32808
Tel: +1 407 293 1626
http://www.catrike.com

BiGHA
4314 SW Research Way
Corvallis OR 97333
Tel: +1 541 738 4340
http://bigha.com/

BikeE
(Not currently manufactured; however, there is a website dedicated to this popular line of bikes: http://www.simplecom.net/poleary/.)

Bike Friday
3364 W. 11th Ave.
Eugene, OR 97402
Tel: +1 800 777 0258
http://www.bikefriday.com

Bilenky Cycle Works, Ltd.
5319 N. Second St.
Philadelphia, PA 19120
Tel: +1 215 329 4744
http://www.bilenky.com

Boulder Bikes, LLC
P.O. Box 1400
Lyons, CO 80540
Tel: +1 303 823 5021
http://www.boulderbikes.com

Burley Design Cooperative
4020 Stewart Road
Eugene, OR 97402
Tel: +1 541 687 1644
http://www.burley.com

Cannondale Corp
16 Trowbridge Drive
Bethel, CT 06801
Tel: +1 800 245 3872
http://www.cannondale.com/bikes/02/
cusa/model-2BM.html

Crank It LLC
47709 N. Shore Drive
Belleville, MI 48111
http://www.crank-it.com

Cycle Genius Recumbents
6215-B Evergreen St.
Houston, TX 77081
Tel: +1 713 666 2453
http://www.cyclegenius.com

Earth Cycles
1500 Jackson St NE
Minneapolis, MN 55413
Tel: +1 612 788 2124
http://www.earth-cycles.com
Earth Traveler
511 South Main Street
Moscow, ID 83843
Tel: +1 208 882 0703

Easy Racers Inc.
P.O. Box 255-W
Freedom, CA 95019
Tel: +1 831 722 9797
http://www.easyracers.com

Haluzak
70 W. Barham Ave.
Santa Rosa, CA 95407
Tel: +1 707 544 6243
http://www.haluzak .com

Human Powered Machines
Center for Appropriate Transport
455 West First Ave.
Eugene, OR 97401-2276
Tel: +1 541 343 5568
http://www.efn.org/~cat/html/human.htm

Human Powered Products
23825 East Euclid Avenue
Otis Orchards, WA 99027-9748
Tel: +1 509 226 0317
http://www.asisna.com/hppbikes/

Infinity
8433 E McDonald Dr
Scottsdale, AZ 85250

Landstrider Sport Trikes
1120 Delno Street
San Jose, CA 95126
Tel: +1 408 727 2568

Lightfoot Cycles
179 Leavens Road
Darby, Montana 59829
Tel: +1 406 821 4750
http://www.lightfootcycles.com

Lightning Cycle Dynamics
312 9th St.
Lompoc, CA 93436
Tel: +1 805 736 0700
http://www.lightningbikes.com

Linear Manufacturing Incorporated
32744 Kestrel Avenue
Guttenberg, Iowa 52052
Tel: +1 319 252 1637
http://www.linearrecumbent.com

Longbikes (formerly Ryan)
8160 Blakeland Drive
Unit D
Littleton, CO 80125
Tel: +1 303 471 6700
http://www.tandembike.com

Mirage Tricycle Company
P.O. Box 185
8905 S. Patricica Blvd.
Oak Creek, WI 53154

Organic Engines
661 Industrial Dr.
Tallahassee Fl, 32310
Tel: +1 850 224 7499
http://www.organicengines.com

PEDAL'N'GO Recumbent Cyclery
Post Office Box 66265
Los Angeles, CA 90066
Tel: +1 310 572 1399

Penninger Recumbents
950 State Avenue
St. Charles, IL 60174
Tel: +1 630 377 1696
http://www.penninger.com

RANS Inc.
4600 Hwy. 183 Alt.
Hays, KS 67601
Tel: +1 785 625 6346
http://www.ransbikes.com/
Recumbent Barn Inc.
205 Beryl St
Redondo Beach, CA 90277
Tel: +1 310 320 1096

Reynolds Weld Lab
134 Rockingham Road
Derry, NH 03038
Tel: +1 603 432 7327
http://www.reynolds-weldlab.com

Rhoades Car
http://www.4wc.com

RoadRunner
Road and Trail Cyclery
1569 Airport Road
Oxford, GA 30267
Tel: +1 770 787 8193

Rotator Recumbent Bicycles
3200 Dutton #215
Santa Rosa, CA 95407
Tel: +1 707 591 0915
http://www.rotatorrecumbent.com

S & B Recumbents
c/o Jack Baker
1607 East 126th Street
Compton, CA 90222
Tel: +1 310 762 2243
http://home.pacbell.net/recumbnt

Sidewinder Recumbents Inc.
334 Descanso Ave.
Ojai, CA 93023
Tel: +1 805 640 0504
http://www.sidewindercycle.com

Special Purpose Vehicles
561 Windsor Street
Somerville, MA 02143
Tel: +1 617 776 3103
http://www.darbydesign.com/~spv/

Sun Bicycles
c/o J&B Importers
PO Box 161859
Miami, FL 33116-1859
http://www.sunbicycles.com/

TerraCycle, Inc.
3450 SE Alder
Portland, OR 97214
Tel: +1 503 231 9798
http://www.terracycle.com

Trailmate
2359 Trailmate Drive
Sarasota, FL 34243
Tel: +1 941 755 5511
www.trailmate.com

Trek Bicycle Corporation
(not currently producing their recumbent)
1170 Universal Blvd
Whitewater, WI 53190-1467
Tel: +1 262 473 8735

Turner Enterprises
P O BOX 18421
Tucson AZ 85731
Tel: +1 520 290-5646
http://www.turnerrecumbents.com/

Velogenesis, Inc.
9654 North Kings Hwy #234
Myrtle Beach, SC 29572
Tel: +1 843 497 2503
http://www.velogenesis.com/

Vision Recumbents
6304 215th St. SW
Mountlake Terrace, WA 98043
Tel: +1 425 673 2448
http://www.visionrecumbents.com

Volae Recumbents
1314 Third Street
Stevens Point, WI 54481
Tel:+1  715 340 1133
http://www.volaerecumbents.com

Werner Advanced Bicycle Designs
P.O. Box 2006
Bridgeview, IL 60455
Tel: +1 815 464 5284
Wicks Aircraft Supply
410 Pine Street
Highland, IL 62249
Tel: +1 618 654 7447
http://www.wicksaircraft .com

WizWheelz
529 W. Clinton St.
Hastings, MI 49058
Tel: +1 616 940 1909
http://www.wizwheelz.com

X-Eyed Design (Bacchetta)
251 6th Avenue N.
Tierra Verde, FL 33715
Tel: +1 785 623 2808
http://x-eyed.com

## *Australia*

Flying Furniture Cycles
Tel: +61 (0) 2 95502805
http://www.flyingfurniture.com.au/

Freedom Human Powered Vehicles
478 Whitehorse Rd
Mitcham 3132
Melbourne
Tel: +61 (0) 3 98748033
http://home.internex.net.au/~freedhpv/

Greenspeed
69 Mountain Gate Drive
Ferntree Gully
VIC 3156
Tel: +61 (0)3 9753 3644
http://www.green-speed.com.au

Hotmover
P.O. Box 180
Paddington
Brisbane
Queensland 4059
Tel: +61 (0) 7 3319 6047
http://www.hotmover.com

LoGo Trikes and H.P.V.s
5b Whyalla Court
Bibra Lake
Western Australia 6163
Tel: +61 (0) 8 9434 6722
http://www.logotrikes.com/

Michael Rogan
678 Stumpy Gully Road
Hastings
Victoria 3915
Tel: +61 (0) 5983 5886
http://mrrecumbenttrikes.com/

Trisled Recumbents
57 Boundary Road
Dromana
Victoria 3936
http://www.trisled.com.au

Wilson Bikes
Fact 2/12 Alleen Avenue
Heidleberg Heights 3081
Melbourne
Tel: +61 (0) 3 9458 5911
http://www.wilsonbike.com

### Austria

MCS Maderna City Scooter
Paris Maderna KEG Zeltgasse 12
A-1080 Wien
Tel: +43 676 422 77 32
http://www.mcsbike.com

### Brazil

Pedro Zöhrer
Rua Triunfo, 41
Rio de Janeiro - RJ - Brasil
http://www.geocities.com/zohrer/

### Canada

Cambie Cycles
3317 Cambie Street
Vancouver, B.C. V5Z 2W6
Tel: +1 604 874 3616
http://www.cambiecycles .com

CCM  (Mikado, Evox, Quetzal, Procycle)
9095 25th Ave.
St. Georges
Beauce, Quebec G6A 1A1
Tel: +1 418 228 8934
http://www.evoxcycle.com
http://www.quetzal.ca

Recumbent Technologies Inc.
102 Larkin Drive
Nepean, Ontario K2J 1C1
Tel. +1 613 825 2230

Varna Innovation and Research Corporation
RR2, Site 54, C 13
Gabriola Island, BC  V0R 1X0
Tel: +1 250 247 8379
http://www.varnahandcycles.com

YIKE
Pi Manufacturing Inc.
86 Arthur Street North
Guelph, Ontario  N1E 4T8
Tel: +1 519 824 3869
http://www.wicycle.com/sun.html

### Czech Republic

Azub
Alesˇ Zemánek
U Olsˇavy 1102
68801 Uhersk‡ Brod
http://www.azub.cz/english/index.html

### Denmark

Hjordt / Bjällby
Hjordt Specialcykler
Granstien 4
Bregninge
DK-5700 Svendborg
Tel: +45 62 22 62 31

LEITRA ApS
Box. 64
DK-2750 Ballerup
Fax: +45 48 18 33 77
http://www.leitra.dk

---

## *Germany*

Aiolos Liegedreiraeder
Goethestrasse 7
D-10623 Berlin
Tel: +49 (0) 30 31 80 60 13
http://www.aiolos.de

AnthroTech Leichtfahrzeugtechnik
Rothenbergstr. 7
D-90542 Eckental-Frohnhof
http://www.anthrotech.de

Brompton Recumbent Conversion Kit
Juliane Neuss
Haferberg 2
D- 21059 Glinde
Tel: +49 (0) 40 710 951 04
http://www.tu-harburg.de/~skfcz/Brekki/
brekki_en.html

Cab-Bike
Reinhold Schwemmer
Strohm͵hle
D-35444 Biebertal
Tel: +49 (0) 641 35495
http://www.cab-bike.com

DALLIegeraeder
Muenchenerstrasse. 8a
D-85391 Allershausen
Tel: +49 (0) 8166 8572

FluxFahräder
Kreuzbreitlstraße 8
D-82194 Gröbenzell
Tel: +49 (0) 8142 53180
http://www.flux-fahrraeder.de/

Go-One
Beyss Kunststofftechnik
Muehlensteeg 5
D-47638 Straelen
Tel: +49 (0) 2834 / 6198
http://www.go-one.de

Hase Spezialraeder
Karl-Friedrich-Strasse 88
D-44795 Bochum
Tel: +49 (0) 2 34 9 46 90 50
http://www.hase-spezialraeder.de

HP Velotechnik
Goethestrasse 5
D-65830 Kriftel
Tel: +49 (0) 61 92 4 10 10
http://www.hpvelotechnik.com

Lohmeyer Leichtfahrzeuge
Geistingestraße 31
D-53773 Hennef
Tel: +49 (0) 22 42 909924
http://www.leichtfahrzeuge.de/

Noell Fahrradbau
Fischerweg 6
D-36041 Fulda/Kaemmerzell
Tel: +49 (0) 661 54836
http://www.noell-fahrradbau.de

Ostrad Fahrraeder
Winsstrasse 48
D-10405 Berlin
Tel: +49 (0) 30 44 34 13 93
http://www.ostrad.de/ostrad/liegerader.html

Quantum-Liegeraeder
Fasanenweg 25
D-25364 Bokel
http://www.quantum-liegeraeder.de

Radius
Liegerad Muenster GmbH
Borkstrasse 20
D-48163 Muenster

Tel: +49 (0) 1805 723487
http://www.radius-liegeraeder.de

Senkels GmbH
Mariendorfer Damm 168
D-12107 Berlin
Tel: +49 (0) 30 70 60 00 63
http://www.senkels.de

Speedbike
Kramer & Kislat GmbH
Am Stadtpark 43
D- 81243 München
Tel: +49 (0) 1718828176
http://members.aol.com/speedbikev/

THORAX Fahrzeugentwicklungs GmbH
Postanschrift
Kolpingweg 5a
D-52382 Niederzier
Tel: +49 (0) 241 4015200
http://www.thorax.de

Tripendo
LW Composite GmbH
Industriestrasse
D-35683 Dillenburg
Tel: +49 (0) 27 71 392 492
http://www.tripendo.com

Veloladen (Scooterbike, Velvet)
Veloladen Liegeraeder
Stegerwaldstrasse 1
D-51427 Bergisch Gladbach
Tel: +49 (0) 2204 61075
http://www.veloladen.com
http://scooterbike.com/start-e.html

Viento
Forschungsbuero Senkel
Bachgasse 7
D-97294 Unterpleichfeld
Tel: +49 (0) 9367 98 17 00

VOSS (BevoBike)
Voss Spezialrad GmbH
Tel: +49 (0) 48 21 7 80 23
http://www.voss-spezialrad.de

ZOXbikes
Michael-Vogel-Strasse 3
D-91052 Erlangen
Tel: +49 (0) 91 31 7 19 73 21
http://www.zoxbikes.de

## Italy

DOLCE VITA
Via Aspesi 164
21017 Samarate (VA)
Tel. +39 (0) 331 234096
http://www.dolcevita-bike.it

Karbyk
ARES GROUP
via Guglielmo Marconi, no 18
33010 Reana del Rojale (UD)
Fax: +39 (0) 432 857504
http://www.karbyk.com

## Japan

ST Manufacturer Inc. (linear drive)
5-6-5 Mure Mitaka
Tokyo  181-0002
Tel: +81 (0) 422 46 0491
http://www.stmfr.co.jp/STMFR/
recumbent.html

## Lithuania

Aistis Putna
Setos 92a
Kedainiai 5030
Tel: +370 8 257 61543

## Mexico

Go-Ze! Industries
Carlos Gomez
Tel: +52 (0) 11 525 2546911
http://members.tripod.com/~recumbentes/
index1.html

## The Netherlands

Advanced Cycle Engineering
Weurden 60
7101 NL Winterswijk
Tel: +31 (0) 543 530905
http://www.ligfiets.net/ace/

Alligt
Vogelplein 4c
5212 VK Den Bosch
Tel: +31 (0) 73 6911388
http://www.alligt.nl/

Challenge
Anklaarseweg 35-37
7316 MB Apeldoorn
Tel: +31 (0) 55 521 24 05
http://www.challengebikes.com

Dutch Speed Bicycles (conversion kit)
http://www.dutchbikes.nl/uk.htm

Flevobike
De Morinel 55
8251 HT Dronten
Tel: +31 (0) 321 337200
http://www.flevobike.nl

J & S Fietsdiensten
De Vecht 28
8253 PH Dronten
Tel: +31 (0) 321 332717

M5 Ligfietsen en Handbikes
Nieuwe Kleverskerkseweg 23
4338 PP Middelburg
Tel: +31 (0) 118 628759
http://www.m5-ligfietsen.com

Nazca Ligfietsen
Castorweg 48
7556 ME Hengelo
Tel: +31 (0) 74 2592886
http://www.ligfiets.net/nazca/

Optima Cycles
Gierstraat 55-57
2011 GB Haarlem
Tel: +31 (0) 23 5341502
http://www.optima-cycles.nl

Rainbow
Barloseweg 28-1
7122 PW Aalten
Tel: +31 (0) 543 451677
http://www.rainbowligfietsen.nl

Roundabout
Hugo de Groot VOF.
Burg. Seinenstraat 57
9831 PV Aduard
Tel: +31 (0) 50 4031904
http://www.hugodegroot-vof.nl

Sinner
Walkumaweg 7
9923 PK Garsthuizen
Tel: +31 (0) 595 464318
http://www.sinner.demon.nl

Ligfiets Shop Tempelman
De Morinel 53
8251 HT Dronten
Tel: +31 (0) 321 337200
http://www.ligfietsshop.nl

Thijs Industrial Designs (row-bike)
Koorkerkstraat 10
4331 AW Middelburg
Tel: +31 (0) 118 634166
http://www.rowingbike.com

Velomobiel (Quest, Mango and Alleweder)
De Vecht 28
8253 PH Dronten
Tel: +31 (0) 321 332717
http://www.velomobiel.nl

Wiegers Wheels
Korn 19
4271 BM Dussen
Tel: +31 (0) 416 391420
http://www.xs4all.nl/%7Ewiegers/

Zephyr Ligfietsen
Danny Siepman
Postbus 27
4486 ZG Colijnsplaat
http://www.zephyr.nl/

### New Zealand

VeloCity (NZ)
Tel: +64 3 348 4812
http://www.southern.co.nz/~velocity/

### Russia

AS Engineering
ykpro@aha.ru
http://www.aha.ru/~ykpro/

Berkut
mvv-toma@mtu-net.ru
http://berkut-trikes.com/

### Switzerland

Birkenstock Bicycles
Stampfstrasse74
CH-8645 Jona
Tel: +41 (0) 79 428 20 08
http://www.speedbikes.ch

### United Kingdom

Inspired Cycle Engineering (ICE)
Bickland Water Road
Falmouth
Cornwall TR11 4SN
Tel: +44 (0) 1326 378848
http://www.ice.hpv.co.uk

MicWic Ltd.
12 Oaklands Industrial Estate
Braydon
Swindon
Wiltshire  SN5 0AN
Tel: +44 (0)1793 852484
http://www.swindonlink.com/MICWIC/

Orbit Cycles
Unit 18
City Road Trading Estate
295 City Road,
Sheffield  S2 5HH
Tel: +44 (0) 114 275 6567
http://www.orbit-cycles.co.uk

Pashley Cycles
Stratford-upon-Avon
Warwickshire  CV37 9NL
Tel: +44 (0) 1789 292 263
http://www.pashley.co.uk

Ultimate Bikes
Brazenhead
Bottom Lane
Sulhamstead
Berkshire  RG7 4BJ
Tel: +44 (0) 118 9305250
http://www.ultimatebikes.com

Windcheetah
Advanced Vehicle Design
L&M Business Park
Norman Road
Altrincham
Cheshire  WA14 4ES
Tel: +44 (0) 161 928 5575
http://www.windcheetah.co.uk

# Recumbent Dealers

Absolutely Recumbents, 2104 Charlevoix Street NW, Albuquerque, NM 87104; Ph: 505 243 5105; www.absolutelyrecumbent.com

Aerospoke, 1200 Holden Ave., Milford, MI 48381; Ph: 248 420 0577; www.aerospoke.com

Alan's Family Bike Shop, 1220 South Coast Hwy, Oceanside, Ca. 92054; Ph: 760 722 3377; www.alansfamilybikeshop.com

Alfred E. Bike, 320 E. Michigan, Kalamazoo, MI 49007; Ph: 616 349-9423; www.aebike.com

Angletech, 318 N. Hwy 67, Woodland Pk, CO 80866; ph: 719-687-7475; angletechcycles.com

Atlantic Bicycles, 6350 W Atlantic Blvd., Margate, FL 33063; ph: 954 971 9590; www.atlanticbicycle.com

Basically Bicycles, 88 Third St., Turner Falls, MA 01376; ph: 413-863-3556; basicallybicycles.com

Best of Bents, 7580 Grant Pl., Arvada, CO 80002; ph: 303 463-8775; www.bestofbents.com

The Bicycle Man, 570 Main St., Alfred Station, NY 14803; ph: (607) 587-8835; bicycleman.com

Bicycle Spokesman (Ontario, CAN), http://www.bikeroute.com/Bicycle-Spokesman

B.I.E.R. Fahrradstudio, Zwei plus zwei Oesterreich, Jaegerhausgasse 20, A-2500; ph: +43 2252 47690; www.fahrradstudio.at

Bicycle Outfitters, 11198 70th Ave. N., Seminole, FL 33772; ph: 727.319.2453; bicycleoutfitters.net

Bicycle Spokesman, 10212 A.Yonge St., Richmond Hill, Ontario L4C 3B6 Canada; ph: (905) 737-4343; bikeroute.com/BicycleSpokesman

The Bicycle Work Shop, 1638 Ocean Park Blvd, Santa Monica, CA 90405; ph: 310-450-3180; www.recumbentbikes.info

The Bike Barn, NW Sixth at Elm, Ogden, IA 50212; ph: 515-275-2981; www.thebikebarn.com

Bike Corral, 605 S 30th St., Heath, OH 43056; ph: 740-522-2708; recumbentsforsale.com

Bike Easy, 734 9th St. W. #8, Columbia Falls, MT 59912; www.bikeeasy.com

The Bike Hub, 1025 N. Broadway, DePere, WI 54115; ph: 920-339-0229; thebikehubonline.com

Bike Path Outfitters Inc., 843 N. Madison, Rockford, IL 61107; ph: 815-968-2543; bikepathoutfitters.com

The Bike Rack, 37 W. 610 Campton Hills Rd., St. Charles, IL 60174; ph: 630-584-6588; thebikerack.com

Bike Zone, 4702 Virginia Beach Blvd., Virginia Beach, VA 23462; ph: 757-497-7971; www.bikezoneva.com

BikeFix, 48 Lambs Conduit St., London, England WC1 England; www.bikefix.co.uk

Bikes@Vienna, 128-A Church St, Vienna, VA 22180; ph: 703-938-8900; bikesatvienna.com

Brown Dog Cycles, 2125 4th Street, Port Townsend, WA 98368; ph: 360 385-6695

Calhoun Cycle, 3342 Hennipen Ave. S., Minneapolis, MN 55048; ph: 612-827-8000; calhouncycle.com

Cambie Cycles, 3317 Cambie St., Vancouver, BC V5Z 2W6 Canada; ph: 604 874 3616; cambiecycles.com

Canalside Bicycle Shop Tandem/Recumbent Center, 3187 Chili Avenue, Rochester, NY 14624; ph: 716-889-7790; www.canalsidebikes.com

Center For Appropriate Transport, 455 W 1st Ave., Eugene, OR 97401; ph: 541.344.1197; www.efn.org/~cat/

College Park Bicycles, 4360 Knox Road, College Park, MD 20740-3171; ph: (301) 864-2211; bike123.com

Cycle Scene, 2893 Johnson Drive, Ventura, CA 93003; ph: (805) 650-9338; www.cyclescene.com

Cyclogical Recumbents, Owatonna, MN 55060; ph: 507 456 6177; cyclogicalrecumbents.com

Dick's Recumbent Cycles, 7685 Heritage Road, Eden Prairie, MN 55346; ph: 612 949 3781

Easy Street Recumbents, 4507 Red River St., Austin, TX 78751

Falmouth Recumbent Cycles, Ste. B. 161 John Roberts Rd., So. Portland, ME 04106; ph: 207 781 4637; www.seis.com/~Mdoyle/

Fools Crow Cycles & Tours, 1046 Commercial Dr., Tallahasse, FL 32310; www.foolscrow.com

Free Flite Bicycles, 2949 Canton Rd Suite 1000, Marietta, GA 30066; ph: 770-422-5237; www.freeflite.com

Future Bike, 31 Fortune Dr. Kiosk #2, Irvine, CA 92618; ph: 949 753 0616

FutureCycles, Friends Yard, Forest Row, East Sussex, England RH18 5EE England; ph: +44 (0) 1342 822847; www.futurecycles.co.uk

Gear to Go, 850 W. Clinton, Elmira, NY 14905; www.gtgtandems.com/

Go-Bent Recumbent Bikes, One Fifth Street Suite 110, Wenatchee, WA 98801; ph: 509 667-7777; www.gobentbikes.com

Gold Country Cyclery, 3081 Alhambra Dr. Suite 103, Cameron Park, CA 95682; ph: 530 676-3305; www.tandems-recumbents.com

Hampton's Edge Trailside Bikes, 9550 E. Atkinson Ct., Floral City, FL 34436; ph: 352-799-4979

HDK Cycles / Denbigh, 467-B Denbigh Blvd, Newport News, VA 23608; ph: (757) 877 5419,

HDK Cycles / Hampton, 1921 N. Armistead Ave., Hampton, VA 23666; ph: (757) 827-0606

Health Cycle, 4679 Leavenworth St., Omaha, NE 68106; ph: (402) 558-6348; www.health-cycle.com

Heartland Cycle & Fitness, 447 N. Oliver, Wichita, KS 67208; ph: 316-682-4144

High Gear Cyclery, Inc., 1834 N. Main Street, Longmont, CO 80501; ph: 303-772-Gear; www.highgearbike.com

Hoigaard's, 3550 South Highway, St. Loiuis Park, MN 55426; ph: 952-929-1351 F; hoigaards.com

Holt Pro Cyclery, 2230 North Cedar, Holt, MI 48842; ph: 517-694-6702

Hostel Shoppe, 929 Main St., Stevens Point, WI 54481; ph: 800 233-4340; hostelshoppe.com

Jay's Pedal Power Bikes, 512 E. Girard Ave., Philidelphia, PA 19125; ph: 215-425-5111; www.jayspedalpower.com

Kinetics, 15 Rannoch Drive, Bearsden, Glasgow, G61 2JW Scotland; ph: +44 (0)141 942 2552; www.kinetics.org.uk

Kirk's Bike Shop, 619 Main St., Ramona, CA 92065; ph: 760-789-4111

Laid Back Tours, 625 Hagen Ave., New Orleans, LA 70122; ph: 504-488-8991; laidbacktours.com

Lakewood Ski & Sport, LLC, 15684 Hwy. 32, Lakewood, WI 54138; ph: 715-276-3071

M5 Ligfietsen en Handbikes, Nwe. Kleverskerkseweg 23, 4338 PP, Middelburg Netherlands; ph: +31 (0)118 628 759

Mill Race Cycling, 11 E. State St., Geneva, IL 60134; ph: (630) 232-2833; www.millrace.com

Mt Airy Bicycles, 4540 Old National Pike, Mt. Airy, MD 21771; ph: 301 831-5151; bike123.com

Neighborhood Transportation, 501 N. Liberty Street, Winston-Salem, NC 27101; ph: 336-722-7727; www.ntransportation.com

NorthEast Recumbents, 9 Wayland Drive, Verona, NJ 07044

People Movers, 980 N. Main St., Orange, CA 92667; ph: 714 633 3663; www.recumbent.com

Peregrine Bicycles, 11 Commerce Ct., #7, Chico, CA 95928; ph: 877-729-2453; pbwbikes.com

Planetary Cycles, 4004 S. Braeswood, Houston, TX 77025; p: 713 668-2300; planetarycycles.com

Power On Cycling, 4705 Water Lark Way, Valrico, FL 33594; ph: (813) 661-6762; www.poweroncycling.com

Prairie Designs / HPV Supply, 21806 S. Broadacres Rd., Pretty Prairie, KS 67570

Prestige Cycles, 36558 Moravian, Clinton Township, MI 48035; www.prestigecycles.com

Rapid Transit, 1900 W. North Ave., Chicago, IL 60622; ph: 773-227-2288; rapidtransitcycles.com

R-D Bike Shop, 128 Second Street NW, Barberton, OH 44203; ph: 330-848-2453, http://www.rdbike.com

Recumbent Bike Riders, 1306 S. Atherton St., State College, PA 16801; ph: 814-234-4636

Recumbent Brothers Cycles, 15180 Russel Drive, Peyton, CO 80831; ph: 719-683-2713

Recumbent Central, 6522 No. 16th St.mayer@amug.com, Phoenix, AZ 85016; ph: 602-230-2393; www.recumbentcentral.com

Recumbent Rider, 88 East Main Street, Mendham, NJ 07945; ph: 973-543-0177

Recumbent shop Amsterdam, Waterspiegelplein 10 - H, 1051 PB Amsterdam, The Netherlands; ph: (+31) 20 686 93 96; www.ligfietswinkel.nl

Recyclist, Inc., 1178 Valley Rd., Menasha, WI 54952; ph: 920 830 1007

Richard's Cyclery, 11943 Valley View St., Garden Grove, CA 92845; ph: 714.379.2717

Ride South Recumbents, LLC, 216 B Avalon Circle, Brandon, MS 39047; ph: 601-992-2490; www.ridesouth.com

Saybrook Cycle Works, 210 Main Street, Old Saybrook, CT 06475; ph: (860) 388-1534, saybrookcycleworks.com

Specialty Cycling, 1712 North Nye St., Toledo, OR 97931; ph: 541 336 5259; www.teleport.com/~hburos/

Speed Merchants, 106 E Bridge St., Rockford, MI 49431; ph: 616 866 2226; speedmerchants.com

Springdale Bicycle, 212 E. Emma, Springdale, AR 72761; ph: 479-751-5318

Stillwater Recumbents, 459 Poplar St., Old Town, ME 04468; ph: 207-827-6461

Stress Management Recumbent Cycles, 10609-B Grant Rd., Houston, TX 77070; ph: 281 890 8575; www.stresscontrol.com/recumbents/

Tailwind Cycling and Fitness, 3723 SW Plaza Drive, Topeka, KS 66609; ph: 785-266-1166

Tom's Bike Annex, 624 Market St., Mt. Carmel, IL 62683; ph: 618 262-4088; bikeroute.com/BikeAnnex

Triketrails, 1621 McEwen Drive, Unit 24, Whitby, Ontario L1R 2L6; ph: 1 866 587-4537; www.triketrails.com

Tri-Sled HPV's, 257 Boundary Rd., Dromana, Victoria 3936 Australia; ph: +61 359810337; www.trisled.com.au

True Wheel Cycling, 400 N. Main, Hailey, ID 83333; ph: none

Two Wheel Drive, 1706 Central SE, Albuquerque, NM 87106; ph: 505-243-8443; www.twowheeldrive.com/bicycles

Tyger's Recumbent Cycles, 510 W. Main, Dakota, IL 61081; ph: (815) 449-2203

Valley Bike & Fitness, 127 N. Washington St., Crawfordsville, IN 47933; ph: (800) 730-9021; www.valleybikes.com

Village Cycle Sport, 1313 N. Rand Road, Arlington Heights, IL; ph: (847) 398-1650; www.villagecyclesport.com

Village Cyclery, 148 N. Grand, Schoolkraft, MI 49087

Wheel and Sprocket, 5722 S. 108th St., Hales Corner, WI 53130; ph: 414-529-6600, www.wheelsprocket.com

The Yellow Jersey, 750 blv. Decarie, Ville St-Laurent, Quebec, Cananda; ph: 514 747-2466; www.promocycle.net

## Accessory Websites

(also see dealer & manufacturer listings)
ATOC (car racks): http://www.atoc.com
Bike Parts: http://www.bikepartsusa.com
Mueller Windwrap Fairings: http://www.windwrap.com
Power On Cycling (components & accessories): http://www.poweroncycling.com
Zzip Designs (fairings): www.zzipper.com. POB 14, Davenport CA 95017. Ph 888-946-7276.

## Recumbent Associations

### *HPVA*

The Human Powered Vehicle Association (HPVA) is dedicated to promoting improvement, innovation and creativity in the design and development of human-powered transportation (http://www.ihpva.org/). (Much of this Appendix info is courtesy of their online Source Guide.) Members receive 4 issues a year of *HPV News*, 2 issues a year of *Human Power* (technical journal), discounts on books, papers and other items. (You can join online.) US dues: $32; HPVA Membership, PO Box 1307, San Luis Obispo, CA 93406-1307; Jean Seay, exec-vp@ihpva.org.

### *BHPC*

British Human Power Club membership and newsletter contact: Dennis Turner, 7 West Bank, Abbot's Park, Chester, CH1 4BD, Telephone: +44 (0)1244 376665. The BHPC website describing their many services, events and publications can be found at http:/

/www.bhpc.org.uk. (The worldwide list of bike and trike makers is provided in this Appendix in part by courtesy of the British Human Power Club.)

### American Club Websites

IHVPA: http://www.ihpva.org

Chicagoland (Ed Gin): http://www.mcs.net/ ~gkpsol

Michigan Wolver-Bents: www.lmb.org / wolbents

Minnestota: http://www2.bitstream.net/ ~mstonich

New York (western): http://bluemoon.net/ ~padelbra/the_recumbenteers.htm

New York (metro): http://www.recumbents .com/mars

Oregon HPV: http://home.pacifier.com/ ~poper/

Ontario Canada (southern): http://www.hpv .on.ca/

Texas (North): http://www.rbent.org/

Washington (Kent Peterson): http:// www.halcyon.com/peterson/bentkent.html

Wisconsin (SE): www.recumbenteers .com/

WISIL (Wisc./Ill.): pro website offers news, photos, reports; www.wisil.recumbents.com

### Worldwide HPVA Affiliates

*Australia*
Contact:, Tim Smith
e-mail: [timotsc@globalfreeway.com.au]
Homepage: http://sunsite.anu.edu.au/community/ozhpv/index.htm

*Belgium*
Contact: Jan Van Dyck,
e-mail: zandhoven.pob@bib.vlaanderen.be
Homepage: http://home2.freegates.be/ hpvbelgium/

*Denmark*
Contact: Curt Bjaellby,
e-mail: dcf@inet.uni-c.dk
Homepage: http://www.dcf.dk/hpv

*Finland*
Contact: Tomas Lindén,
 <tlinden@pcu.helsinki.fi>

*France*
Contact: Emmanuel Delannoy,
e-mail: <emmanuel@bikeeden.com>
Homepage: http://www.ihpva.org/chapters/france/

*Germany*
Contact: Christian Meyer,
e-mail: <c.meyer@snafu.de>
Homepage: http://www.hpv.org.

*Great Britain*
Contact: David Cormie,
e-mail: <Cormie@btinternet.com>
Homepage:http://homepages.tesco.net/ ~john.olson/BHPC/

*The Netherlands*
contact: Ben Wichers Schreur,
e-mail: <wichers@knmi.nl>
Homepage: http://www.ligfiets.net/nvhpv

*Switzerland*
Contact: Theo Schmidt,
e-mail: <tschmidt@mus.ch>
Homepage:http://www.futurebike.ch

*Sweden*
Contact: Mats Nilsson,
email: mats.nilsson@uhregn.mil.se
Homepage:http://hpv-sverige.just.nu//

*North America*
Contact: Paul Gracey,
email: pngracey@aol.com
Homepage: http://www.ihpva.org/hpva

# Recumbent Publications

*Recumbent Cyclist News* is the #1 magazine for anyone who has or wants a recumbent bicycle. Visit recumbentcyclistnews.com. $8 sample issue (current issue only) via First Class mail. $20 for three most recent issues via Priority Mail. RCN PO Box 2048 Port Townsend, WA 98368. (The dealer list in this Appendix is provided in part by courtesy of *RCN*.)

*'BentRider Online Magazine* is the major online HPV news and product resource, at www.bentrideronline.com.

*Easy Riders Recumbent Club* magazine is a fine B&W mag all about 'bents, with an emphasis on Easy Racers. Full of photos, trip and event stories, race reports and equipment news. 48 pages. $10 to ER owners/$15 non-owners to: Connie McAyeal, 28009 NW Dorland Rd., N. Plains, OR 97133.

The WISIL club website (WISIL.recumbents.com) and Recumbents.com, both hosted by Warren Beauchamp, offer the best online coverage of HPV racing and homebuilding.

*Velo Vision* is the major UK magazine covering cycling alternatives. £6.50(UK)/ £8.50(US) an issue. St Nicholas Fields, Bull Lane, York, YO10 3EN, UK, Tel/Fax: +44 1904 438 224; www.velovision.co.uk. Available from Calhoun Cycle in the US.

*Encycleopedia* publishes the only ad-free alternative cycle buyer's guide and HPV video series! More at encycleopedia.com. £12.00(UK)/£23.95(US). Encycleopedia Ltd, PO Box 317, Stockport, SK2 7YH, England.

*Recumbent UK* is a recumbent-only magazine; biannual. £10($17.50 US). Recumbent UK, The Laurels, Church Hill, Olveston, BS35 4BZ UK; www.recumbentuk.hpv .co.uk.

*E-Bent* is an online zine on recumbent biking; http://www.E-bent.com.

# Books

### Bicycle Technology

Abbott, Allan/Wilson, David Gordon: Human-powered Vehicles. Publisher: Human Kinetics Publishing, Ph: 1-800-747-4457, 217-351-5076. 1st edition 1995, 288 pages, 8.5x11", $45. ISBN 0-87322-827-8.

Brandt, Jobst <jbrandt@hpl.hp.com>: The Bicycle Wheel, Palo Alto/CA: Avocet Inc., 3rd Edition 1993. ISBN 0-9607236-6-8.

BHPC: "So you want to build an HPV?" 50 pages, booklet. £4.50/$7US. Dennis Turner, BHPC Membership Secretary, 7 West Bank, Abbot's Park, Chester, CH1 4BD, UK

Hadland/Hadland: Moulton Bicycle. Sold only by the Moulton Bicycle Club; send £9 + cost of add'l postage, cheque payable to'Moulton Bicycle Club' to: Malcolm and Jenny Lyon; 2 The Mill, Mill Green, Turvey, Bedfordshire MK43 8ET, UK.

Kolin, Michael J./de la Rosa, Denise M.: The Custom Bicycle. Rodale Press, Emmaus PA, 1979, ISBN 0-87857-254-6.

Schmitz, Arnfried: Human Power—the forgotten energy. (Memoir of HPV racing.) Available via bikefix.co.uk. Tony Hadland, publisher. 12.95£. ISBN 0-9536174-1-6.

Sharp, Archibald: Bicycles & Tricycles - An Elementary Treatise on Their Design and Construction. London 1896, Reprint Cambridge: MIT Press 1984. 533 Seiten. ISBN 0-262-19156 (paperback), 0-262-69066-7 (hardcover), available via IHPVA, $15.

Whitt, Frank Rowland/Wilson, David Gordon: Bicycling Science - Ergonomics and Mechanics. Cambridge, Mass., MIT Press [1974], 2nd Edition 1982. ISBN 0-262-73060-X. 247 pages illus. 21 cm.

Wright, Robert: Building Bicycle Wheels. World Publications, PO Box 366, Mountain View, CA ( ). ISBN 0-89037-106-7, 1977.

### Frame Building

Anonym: The Oxyacetylene Handbook, 3rd Edition, Union Carbide Corporation, Linde Division, New York, NY; ISDN 0-914096-10-9, 1976.

Anonym: The Proteus Guide to Frame and Framebuilding Products, Proteus Design, Inc, 9225 Baltimore Blvd, College Park, MD 207040 ( ).

Paterek, Tim: The Paterek Manual for Bicycle Framebuilders, Framebuilders Guild: River Falls WI 54022  , 1986, suppl. version. $79.50.

Talbot, Richard P.: Designing and Building Your Own Frameset - An Illustrated Guide for the Amateur Bicycle Builder, The Manet Guild, 1st edition 1979: ISBN 0-9602418-1-7, 2nd edition 1984: ISBN 0-9602418-3-3, 160 pages.

### Related Topics

Costin, M./Phipps, D.: Racing and Sports Car Chassis Design, Robert Bentley, Inc, 872 Massachusetts Avenue, Cambridge MA 02139 ( ), ISBN 0-8376-0296-3, 1965.

Mellin, Bob: Railbike, Cycling on Abandoned Railroads. Balboa Publising, 11 Library Place, San Anselmo, CA 94960, Ph: +1 415 453 8886 Fax: +1 415 453 8888, $16.95 US, $22.95 CAN + $3 shpg.

Milliken, D. L./Milliken, W. F.: Race Car Vehicle Dynamics. ISBN 1-56091-526-9, Hardbound US $85.

### CD-ROM's

Oliver Zechlin offers a unique line of three fascinating HPV CD's—with editions for 1996, 1997 and 1999. Here's a quote from his intro to this enormous, helpful project:

"In spring of 1996 the worlds' first CD about HPV's was born.

"The whole project started with a slideshow I was asked to do about the WCC in Lelystad, Netherlands. After reviewing the pictures, I thought it would be great to share them with other recumbent-enthusiasts.

"I call this series 'a collection of data about land-, water- and aircraft,' and nothing more it is. Each CD contains thousands of pictures, endless text-files, QuickTime-movies...and much, much more." —O.Z.

In the US, 96/97/99 CD-ROM's $10 ea. HPVA members; $17.50 ea. non-members. Send to: HPVA Membership (CD-ROM's) PO Box 1307, San Luis Obispo, CA 93406-1307; Jean Seay exec-vp@ihpva.org

Deutschland: 30 DM ea., US$13, postpaid. Oliver Zechlin, Rudolf-Breitscheid-Str. 10, D-90547 Stein / Fax : +49 (0)89 722 28154 email: hpv-cd@liegerad.com http://www.liegerad.com

# Homebuilder Websites

Bentech: http://members.aol.com/domerie/bentech.htm

Homebuilder Projects: http://www.rqriley.com

Ed Gin Fairings: www.mcs.net/~gkpsol

Joe Kochanowski's Amazing Homebuilt Bents and HPVs: outsideconnection.com/gallant/hpv/joe/

LaDue Homebuilder: http://www.radiks.net/~ladue/

Steve Robson Homebuilder: http://www.xcelco.on.ca/~stevbike/

# Recumbent Plans

Bentech Plans, P.O. Box 198, McKean, PA 16426; domerie@aol.com

Greenspeed (see other listing) trike plans (Ferndale, AU)

Ground Hugger Bent Plans P.O. Box 12294, Scottsdale, AZ 85267-2294; http://www.rqriley.com/bike.html

LaBent by LaDue, kit or plans, 1607 S. 84th St., Lincoln, NE 68506; http://www.radiks.net/~ladue/

M12 Aerocoupe Vehicle, kit by Blue Sky, 1929 W. 25th Pl., Eugene, OR 97405; http://www.blueskydsn.com/order.html

Practical Innovations, free trike plans (Morgan Hill, California US); rhorwitz@flash.net

Recumbent Bike Project by Mike Wolfe; http://home.inreach.com/wolfman/recumben.htm

Tour Easy Licensed Plans. $35 (includes a $10 fee sent to Easy Racers Inc.); Cornel Ormsby, 2735 Burnham Ave., Las Vegas NV 89109-1703; members.aol.com/OrigamiTB

Tricanter Mk VI, trike (Christchurch, New Zealand)

Trice plans ICE (Cornwall, England); http://www.ice.hpv.co.uk

Varna 2- and 3-wheel recumbents, plans, also hand-power (see other listing)

WISIL club pro-quality website offers dozens of detailed project reports; http://www.wisil.recumbents.com

# Personal & Misc. Websites

Bike Rod & Kustom: bikerodnkustom.com

Easy Racer Club: http://www.geocities.com/e_r_r_c/

Eric Vann's page: http://www.beezodogs-place.com

Computing Across America: http://www.microship.com/

Coroplast material: http://coroplast.com

Handcycling: http://www.handcyclequest.com; http://www.handcycling.com

Human Power Boats: http://www.Human-PoweredBoats.com

National Bicycle Greenway: http://www.bikeroute.com (Martin Krieg)

Recumbents.com: Warren Beauchamp's wide-ranging yet detailed 'bent resource site

Recumbent History: http://www.physics.helsinki.fi/~tlinden/winforb.html

Unusual HPVs: http://www.geocities.com/rcgilmore3/

Velomobiles: http://www.velomobile.info

# Acknowledgements

*I'd like to thank the following people for their cooperation and contributions.*

Ewald Fehlau, Clara Fehlau, Axel Fehlau, Jasmin Fischer, Martin Sörensen, Werner Stiffel, Martin Staubach, Caroline Schemensky, Michael Pohl, Michael Malich, Angela Molclenhauer, Andreas Pooch, Gisela Daubitz, Francine and Georges Mochet, Jürg Hölzle, Gottfried Graupner, Johannes Dychhoff, Frau Rinkowski, Manfred Kops, Klaus Schroder, Manfred Harig, Michael Bollschweiler, Olaf Muller, Karin Knauf, Klaus Bartelt, Ulrich Troyer, Wolfgang and Andre Gronen, Herrn Steinhach, Mike Burrows, Frangoise and Bernard Magnouloux, John Kingsbury, Jurgen Reimann, Christian-Uwe Mischner, Peter Bruggen, Palle Lindvig Frederiksen, Thorsten Rähse, Christine Ahrendt, Ulrich Knaack, Jon Schwartz, Matt Weaver, Ingo Kollibay, Gardener Martin, Arnfried Schmitz, Walter Eubus, Marek Utkin, Andreas Fuchs, Paul Atwood, Rick Pope, David Gordon Wilson, Chester Kyle, Mats Nilson, Andrew Letton, Paul Rudin, Jonathan Woolrich, Paul Craig, Brett Poirir, Hanz Scholz, Bernhard Klar, Wolfgang Scholz, Wolfgang Schoppe, Paul Pancella, Paul Goodrich, Peter Eland, Bryan Ball, Robert Bryant, and many others.

*...And these firms and organizations:*
Recumbent Cyclist News, Recumbents.com, BentRiderOnline.com, VeloVision, IHPVA, BHPC, Veloladen, Vam Bike, Liegeraddatei, HPV Deutschland, Moby Dick Verlag, Bundesanstalt fur Strassenwesen, Bundesminister fur VerEehr, ADFC, SWF 3, Atari, Coca Cola, Bieletelder Verlagsanstalt, Foto Hauser, IGP, den Herstellern, Beratungsstelle fur Verkehrstragen des Landes NRW, BDR, HPV France, NHPVA, Danemark HPV, DTU, Futurebike, Berliner MUSCUm fLir Technik und Verkehr, Einbecker Fahrradmuseum.

I apologize if I forgot anybody. If this is the case, it must have happened accidently. The order here, furthermore, does not reflect any priority, but is simply random.
—*Gunnar Fehlau*

*"Flux": The Flux is available with suspension, which is comfortable and extends the range of things the bike can do. (photo: Flux)*

# Glossary of HPV Terms

## *Frame types:*

*recumbent*: a type of cycle ridden while laying back, with weight on butt and back, with feet raised; to go "feet first"

*prone recumbent*: also called 'belly bike'; type of bike that supports rider laying down on belly; travels head first

*'bent*: recumbent

*LWB*: long wheelbase, a 'bent with front wheel ahead of crank

*MWB*: medium wheelbase, or Compact; typically city bikes

*SWB*: short wheelbase, a 'bent with front wheel behind crank

*adjust on the fly*: a change made while riding

*adjustable recline*: seat back and base angles can be changed

*boom*: frame tube that holds crank with a SWB bike

*bottom bracket (crank) height*: how high off the ground is the crank bottom bracket axle center

*chipmunk position*: riding with narrow OSS handlebars close to chest

*closed position*: seat and crank heights are set up so that rider gets power right in front of chest area, as in a racing upright bike while riding in the drops; can push hard against seat back; associated with low seat, high crank, upright seat angle

*derailleur sprout*: frame tube that supports front derailleur on an SWB bike

*hardshell seat*: a solid seat with any padding attached directly to seat

*heel-strike*: amount that heel overlaps front wheel when turning a SWB bike

*idler pulley*: a pulley that tensions and/or controls chain

*intermediate drive*: a two-chain set-up with a cogset (and sometimes a shifter) between crank and rear wheel gearing

*landing gear*: "training wheels" which are lowered from an unstable HPV to allow for reliable start-ups, stops and dismounts

*low-racer*: a 'bent with a seat low enough that one can easily support oneself at a stop with a hand on the road; seat-base is generally below axle height

*mesh/sling seat*: a seat made of a frame with fabric suspended from framing to support rider

*monotube frame*: a large diameter tube is the main frame for a bike

*open position*: seat and crank heights are set up so that rider finds power in lower, more extended range of motion; if push hard, rider tends to rise off seat base; associated with low crank height, reclined seat back

*pedal steer*: if crank area is flexible, pedaling hard can cause steering shifts

*pivoting steerer stem*: the handlebar stem pivots forward to allow rider to easily get on and off of bike

*recline*: how far back a seat-back is reclined from the vertical (90 degrees is laying flat back)

*return-side*: the low-tension part of the chain which goes back from crank to gears

*seat stays*: tubing that supports the seat back, often attached to rear drop-outs

*space frame*: frame made of triangulated tubing, as in a diamond frame bike

*strong-side*: the part of the chain which is under pedaling tension, being pulled from gears to crank

*toe-strike*: amount toe overlaps front wheel when turning a LWB bike

*tub bike*: faired HPV where the fairing acts as the frame

*velomobile*: practical, all-weather HPV that performs functions of a car for short trips

### Steering:

*ASS*: above seat steering

*OSS*: over seat steering (a "tidier" term than ASS)

*USS*: under seat steering

*top steering*: another term for OSS, ASS

*direct steering*: handlebar is attached to fork steerer tube

*indirect steering*: handlebar is attached to pushrod or cable which in turn is connected to fork assembly for steering

*fork-flop*: how much a front wheel tips over and front end drops, as handlebar is turned; relates to relaxed head-tube angle; makes a force to continue turning that must be resisted by rider

*heavy steering*: handlebars require firm control but don't change bike direction as readily

*pushrod*: rod attached from handlebar to fork assembly in indirect steering

*tiller*: how much a handlebar moves from the centerline as it is turned

*twitchy steering*: very light handlebar pressure where small movements quickly change bike direction

### Drive trains:

FWD: front wheel drive

RWD: rear wheel drive

flex-chain FWD: type of FWD where chainline twists between crank and gears during steering; also called "rigid" because frame doesn't pivot.

pivoting FWD: "swinging" FWD where crank and gears stay in constant relation during steering; pivot is usually located at the headtube, but can be located farther back, so that bike acquires "leg steering" properties

### Misc:

*bodysock*: a stretch fabric fairing attached to the cyclist

*Coroplast*: thin, colorful, cheap, light, rugged, corrugated plastic paneling popular for low-tech, quicky hobbyist fairings

*fairing*: a device to shield a rider from the wind, giving higher speeds

*foot trap*: what happens when foot falls from pedals of 'bent while under way and foot gets grabbed by pavement then pulled back under seat: avoid!

*nosecone*: a front fairing

*recumbent butt*: painful temporary rear condition for untrained rider, often associated with prolonged riding with more weight on butt than on back; due to support pressure on the same muscles as are used in riding

*recumbent foot*: painful temporary condition for untrained rider, usually associated with prolonged riding with elevated feet

*tailbox*: a rear fairing, often includes cargo area

*wheelcover*: a disk fairing for a wheel, covering the spokes

# Index

# Out Your Backdoor Press Catalog

## What is OYB?

It's a resource for otherwise unobtainable books and other media at a high level of cultural development, redundant to no others. These titles have an integrity which is hard to find. As a result, hopefully you'll be inspired to set aside some subject biases. If you don't like bike books, ski books, religion books, or even novels, don't fret. These aren't like that. Bikers *rave* about my ski book, for instance. OYB books are cross-training for the brain. Even when they're about specific topics, they're general interest because they build from the roots and include all of life, working against fragmentation and alienation. I've read most of what's been done in these areas, found something lacking, backtracked to the writer who fills that need (often unknown or out-of-print)...and publish it for you. A few years ago this could *not* have happened. Thank you, Internet, for breaking down barriers set up by the book trade. Thank you, short-run printing innovations. Get your hands on an OYB title and you know you have something worth reading. Be the first on your block. If you know of similar topics or books that need help, let me know. I've done the *OYB* zeen since 1991, a large website since 1995, and OYB books since 1997. Visit OutYourBackdoor.com to discover far more than publishers usually deliver: a line of downloadable music, travel forums, stickers, and book/zeen reselling. And sign up for the next issue of the new "catazeen." —*Jeff Potter, publisher*

## Topics

- Outdoor Culture
- Local Culture Ruminations
- OYB Magazine & Anthologies
- Fiction
- Underground Literary Alliance
- Philosophy
- Music & More

## How to Order

Most titles approx. $15 (see listings). Send cash, check, or MO. Credit cards accepted.

Mail orders: OYB Press, 4686 Meridian Rd., Williamston MI 48895

Phone orders: 1-800-763-OYBD (6923)

Online orders: OutYourBackdoor.com

Retail/group orders: 40% off multiple copies.

Publisher: Jeff Potter, jp@outyourbackdoor.com

All titles in "Books in Print" and available via Amazon, Barnes&Noble, and Borders, who take more than half the proceeds. Best to order direct from me!

Many titles available to the retail trade from the following wholesalers: Baker & Taylor, Partners, AlpenBooks, Great Outdoors.

## Outdoor Culture

### *Momentum: Chasing the Olympic Dream*

AUTHOR: Pete Vordenberg   ISBN: 1892590565 PAGES: 200 LISTPRICE: $17.95 DESCRIPTION: "The best XC ski read, ever." (*Master Skier* magazine) An inside look at life as an elite XC skier. Vordenberg is a 2X-Olympian, Natl Champ and a current US Team Coach. The most interesting picture to date on what it's like to ski...and live...really fast. (With dozens of black&white photos.) Vordenberg says: "We have seen the Olympics through the filter of mass media. But at the edge of the screen there is another figure. When the camera zooms out you can see

him, almost too small to recognize. This is the story of the figure at the edge of your screen. It's a voyage following the pursuit of my dream to win an Olympic gold medal. It travels the world, crossing from childhood to the precipitous edge of adulthood. It shares the quixotic humor, excitement, and poignancy inherent in the pursuit of dreams. It is not a retelling of the little engine that could. Rather, it

is about why the little engine even tried." RE-
VIEWS: "The marvel of Vordenberg's book is that
it appeals to the non-skier as well as to ski racers
past and present. Healthy doses of self-revelation,
touches of *On The Road*, and remarkable insights
make this a unique book. It's supposedly about skiing—but it's more about life and seizing it." —Bob
Woodward, veteran XC ski journalist. "The most
compelling athlete's book I've ever read. It may not
have the drama of Lance's return from near death,
but it's got as much guts and more real life.
McKibben's *Long Distance* is a bit more polished,
but Pete's book is much more compelling. Pete is
the real thing." —Ken Salzberg

### The Recumbent Bicycle

AUTHOR: Gunnar Fehlau ISBN:1892590581
PAGES: 192 LISTPRICE: $19.95 DESCRIP-
TION: Here's the first complete book about a whole
amazing, creative side of bicycling: recumbents and
HPVs. Enjoy! This book covers Features, History,

Racing, Tour-
ing, Physics,
Construction
and much
more, as regards
the colorful, di-
verse world of
recumbents
and HPVs.
Many great
black&white
photos, full
color 12-pg
center spread.
REVIEWS:
"A super book,
full of photos, wisdom on every aspect of
recumbents, and resources for riders and builders
alike!" —D. G. Wilson, author *Bicycle Science*. "The
best, most complete book on recumbents and HPVs
ever written!"—Warren Beauchamp, editor
Recumbents.com. "No other book deals with recumbent bicycles in this breadth and depth. It also
helps that it is extremely readable and full of cool
pictures. Well-suited to anyone who might be interested in these bikes, even if they have no previous knowledge."—P. Pancella.

### A Dirt Road Rider's Trek Epic

AUTHOR: Victor Vicente of America
ISBN:1892590506 PAGES: 100 LISTPRICE: $15
DESCRIPTION: If you're a bike buff, you know
how rare bike literature is. Here's a bit of story-
telling to savor, *A Dirt Road Rider's Trek Epic* by
Victor Vincente of America, a bike cult guru hero.
This book presents the many media offerings of a

unique *victor*. The
*Epic* is showcased
in this volume
along with media
reprints from
VVA's heyday as
first US road rac-
ing champion,
first modern-era
Euro winner, first
ultra-distance
record holder, and
early mountain-
bike innovator,
dirt guru, events

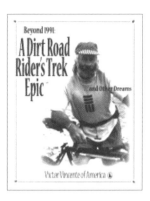

host and then some. Illustrated with his own art
from many projects, including bike-making, coin
art, posters, and stamps. Sports today seem one-
dimensional: why? Here's a fantastically different
take: the world of a champ who explores widely.
Among many surprises, you'll find that offroad
riding offers a treasure of lore and insight. Our author has mined a wondrous chunk of life. His no-
torious So. Calif. newsletter was the first home of
his prose-poem about days and nights in the natural and cultural outback.

### Fold-It!—The World of the Folding Bicycle

AUTHOR: Gunnar Fehlau ISBN:1892590573
PAGES: 150 LISTPRICE: $19.95 DESCRIP-
TION: The world's only book with everything you
need to know about folding bikes. Covers history,
development, features and the various models offered, with pro's and con's. With so much new technology readily available, the scene is booming, and
the future of the folding bike never looked better!
Elegant established models are still inspiring and
holding their own, while gorgeous new models are
coming out to challenge rigid bikes in every way—
but especially in convenience! Find out for yourself. *(Due to be released April, 2004.)*

### DreamBoats: A Look at Small Boats in the Heritage of Seafaring Peoples

*Memories, Ex-
planation and In-
novation with
Coastal Craft,
Junks, Dhows,
Outriggers &
More... in the eyes
of an old salt.* AU-
THOR:
Richard Carsen
ISBN:1892590549
PAGES: 80
LISTPRICE: $10

LISTPRICE: $10 DESCRIPTION: There aren't any books about the exotic sailboats of sea-faring peoples for the lay reader. And there sure aren't any on how and why they do what they do and how their methods might help the average backyard boater. 3rd World sailing: who'da thunk it? Richard Carsen did. He's 83 and traveled the world. He writes up his experiences with indigenous boats and rigs in the magazine *Messing About in Boats*. This book is a compilation of Carsen's columns as they appeared in *MAIB*. The anthropology of boats is fascinating and relevant: Western boating developed with expendable crews for maximum profit; 3rd World boating is about sustainability, family, and bringing 'em back alive with enough to live on. It still works this way. Whose heritage or reality seems better to you?

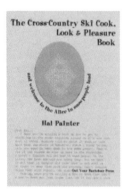

### The Cross Country Ski, Cook, Look & Pleasure Book

*(Out of Print: some dealer copies available.)* AUTHOR: Hal Painter ISBN:1892590514 EDITION: 2 PAGES: 154 LISTPRICE: $20 DESCRIPTION: Reprints and originals available of this 60's-style classic. A unique literary art book on cross country skiing capturing the spirit of the outdoor culture heyday in the US. Zen and the art of skiing. An antidote to consumerism in skiing and an energetic attempt to reconnect skiing with its roots in fluidity, friendship and just plain fun.

### The Captain Nemo Cookbook Papers

*Everyone's Guide to Zen and the Art of Boating in Hard Times Illustrated, A Nautical Fantasy (Out of Print: some dealer copies available.)* AUTHOR: Hal Painter ISBN: 1 8 9 2 5 9 0 5 5 2 2 PAGES: 135 LISTPRICE: $20 DESCRIPTION: Reprints and originals available of this comic 60's look at boating through the eyes of a variety of escapees

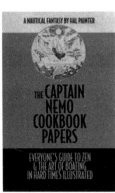

from the rat race. Zen nuggets, marina etiquette, boat fixer-uppers and an appearance by a wildly mythic hero of boating all combine for a rare literary addition to the boating bookshelf. A great period piece that offers wit and antidotes to the consumerism that's overwhelming modern boating.

# Local Culture Ruminations

### Growing Up in Freewayexitville: Making Somewhere from Nowhere in Okemos, Michigan

AUTHOR: Potter, Jeff PAGES: 100 LISTPRICE: $15 DESCRIPTION: Essays written about the author's hometown—a faceless, transitioning rural-suburb of professors, professionals, mall-rats, and mini-malls. A rare look at the 'here' which is taking over America. 'Here' is a traffic-packed sector smashed out of the rural countryside in the last 30 years. But it's also a place with hidden natural and cultural distinctions. How can it survive the

onslaught of speculation? That's the drama. Potter offers practical methods which can be used to create Somewhere out of the Nowhere foisted on us by our best and brightest. A candid, polite, unpublishable point of view unseen before. The average, nonacademic view. It's intended to raise the level of discussion by taking it away from the elite, experts, specialists and those who hope to separate people from each other for their advantage.

## *Out Your Backdoor:* The Magazine of Homemade Adventure, Modern Folkways and Cultural Rescue

### Anthology Volumes 1 & 2

Vol. 1 is a 200-page collection of issues #1-8, $20. Vol. 2 is the huge 75-page issue #9, $5.

*OYB* has been covering the neglected aspects of modern folk culture since 1991. The latest issue is Vol. 2 of the anthology. The previous 8 issues form Vol. 1.

*OYB* is the back porch of culture, where people hang out helping each other find the nifty things that people really do. (The front door being for salesmen and authorities.) *OYB* revives the jaded, helps those who've 'been there, done that' to get to the next level. *OYB* is for all-rounders and generalists, like most people are. It works against the alienating specialties that society uses to split us from ourselves and each other. It creatively explores all sorts of things, including: biking, books, boats, movies, zines, religion, skiing, fishing, hunting, garage sales, getting by, making do. Get the picture? Big website at OutYourBackdoor.com.

### *OYB #10 to be published early 2004.*

*OYB* magazine will be publishing again as of 2004, and will accept subscriptions starting with issue #10. $10 for 4 issues, biannual or quarterly, 24 pages. OYB, 4686 Meridian Rd., Williamston MI 48895.

## Fiction

## The Novels of Jack Saunders

### *General Description of Jack's Style...*

In no-holds-barred "Florida writer" tradition, Jack Saunders writes stories about publishing, academia and everyday life, about what it's like to work and succeed while being true to oneself and one's family and culture. He writes honestly and creatively, and that's the understatement of the year—yet it's accessible, fits like a shoe. Tastes like coffee (being an acquired taste, a step up). He writes with encyclopedic insight about how this effort relates to the world around him, other authors, books, movies, music, Florida, cooking, his life, work, business, progress. In folk vernacular with local color that won't quit. Jack names names, uses cultural artifacts in his poetry so superbly you'll be spurred to rent movies, read books, listen to music that you never would've otherwise. Heck, you'll get new appreciation for boxing and baseball..and everything else. (Sailing? Farming?) Folky yet also a linguistic eye-opener. It's that big. It's all about someone trying to do their best in the modern world, to write honestly. Give it a try and see where it gets you, is one of his motifs. Each book is a slice of a larger ouevre (ahem, can you say forklift pallet?)--with letters, memoir, poetry and essay all playing off each other. In the end, though, "it's just stories." Jazz and the blues. In the mainstream of American outsiders: Whitman, Melville, Faulkner, Kerouac, Miller, Algren, Thompson, Bukowski, MacDonald, Willeford, Burke, Hiassen and Finster. As he says, the Cracker spirit lives on and a country boy will make do. Except for insiders, he is entirely unknown. But he's been working close, prolific and giving it his all for 25 years now. Why haven't you heard of him? Find out...

### *General Reviews of Jack's Books...*

In Jack Saunders our generation is extremely lucky to have a powerful and determined writer, an honest writer. A Diogenes not merely of words, but of provocative thoughts. From his hideaway in Florida, like a super-energized lobster, Saunders lashes out at the sickening hypocrisy which is deadening our senses and rotting our souls. It is Saunders' adamant, boneheaded, determined persistence that is his great strength, his great gift to a society staggering in its own materialistic greed. Saunders is America at its best. He spells out what spirit is all about. And humanity. How do we live? When do we really come ALIVE? As we should? And deserve? America needs writers with such strength and ferocity and independence and integrity, not all those greedy little word-mongers contemplating their private parts on every supermarket shelf. Saunders is more than a literary volcano. He is a live, writhing, crackling wire. Spewing sparks in all directions. Creating and developing a brighter, newer world. —*Raymond Barrio*

As exasperating and slippery a "read" as they come. This work is totally unpretentious (and thus honest) and yet its theme is the total unrelenting pretension of a life. That life is excruciating and unavoidable, unedited and ambiguous, squalling and scrawling, elegant and vulgar, ordinary and completely out of the ordinary. Read it; you'll never forget it. —*John M. Bennett*

I have a hunch your stuff is wild and terrific and keeps going off the rails. I have no better explanation for why you don't find publishers, since you certainly write well enough sentence for sentence and paragraph for paragraph. —*Norman Mailer*

This is some very clever writing...rings true to my own wars with the publishers—good luck! —*Theodore Roszak*

All fine hard hitting work. The works of Jack Saunders give us hope. Hope that our lives won't be horrible wasted foolishness. Even when it seems that hope is all we have left, if you feel you can live a fuller life and spend your days in a more profitable way for yourself AND MANKIND you should read Jack Saunders for a ray of hope and a great deal of enjoyment and amusement. OK it rings so true that you'll forget you're reading & think you're talking to yourself. —*Larry Schlueter*

Hey it broke me up—I imagined someone calling here and asking what I was crying about. I was not crying, kid. I was laughing at Jack Saunders' new movie. —*David Zack*

Nothing studied about this one. He just knows. And does. It hangs together, flows together, makes a lot of sense. Cooking like a Tasmanian Dervish. All I can do is tip my hat. —*Carl Weissner*

Jack Saunders is an American original and his life is an open book. His dedication and commitment are evident throughout, and his abundant energy enlivens every page. —*Lawrence Block*

## Screed

AUTHOR:Saunders,Jack,L ISBN: 0912824247 LISTPRICE: $15 DESCRIPTION: Stories about life and dealings with the fine arts scene, as world literature. REVIEWS: Thanks for the copy of *Screed*. I liked it very much. In fact, I've been reading it aloud to my wife in bed at night. You write in a kind of natural, organic, free-flowing and perfectly lucid style that I much admire. —*Edward Abbey* Dear Jack: Thanks for *Screed*. It's good diatribe. The reason I know is that diatribe makes me feel better. And I felt better reading it. —*Walker Percy* Thanks for Screed. Nicely done. He rolls on. —*Charles Bukowski*

## Evil Genius

AUTHOR: Saunders, Jack L. ISBN: 1892590298 PAGES: 277 LISTPRICE: $15 DESCRIPTION: Mortgages house and gives self Evil Genius Award, first prize ever won. Many cultural reviews. Stories of his days in archeology and grad school, fun with The System, as world literature. REVIEWS: In my library the novels of Jack Saunders go right next to MOBY DICK, ISLANDIA, and THE RECOGNITIONS. EVIL GENIUS is an astonishing feat—like watching a man lay eight hundred miles of track single-handed, without ever once stopping, or faltering, or resorting to adjectives. —*Dr. Al Ackerman* Thank you for sending me EVIL GENIUS, which I

read last night. I didn't really want to stay up so late, but the book moved forward with a momentum that was overpowering and almost tragic. Your fiction can also be very annoying—which is a virtue, I think. —*Richard Grayson* I am very pleased at the way you handled the tale of your life in EVIL GENIUS. It owes something to Henry Miller, but every writer owes a debt to those before them and those in turn were helped by their predecessors. No one is an absolute original, but you come close. —*William Eastlake* Words for *Evil Genius*? I took nearly a year out of my own writing time to work on SCREED, on its production, what more need to be said for how I feel about your worth? You're a diamond in the rough, Jack. You've got an intrinsic worth worth more than the realized worth of about 99% of the writers in this country lumped together.

If you feel in your heart of hearts that what you're doing is what you must do, then that's settled. Settled with nothing further implied. I'd say your chances of being treated with any sort of kindness, your chances of being recognized for your intrinsic worth, are worse than mine, and mine are Virginia slim. —*John Bennett*

## Open Book

AUTHOR: Saunders, Jack L. ISBN: 1892590301 PAGES: 250 LISTPRICE: $15 DESCRIPTION: Covers what happened to *Evil Genius*, how he goes from bad to worse: who would follow up *EG* with another book? None but a blockhead. Stories about working life after college, as world literature. REVIEW: Thanks for *Evil Genius* and *Open Book*; I enjoyed both of them, and asked my publisher to send you my new book, *Sideswipe*, when it comes out in Feb. In 1957, Theodore Pratt

told me that Delray Beach was a better town than N. Y. for a writer. "If you stay in Florida," he told me, "you'll never run out of things to write about." He was right, of course; I never have, and you won't either. My most productive years were from age 50 to 55, and I'm sure that yours will be too. —*Charles Willeford*

## Common Sense

AUTHOR: Saunders, Jack L. ISBN: 1892590263 PAGES: 137 LISTPRICE: $15 DESCRIPTION: Book 1 of a 2-book series, Jack Saunders writes stories about his efforts to acculturize IBM during the early days of the PC so they wouldn't get left behind by a competitor more in tune with the times...it didn't work. (*Full Plate* is Book 2.) An open discussion with his superiors asking how a committee system which rewards buck-passing could ever recognize innovation. "This is the only treaty I will make." World literature.

## Full Plate

AUTHOR: Saunders, Jack L. ISBN: 1892590271 PAGES: 76 LISTPRICE: $15 DESCRIPTION: Part 2 of a 2-part series. Jack Saunders writes stories about his efforts to acculturize IBM during the early days of the PC so they wouldn't get left behind by a competitor more in tune with the times...it didn't work. (*Common Sense* is Book 1.) "A Contract between Dem and Ashola." World literature.

## Forty

AUTHOR: Saunders,Jack,L. ISBN: 0945209010 LISTPRICE: $15 DESCRIPTION: Stories about Jack's efforts to enter the Buddhists' "Stage 4" of writing: to give it up, then see what happens. Plenty of culture and bluegrass reviews and overview of life on the edge, with kids, as world literature.

## Blue Darter

AUTHOR: Saunders, Jack L. ISBN: 1892590255 PAGES: 85 LISTPRICE: $15 DESCRIPTION: An aggressive, tricky fast pitch: "Rare back and hurl your blue darter at their ear." Stories from Jack's youth. World literature.

## Lost Writings

AUTHOR: Saunders, Jack L. ISBN: 189259028X PAGES: 158 LISTPRICE: $15 DESCRIPTION: "Minor chord: Bigfoot sidles into the shadows." Fiesty writings, as world literature.

# Other Fiction

## Potluck

AUTHOR: Rudloe, Jack ISBN: 1892590375 PAGES: 264 LISTPRICE: $14.95 DESCRIPTION: Hard times and opportunity collide on the high seas. *Potluck* is a page-turning thriller about a decent captain who decides, in extremity, to take a big risk. It's the only realistic picture of small family commercial fishing on the Gulf Coast of Florida and the problems and temptations that confront it. Corrupt forces on all sides are pushing this stalwart breed of Americans

into desperation or extinction. But they still do their best to feed us. If you've ever wondered what the lives are like behind the few fishing boats you still see along the coast, look no further. A rare look at the broad and surprising impacts of drug smuggling, mis-guided regulation and realtor greed along the coast. Author Rudloe is the pre-eminent conservationist of the Florida Gulf Coast, author of highly regarded naturalist books, and operator of the only independent (and thus frequently bureaucratically besieged) marine institute in the region. REVIEW: "Jack Rudloe's non-fiction account of living on the Gulf Coast, *The Living Dock at Panacea*, is a Florida classic that ranks with *Cross Creek*. In *Potluck*, Rudloe proves he can handle fiction with the same energy and insightful style."—Randy Wayne White (*Shark River, Sanibel Flats*)

### Tales From the Texas Gang

AUTHOR: Blackolive, Bill ISBN: 1892590387 PAGES: 339  LISTPRICE: $21.95  DESCRIPTION:  Wild Bill's writing is in the tradition of  Melville...and Keroauc and Castenada and Abbey. It's a bit like Cormac McCarthy as well, only more realistic, authentic and candid. If you like the thrust of those other writers, you'll be thankful for *Tales From the Texas Gang*. It's one of the rare significant additions to American literature. And it's based on real life, and a real life gang. It's set in the late 1800s. It's an outlaw gang gunfighter novel...but so much more. (*Previous printing available. Due out Fall 2004.*)

### The Emeryville War

AUTHOR: Blackolive, Bill ISBN: 1892590395 PAGES: 109  LISTPRICE: $12.95  DESCRIPTION:  If you liked *Confederacy of Dunces*, you'll like this. Only, it's real. An amazing tale of actual life in the fringey, unhip edge of Berkeley in the 60s. You've never seen neighbors, cops and city officials like these, nor an observer like Wild Bill—dogs, barbells, wrecked cars and all. (*Due out Fall 2004.*)

# The Underground Literary Alliance (ULA)

The ULA is an activist group of zeensters and fans of literature who are commited to reviving the literary scene in the U.S. It's the only group remotely like it. Until they showed up, literary culture was apathetically being allowed to sink into complete irrelevance. It's the most exciting literary movement in the country. It has received accolades and scorn for its actions— and both as well for its writing. It has received major articles in top culture and literary media like the *New York Post*, *The Village Voice*, *Black Book* and *The Believer*, as well as major coverage at many websites such as the forum at *The Atlantic Monthly*. The only literary figure who dared meet and explore issues in a public debate with the ULA was George Plimpton (bold to the end). Its mission is to expose and repair the current disaster in U.S. literature. It insists that a wider more realistic view which is more inclusive and populist is the key to progress. They say, "The ULA is looking for America's great writers! If we don't do it, no one will. The MFA system has had decades and has come up empty. It's time for a change." The ULA says that out-of-touch elites, with their pointless irony and over-stylizing, have ruined writing for the past couple decades. It offers a wide sample of do-it-yourself writing meant to counteract this trend and help literature become relevant again. Members also appear at major literary events and ask tough questions, such as why two million aires recently won tax-sheltered awards meant for needy writers. Mainstream media has followed up on these challenges. Learn more at their website LiteraryRevolution.com. Members include Jack Saunders, Wild Bill Blackolive and Jeff Potter. Here are some ULA and ULA-member publications:

### "Slush Pile"

Issues 1, 2 and 3. AUTHOR: Steve Kostecke editor; contributions by Karl Wenclas, Michael Jackman and many others. PAGES: Approx. 10 LISTPRICE: $5 DESCRIPTION: From a review in *Zine World*, #19: "SP2 is another fine publication from the ULA, which showcases excellent e amples of non-mainstream writing from the likes of Urban Hermitt, Jack Saunders and Michael Jackman. ... The writing in this issue outshines anything the corporate literature machine can churn out—proving over and over that some of the best writing comes from the underground. I especially liked the personal accounts of gilded literary events crashed by members of the ULA."

## *"Axian Kix," "Destination Absolutely," & "Auslanders Raus"*

AUTHOR: Steve Kostecke. PAGES: Approx. 100 ea. LISTPRICE: $5 DESCRIPTION: Kostecke is one of the best young travel writers writing today, but mainstream publishers won't touch him. This isn't just travel writing. He lived in the bushes while working at Burger King in Germany and has taught English in S.E. Asia the past few years. His tales give insights into where he is like we haven't seen in "travel" writing in awhile. Especially as regards the working, dating and bargirl cultures of various S.E. Asian countries, Kostecke offers an extra-dry view of the entirely different yet totally urban mindsets of these cultures, from someone who immersed then went with the flow. And yet who still retains an American eye. The view exposes them and reflects us.

## *"The Pornographic Flabbergasted Emus"*

Serial novel in 5 zeen issues. AUTHOR: Wred Fright PAGES: Approx. 50 ea. LISTPRICE: $3 ea. DESCRIPTION: A story of a hilarious ever-changing rock band built around a college-town houseful of semi-students who practice their music in a wet basement on pallets to keep them out from electrocution, and who can barely keep jobs and the beer-bong full. They try, though. And try. How many ways can bandmates complicate each other's lives as they try to get along and get a life? ...More than you imagine. Written in rotating confessions from each of the gang. A fresh, non-ironic Gen-X/Y/Z tale.

# Philosophy

### The Integrative Works of Ronald Puhek

Fifth Way Press is an imprint of OYB. It is sponsored by the MIEM, the Michigan Institute of Educational Metapsychology—a fancy way to say "workable religion, philosophy and psychology for living today, inspired by the best of the past." The institute has been represented for 30 years by weekly meetings of quiet, polite folk. Typically these have been people from the 'helping' professions who themselves see that their ways need help. Are in desparate straits. Due to modernism. The "Fifth Way" concept comes from "the Fourth Way" of Ouspensky and Gurdjieff. The previous three ways to attain contact with reality were: the emotional way of the monk, the intellectual way of the yogi, and the physical way of the fakir. These were unified and superceded by the fourth way of the householder, who lives normally in everyday life. The Fifth Way takes the best of all ways without leaving any behind, transcending them all: count your fingers: thumbs up!

If you like Simone Weil, St. Theresa and St. John of the Cross, you'll like Puhek. It's plainly written but maximumly intense philosophy for a modern age. His reflections integrate and build on many works, especially Plato, Sartre, Jung and Freud.

### *Analects of Wisdom*

SERIES: The Art of Living, Book 1 AUTHOR: Puhek, Ronald E. ISBN: 1892590123 PAGES: 118 LISTPRICE: $15 DESCRIPTION: Analects are, literally, "cut readings." In this collection of verses and commentaries, not just the verses but even the commentaries are brief. They all use two devices of higher knowledge: *paradoxical logic* and experiential thinking. Representing the first phase of the soul's transformation in this life, the *Analects* provide instruction in how to live. They establish "rules" whose truth can be tested even by the mind still held captive by the senses. Anyone can understand them without a great development of faith. These stirrings of other-worldly wisdom can work effectively in guiding life in this world. We are of the opinion that the verses themselves may have had more than one author. This is almost certainly true of the commentaries. *Analects of Wisdom* is the first volume of the trilogy, *The Art of Living*.

### *Descent into the World*

SERIES: The Art of Living, Book 2 AUTHOR: Puhek, Ronald E. ISBN: 189259014X PAGES: 175 LISTPRICE: $15 DESCRIPTION: As the middle book of the *Art of Living* trilogy, *Descent into the*

*World* deals with the second phase of development. It is the one hardest to pass through. In the first phase as we launch on our inner journey, hope sustains our spirits. In the third phase, as we draw closer to our destination, we see it distinctly ahead and the joy of anticipation arises. The second phase, however, requires that we return to face the world where we will do our final work. The *Descent* describes this harshest and driest time. Now the comforts of inward meditation leave us. We meditate but return to the world where we must overcome severe tests and avoid deep traps if we are to find in the end the redemption of love.

### The Redemption of Love

SERIES: The Art of Living, Book 3 AUTHOR: Puhek, Ronald E. ISBN: 1892590158 PAGES: 209 LISTPRICE: $15 DESCRIPTION: Love is the greatest, most enduring, most divine blessing on earth. But love is also suffering, and much of what is done in its name makes it appear to be a curse. The Greeks celebrated love in the form of gods such as Aphrodite and Eros; the ancient Christians said, "God is love." As both indicate, love is a powerful spiritual principle in our lives, but any spiritual principle can be corrupted and its power transformed into a malignant force. *The Redemption of Love* seeks to answer how love gets corrupted and how it can be purified and freed to serve its natural function of rescuing human life and redeeming the world.

### A Guide to the Nature & Practice of Seminars in Integrative Studies

SERIES: The Science of Life, Book 1 AUTHOR: Puhek, Ronald E. ISBN: 1892590093 PAGES: 145 LISTPRICE: $15 DESCRIPTION: "Seminars in Integrative Studies" is written to serve a distinct and special kind of learning. Integrative studies focus on searching for a principle of unity or integrity to hold together our knowledge and our life. These studies concern themselves with consciousness and conscience. Consciousness and conscience are different from mere knowledge and value judgments. Consciousness and conscience are comprehensive and integrating instead of single, narrow and analytical. Consciousness integrates your understanding and conscience integrates your sense of the good. We concentrate here not on offering a preliminary and superficial "exposure" to the concept and practice of integrated knowledge. Instead, we address those with a serious commitment to integrative research and to those working together as a permanent community dedicated to integrative studies. Thus, the idea of "seminars" in integrative studies refers not to classes in any ordinary sense of external enrollment but to personal intention, interest, and involvement. Seminars are regular gatherings of those devoted to pursuing integration in knowledge and life. These seminars have formal and informal rules. They require an inner commitment and a desire to grow to knowledge of life through investigating the nature of life using the only concrete and direct perspective we have: our own existence.

### Spiritual Meditations

SERIES: The Science of Life, Book 2 AUTHOR: Puhek, Ronald E. ISBN: 1892590107 PAGES: 166 LISTPRICE: $15 DESCRIPTION: Spiritual Meditations, the second book in the trilogy The Science of Life, is an excursion into the second stage of human spiritual development. Its primary focus is on the practices that will allow us to elevate our understanding so we might better perceive the standard of value that can inwardly bring us peace and outwardly guide us to the best life possible. Integrative knowledge is essential to both and methods of pursuing such knowledge are essential if we are to gain it and live fuller, less violent, and more harmonious lives. None of the methods prevailing today is adequate to the task of arriving at integrative knowledge. This book presents part of the process of an effective response to life.

### The Spirit of Contemplation

SERIES: The Science of Life, Book 3 AUTHOR: Puhek, Ronald E. ISBN: 1892590115 PAGES: 175 LISTPRICE: $15 DESCRIPTION: *The Spirit of Contemplation* is the final book in the trilogy *The Science of Life*. It explores the culminating phase of spiritual development and what needs to happen after the completion of the spiritual exercises associated with meditation. Meditation takes us out of the world; contemplation returns us to it. Meditation renders us unable to live in reality; contemplation realizes the redemption of reality. It is the highest peak of the mountain of spritual growth. The entire trilogy, however, is only the first of two. *The*

*Science of Life* concentrates on the development of spiritual understanding; the second trilogy, *The Art of Living*, will focus on the transformation of life.

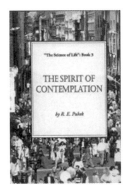

*Note:* The previous six books stand on their own, but they are also parts of two trilogies called *"The Art of Living"* and *"The Science of Life"* which interact together. Each of the three volumes in the trilogies describes development in qualities of soul called hope, faith, and love. The first volume in each trilogy focuses on the inner and outer growth of hope; the second in each, on faith; and the third in each, on love. The twin trilogies are distinct in as much as *"The Science of Life"* deals with the three-step movement to integrity in life by means of an upward and inward journey to knowledge of the integrating good that alone makes a life of integrity possible while *"The Art of Living"* deals with how actually to live in the world with integrity and meaning. The first volume of each trilogy represents how human, not individual, memory stimulates and guides *hope*'s development first upward through group study under rules where the group represents human or universal wisdom and then downward through insightful sayings of inherited wisdom guiding life. The second volume in each trilogy represents the subsequent movement of *faith*. Similarly, this involves first an upward direction by losing illusory beliefs in the realm of visible goods and attending to the timeless or eternal good and then a downward direction in the practical world. Finally, the third volumes represent the movement in *love* upward to the ultimately indefinable Good and downward to living divine love in the world. While each volume can be read independently, there are two additional reading strategies. First, the reader might follow the movement of understanding from one book to the next in the "Science" trilogy and then the movement of life in the world in the "Art" trilogy. Alternatively, the reader might even better follow the path of hope upward in the first book of "Science" and downward in the first book of "Art," then the path of faith upward and downward in the second books of each trilogy, and finally the path of love upward and downward in the third books.

## Meaning & Creativity

SERIES: Blue Trilogy, Book 1 AUTHOR: Puhek, Ronald E. ISBN: 1892590069 PAGES: 118 LISTPRICE: $15 DESCRIPTION: Meaning and Creativity, first book of the Blue Trilogy, explores the illusions of meaning that dominate life today and how to break out of their chains-a vital first step in the process of reality. Life is not worth living if it is not meaningful. Most of the strategies for living today are, however, merely methods of enabling us to endure frightful meaninglessness. They are all mechanical and operate by encouraging us to flee from one meaningless activity as soon as we catch the scent of its decaying character and race to another, equally meaningless. Life becomes a continuous merry-go-round. We move in circles, getting nowhere, but are lost in the illusion that we

are moving along a straight path to greater good-even when we try to use methods that are thought to counteract this. So long have we lived like this that if we would wake up and see our true state, we would be shattered. Nihilism would be our fate. To avoid this catastrophe, we need to prepare ourselves with some understanding of how to live a life of meaning. The only meaningful life is a creative life. This is easy to see once we realize what "creativity" consists of.

## The Abyss Absolute

SUBTITLE: *The Autobiography of a Suicide* SERIES: Blue Trilogy, Book 2 AUTHOR: Puhek, Ronald E. ISBN: 1892590077 PAGES: 146 LISTPRICE: $15 DESCRIPTION: The Abyss Absolute is the second book of the Blue Trilogy. It is the heart and soul of this series. Realizing the meaning-lessness of most of contemporary life and even understanding how we must live if we are to find meaning are not enough. By themselves, these achievements may end in

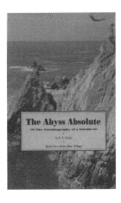

nothing but disillusion-disillusion of the meaninglessness and disillusion with the prospects of finding an alternative-even among those approaches typically thought to bring hope. This is because before we can find a way upward we must first allow ourselves to fall into an abyss so profound that it feels as if it will annihilate us. Courage to enter this abyss is the only hope of escaping the emptiness of contemporary life, but there are dangerous traps along the way.

### Killer Competitiveness

SERIES: Blue Trilogy, Book 3 AUTHOR: Puhek, Ronald E. ISBN: 1892590085 PAGES: 130 LISTPRICE: $15 DESCRIPTION:Killer Competitiveness is the third and last book of the Blue Trilogy. We explored the meaninglessness that dominates life today in Meaning and Creativity, the first book of the series. Then we face a great challenge when we take up a path to meaning in the second book, The Abyss Absolute. This last book accounts for how it is possible for us today to exist so long under meaningless conditions without realizing it. So empty is life without meaning that it could continue only with the help of an extremely powerful illusion. This compelling illusion is generated by competitiveness in nearly everything we do-even in our supposed efforts to cooperate or function independently. Competitiveness generates the illusion of value. Therefore, we do not see the valuelessness of our lives even as we suffer from it.

### Mind, Soul & Spirit

*An Inquiry into the Spiritual Derailments of Modern Life* AUTHOR: Puhek, Ronald E. ISBN: 1892590026 PAGES: 148 LISTPRICE: $15 DESCRIP-TION:The prevailing styles of living today require the "derailment" of our energies. The spirit or energy that life grants us to fulfill our destiny is seized, imprisoned, and then turned away from its natural direction, usually to be amplified for ulterior motives. The various derailments of spirit operate unconsciously upon their victims. We today are particularly vulnerable to blindness here because of our ignorance of the dynamics of spiritual life-even as many of us pretend to spirituality and feel energy which we trust to be helpful. Spiritual knowledge is almost completely absent in all contemporary education, and, as a society, we are

nearly bankrupt spiritually. This book maps out the many ways our spirit gets diverted without our knowing it. We must take back our spiritual birthright.

### The Powers of Knowledge

SERIES: The Crisis in Modern Culture: Book 1 AUTHOR: Puhek, Ronald E. ISBN: 1892590042 PAGES: 83 LISTPRICE: $15 DESCRIPTION: Modern culture is the source of a crisis in civilization. This now world-wide culture is generating increasingly intolerable conditions of human life mostly because of the faulty assumptions built into it that concern our powers of knowledge. Because of these assumptions, we fail today to develop and use the whole range of our powers. Consequently, we find ourselves increasingly unable to perceive, let alone understand, the forces flowing into and out of our lives. We can see that things are bad but not why they are so. We do not see this because the very tools of perception we use are the flawed victims of a culture that renders them inadequate. The Powers of Knowledge (Book I of The Crisis of Modern Culture) explores our powers of knowledge-both those we only partly or wrongly develop and those we entirely neglect. It shows how we may expand our awareness by actualizing all of them in a more integrated way. It illustrates how we can turn aside the forces of destruction that today are reaching critical mass everywhere, even in places we thought were protected.

### Violence

SERIES: The Crisis in Modern Culture: Book 2 AUTHOR: Puhek, Ronald E. ISBN: 1892590050 PAGES: 82 LISTPRICE: $15 DESCRIPTION: This book (Book II of The Crisis of Modern Culture) presents an approach to understanding the specific forms of violence particularly appropriate to contemporary life. It illustrates that most violence today is completely invisible both to those who do it and to those who suffer it. This is because the prevailing concept of violence is inadequate. If our concept of violence encompasses only its physical or sensible forms, we will not see it when it operates even when we think we fight against it in its emotional and especially in spiritual forms. Today the dominant form of violence is spiritual. Today we can even love vio-

lence because we suffer from it in ways we do not see. Today there is violence in our acts of love. We must be concerned, therefore, both about our love of violence and the violence of our love.

## Stephen of the Holy Mountain

AUTHOR: Puhek, Ronald E. ISBN: 1892590018 PAGES: 94 LISTPRICE: $15 DESCRIPTION: An inner journey, outwardly masking itself as a sojourn up the side of a high mountain, Stephen of the Holy Mountain seeks answers to the most perplexing questions that come to those who have awakened from the sleep of ordinary existence. The mysterious figure of Stephen acts as a guide both to the author and to many others who climb Stephen's mountain to find him. His advice is often too harsh for many who think they seek it. Unfailingly kind, however, Stephen does his best to aid all who come to him.

## The Metaphysical Imperative

*A Critique of the Modern Approach to Science* AUTHOR: Puhek, Ronald E. ISBN: 1892590034 PAGES: 135 LISTPRICE: $15 DESCRIPTION: Metaphysical assumptions are and have always been a necessary and unavoidable part of human life. Unfortunately, today we have fallen into the catastrophic belief that our basic perceptions of reality do not rest on metaphysical judgments but are purely "physical." If we use the term "metaphysics" at all, it is only to refer to abstract philosophical ideas or, worse, to half-crazed religious attitudes. Consequently, we have rendered ourselves unable to distinguish between the metaphysical and non-metaphysical aspects of any knowledge and are still less able to judge whether our hidden or flaunted metaphysical assumptions are faulty and, if so, how they might be corrected. The Metaphysical Imperative explores the nature of metaphysical assumptions, how they are all-pervasive, which ones dominate our attitudes today, what their flaws are, and how we might improve them.

## Social Consciousness

*Renewed Theory in the Social Sciences* AUTHOR: Puhek, Ronald E. ISBN: 189259000X PAGES: 202 LISTPRICE: $15 DESCRIPTION: This is a unique study of the theoretical foundations of social science. In particular, it criticizes the practice of applying the methods of the physical sciences to the study of human life. Methods very appropriate to the study of "things" or objects are not appropriate to the study of the human self. When we use such inappropriate methods, we end in making the human self into a thing, and all the knowledge we gain affords us only more power to dominate and suppress the human. These methods violate human freedom and dignity in any use, let alone in their application in fields like psychology, advertising and politics. This study concludes by developing an alternative approach to explanation.

## Matricide

AUTHOR: Lombardi, Vincent L. ISBN: 189259031X PAGES: 287 LISTPRICE: $15 DESCRIPTION: A novel about a crime that shook a small town and hurled a 12-year-old girl into the bizarre world of court-appointed professionals. As she grows up, she's driven to madness, torn between cultures, struggling at the crossroads of what comes next—will it be Brave New World or a new Renaissance?

# OYB Music ...& More

## *(Yes, OYB is also a record label.)*

### *Back Tracks: The Best of Richard Dobson*

ARTIST: Richard Dobson  PRICE: $12 CD; 21 songs; $1 per song download and free samples online at OYB website.  DESCRIPTION: Rich-

ard Dobson is one of the gang who started today's Austin Texas music scene. He says it's "folk and rocking country music." (Say it fast.) I call it great music that I hadn't heard before. I greatly appreciate his tales of work-

ing class heroes and the kind of fun, love and heartache they get up to. Here's what a few other folks have had to say: *"His rhythms and ideas are great. His words are precise and never wasted. He's one of my favorite songwriters."* —Townes Van Zandt  *"Richard Dobson is a great songwriter."* —Steve Earle  *"Richard Dobson is one of the best songwriters in Nashville—make that the whole U.S."* —John Prine  *"Richard Dobson is the Hemingway of Country Music."* —Nanci Griffith

### *Gulf Coast Boys*

AUTHOR: Richard Dobson  PAGES: 177 LISTPRICE: $15  DESCRIPTION: I learned about Dobson's memoir from Jack Saunders. Richard played hard-driving bar music in the 1970s, with the toughest guys around, spending ex-

tremely wild years on the road with the likes of Townes van Zandt as they created the new Texas sound. Between tours Dobson worked on oil rigs and shrimp boats, and hunted and fished for food. This

is a fine story of those days, about a kind and place of culture that isn't published about often. I noticed that Bush Sr.'s oil company came off looking *very* bad from Dobson, who saw it and many more from the dirty inside. After I read *GCB*, I bought Dobson's music (backwards, but it worked out fine).

### *U.K.E.: Comrade Cool*

ARTIST: Bart Casad  PRICE: $12; 11 songs; downloads and samples at my website.  DESCRIPTION: Welcome to U.K.E., the land of Bart! It's socially relevant ukele clever-fest, ensemble-style. (U.K.E. = "ultra kitsch ensemble.") He's a lively, astute singersongwriter. There's great instrumenta-

tion and nifty production values on this album, too. Quirky, with a beat, and country in its bones. Bart is a PhD biochemist, lawyer and singersongwriter with folksy Kansas expressions. Bart and Friends had recorded "Comrade

Cool" a year earlier and played it around Ann Arbor. They also made a couple videos which were aired on MTV. They played some big venues. He then brought the first (and only?) Soviet rock band to the U.S. in 1988. The tape has since sat around, entertaining us. But why keep it to ourselves?

### *Slim McElderry: The Blue Sun*

ARTIST: Slim McElderry  PRICE: $12 CD; 18 songs; $1 per song download and free samples, art and lyrics online at OYB website.  DESCRIPTION: Rich, twangy swamp blues with worldclass lyrics courtesy of Mac's de-

cades of global wandering and busking with his 12-string dobro. It's something like Leadbelly, say. In the vein of Woody. With a Kerouac vibe tossed in. This important music has been hiding under a bushel since the 70s. Here's your chance. Mac also created a "Blue Sun" songbook of over 100 songs and art plus essays on the wandering, loving, radical life fully lived—look for it here soon. He also has a novel waiting to see print that alleges the spirit of Steinbeck's *Cannery Row* ended up in Mac's neck of the woods in a new creative, mythic, scientific collaboration of mysterious but true proportions. Mac is 70+ and still rocks. He lives in a no-electricity barracks in Panacea, Florida.

## Spring Creek Chronicles

AUTHOR: Leo Lovel ISBN: 0970961618 PAGES: 240 LISTPRICE: $15 DESCRIPTION: The subhead says "Stories of commercial fishin', huntin', workin' and people along the North Florida Gulf Coast." By a fiesty storyteller who owns and runs a coastal restaurant with his family, one that they catch the fish for. Artwork by his son. He wrote this book  while his fishing license was suspended by the game wardens. He dedicates it to them. ...And sells thousands of copies of his book along the coast even though no mainstream wholesaler will help him. A rare tale of real life on the coast today.

## Dread Clampitt

CD; 10 songs; on their own label. PRICE: $20 DESCRIPTION: Gulf Coast funky roots music, popular with young and old, locals and cognoscenti. This gang of trailer dwellers and broke-down car owners play the virtuoso swamp tunes that only the truly commited can.

From "Granny Brown":

*I said, "Granny, tell me about the Depression" /*
*She said, "There weren't no such thing. We always lived that way /*
*"We had our pride and our music, weren't supposed to have nothing /*
*"So much fun to be had, quit your cryin' and your fussin'."*

This debut CD hit #2 on the Gulf Coast charts. These artists have played daily (and nightly) since high school, working their way up through parking-lot pick-ins at folkfests to their current loyal following. Balder

Saunders was first-chair trumpet in the All Forces band but prefers his home-built electric mando. Guitarist Kyle Ogle grew up on the local beach spear fishing and surfing. Fiddleplayer Justin Price-Rees is a multi-champ of Australian bluegrass fiddling. Bassist Duke Bardwell was in Elvis's band...really. They play originals, relatives' songs and standards for raving fans. Samples and much more at www.dreadclampitt.com.

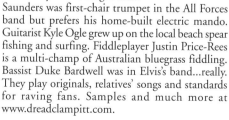

# An OYB corner on Gulf Coast culture? Stay tuned!

The perceptive will notice quite a bit of Gulf Coast homebrew culture popping up in this catalog here and there. —On this spread, and with Jack Saunders and Jack Rudloe in the Fiction section. What's up? Wait and see...there's more to come if I can pull it off. The Gulf is a rich place whose true story hasn't been told yet. Well, not in any accessible way at least. Will the locals finally have their say? The fancy lads at places like Seaside have kept the locals out of sight, over the sand-dunes, in their trailers. An independent publisher might be required in this situation. It's an interesting place: a new frontier with an old culture...which is fast disappearing. But the locals are hanging on between the cracks, as ever. The weather helps. The culture keeps rolling on and building with a well-blended ripeness that might be what we've been missing. We won't know until we get a chance to see it. The food isn't bad either—a *very* good sign a culture is on to something.